资助项目及编号：

2021 年度山东省人文社会科学课题

课题名称 适应与发展：山东高校海外高层次人才职业适应性研究

课题编号 2021-YYJY-04

Chinese EFL Teachers' Feedback on
Task-Based Oral Presentations

王博 著

任务型口语与外语教学的反馈

中国社会科学出版社

图书在版编目（CIP）数据

任务型口语与外语教学的反馈 / 王博著 . —北京：中国社会科学出版社，2024.3

书名原文：Chinese EFL Teachers' Feedback on Task-Based Oral Presentations

ISBN 978-7-5227-3128-5

Ⅰ.①任… Ⅱ.①王… Ⅲ.①外语教学—教学研究 Ⅳ.①H09

中国国家版本馆 CIP 数据核字（2024）第 041618 号

出 版 人	赵剑英
责任编辑	张 湉
责任校对	王志鞠
责任印制	李寡寡

出　　版	中国社会科学出版社
社　　址	北京鼓楼西大街甲 158 号
邮　　编	100720
网　　址	http://www.csspw.cn
发 行 部	010-84083685
门 市 部	010-84029450
经　　销	新华书店及其他书店
印　　刷	北京君升印刷有限公司
装　　订	廊坊市广阳区广增装订厂
版　　次	2024 年 3 月第 1 版
印　　次	2024 年 3 月第 1 次印刷
开　　本	710×1000　1/16
印　　张	16.25
字　　数	260 千字
定　　价	89.00 元

凡购买中国社会科学出版社图书，如有质量问题请与本社营销中心联系调换
电话：010-84083683
版权所有　侵权必究

Abstract

While research on teacher feedback in second language (L2) education has proliferated in recent years, not much is known about how English as a Foreign Language (EFL) teachers provide feedback on students' task-based oral presentations and how EFL students engage with such feedback that they receive from teachers so as to improve their future task performance. Informed by the theoretical perspectives of cognitivism, sociocultural theory, and social constructivism, this study not only investigates the methods used by two EFL teachers to provide feedback on students' oral presentations, but also explores the processes through which six EFL students cognitively, behaviorally, and affectively engage with teacher feedback.

The study adopts a case study approach with a multiple-case design and collects multiple sources of data, including video recordings of oral presentations and teacher feedback sessions, semi-structured interviews, stimulated recalls, reflective accounts, field notes, students' PowerPoint (PPT) slides, and other documents. Two Chinese EFL teachers and six English-majored undergraduates were selected through purposive sampling to participate in the study. Data analysis indicated that the two teachers behaved differently in their choices of what aspects of oral presentations should be focused on and what types of feedback strategies should be used. These differences were shaped by teachers' personal belief systems, students' task performance and emotional states, the Chinese traditional cultural concept of face-saving and the teacher appraisal system. The findings also indicated the complexity of student engagement with teacher feedback. Cognitively, the six students occasionally ignored teacher feedback on purpose, but they were able to notice and understand most of teacher feedback by using cognitive and metacognitive operations as enabling tools to process teacher feedback. Behaviorally, the students all attempted to respond to teacher feedback by either repairing linguistic errors, revising and editing their PPT slides, or improving their presentation delivery. Affectively, students displayed mostly positive attitudes toward teacher feedback and a wide range of discrete emotions were induced by teacher feedback, which were subject to students' self-regulation. Also prominent in the findings were characteristics of teacher feedback practices, students' individual differences, and contextual realities, which jointly influenced the six students' engagement with teacher feedback.

Based on the three theoretical perspectives (i.e., cognitive, sociocultural and social constructive) and the major findings of the present study, an exploratory framework to conceptualize teacher feedback on tasks of oral presentations has been proposed, which serves as a tentative conceptual framework for future research in teacher feedback on EFL oral tasks. This study contributes new knowledge to the research field of teacher feedback and deepens our understanding of the nature of teacher feedback on EFL students' task-based oral performance.

Key words: teacher feedback, student engagement, oral presentations, Chinese EFL teachers

Table of Contents

Chapter 1   Introduction ·· 1
  1.1   Background of the Study ·· 1
  1.2   Purpose of the Study ··· 5
  1.3   Research Questions ··· 6
  1.4   Definition of Key Terms ··· 7
  1.5   Methodological Considerations ··· 8
  1.6   Outline of the Study ·· 9

Chapter 2   Literature Review ··· 11
  2.1   Task-Based Language Teaching ··· 11
      2.1.1   Definitions of Task ··· 12
      2.1.2   Procedure and Principles for Task Design ················· 13
      2.1.3   Task-Based Teaching Frameworks ··························· 15
      2.1.4   A Task-Based Framework of Oral Presentations ········· 17
  2.2   A Multi-Dimensional Theoretical Perspective on Teacher Feedback · 19
      2.2.1   Defining Teacher Feedback ······································ 20
      2.2.2   A Brief History of Teacher Feedback Research ··········· 21
      2.2.3   Teacher Feedback: Cognitive Perspective ·················· 22
      2.2.4   Teacher Feedback: Sociocognitive Perspective ··········· 23
      2.2.5   Teacher Feedback: Social Constructive Perspective ···· 26
  2.3   Empirical Studies on Teacher Feedback in L2 Education ········· 29
      2.3.1   Teacher Feedback Practices: Focus, Function,
           and Strategies ·· 29
          2.3.1.1   The Focus of Teacher Feedback ················· 29
          2.3.1.2   The Function of Teacher Feedback ············· 33

     2.3.1.3 The Strategies of Teacher Feedback ·················· 35
   2.3.2 Teacher Cognitions about Feedback Provision ················ 37
   2.3.3 Student Perspectives on Teacher Feedback ·················· 39
   2.3.4 Effects of Teacher Feedback ································ 40
   2.3.5 Student Engagement with Teacher Feedback ·················· 41
   2.3.6 Context and Teacher Feedback ······························ 44
   2.3.7 Teacher Feedback on Oral Tasks ···························· 46
 2.4 Research Gaps ·· 48
 2.5 A Tentative Conceptual Framework ·································· 49
 2.6 Next Step for Teacher Feedback Research and Practice ················ 51

Chapter 3 Methodology ·· 53
 3.1 Qualitative Case Study ··· 53
   3.1.1 Qualitative Research Paradigm ···························· 53
   3.1.2 Case Study Approach ···································· 55
 3.2 Research Context ··· 57
   3.2.1 Chinese Cultures of Learning ······························ 57
   3.2.2 The Chinese EFL Context ································ 59
   3.2.3 The Institutional and Instructional Contexts ·················· 62
 3.3 Participants of the Study ··· 65
   3.3.1 Selection of Teacher Participants ··························· 65
   3.3.2 Selection of Student Participants ··························· 67
 3.4 The Pilot Study ··· 69
 3.5 Data Collection ··· 70
   3.5.1 Data Sources ·· 71
     3.5.1.1 Classroom Observations ·························· 71
     3.5.1.2 Video Recordings ······························· 72
     3.5.1.3 Semi-Structured Interviews ······················· 73
     3.5.1.4 Stimulated Recalls ······························ 74
     3.5.1.5 Reflective Accounts ···························· 75
     3.5.1.6 Field Notes ··································· 75
     3.5.1.7 Documents ··································· 76
   3.5.2 The Procedure of Data Collection ·························· 77

	3.5.3	Data Triangulation ···································· 79

3.6 Data Analysis ··································· 80
    3.6.1 Analysis of Teacher Feedback ···················· 80
    3.6.2 Analysis of Semi-Structured Interviews, Stimulated Recalls, Reflective Accounts, and Field Notes ···················· 82

3.7 Ensuring Trustworthiness ··································· 85

3.8 Ethical Issues ··································· 87

Chapter 4 Teacher Feedback Practices in Oral Presentations ··············· 89

4.1 Amelia's Feedback Practices ··································· 89
    4.1.1 Feedback Focus: Comprehensive Feedback ·············· 89
    4.1.2 Feedback Function: Praise-Criticism and Criticism-Suggestion ····· 93
    4.1.3 Feedback Strategies: Input-Providing CF, Use of L1, and Nonverbal Feedback ···················· 97

4.2 Gwen's Feedback Practices ··································· 101
    4.2.1 Feedback Focus: Language-Focused Feedback ············ 101
    4.2.2 Feedback Function: Praise-Criticism-Suggestion ··········· 105
    4.2.3 Feedback Strategies: Output-Prompting CF, Use of L1, and Peer/Self-Feedback ···················· 108

4.3 Summary of Chapter ··································· 112

Chapter 5 Student Engagement with Teacher Feedback on Oral Presentations ··································· 113

5.1 Engagement with Teacher Feedback: Student Cases from Amelia's Class ··································· 113
    5.1.1 Deng: A High-Proficiency Student's Engagement with Teacher Feedback ··································· 113
        5.1.1.1 Deng's Background ··································· 113
        5.1.1.2 Deng's Engagement with Teacher Feedback ········ 115
    5.1.2 Wang: An Intermediate-Proficiency Student's Engagement with Teacher Feedback ··································· 120
        5.1.2.1 Wang's Background ··································· 120

     5.1.2.2 Wang's Engagement with Teacher Feedback ········ 122
   5.1.3 Li: A Lower-Proficiency Student's Engagement with
     Teacher Feedback ··· 129
     5.1.3.1 Li's Background ·································· 129
     5.1.3.2 Li's Engagement with Teacher Feedback ············ 131
 5.2 Engagement with Teacher Feedback: Student Cases
   from Gwen's Class ··· 137
   5.2.1 Wu: A High-Proficiency Student's Engagement with
     Teacher Feedback ··· 137
     5.2.1.1 Wu's Background································ 137
     5.2.1.2 Wu's Engagement with Teacher Feedback············ 137
   5.2.2 Chen: An Intermediate-Proficiency Student's Engagement
     with Teacher Feedback ·· 141
     5.2.2.1 Chen's Background ······························ 141
     5.2.2.2 Chen's Engagement with Teacher Feedback ········ 142
   5.2.3 Han: A Lower-Proficiency Student's Engagement with
     Teacher Feedback ··· 147
     5.2.3.1 Han's Background································ 147
     5.2.3.2 Han's Engagement with Teacher Feedback ··········· 148
 5.3 Factors Influencing Student Engagement with Teacher Feedback··· 152
   5.3.1 Learner Individualization ··· 152
   5.3.2 Characteristics of Teacher Feedback Practices ················ 154
   5.3.3 Teacher-Student Interactional Patterns and Interpersonal
     Relationships··· 155
   5.3.4 Teaching Agenda ··· 157
 5.4 Summary of Chapter ·· 159

Chapter 6 Discussion ·· 161
 6.1 Understanding Teacher Feedback on Oral Presentations
   in the Chinese EFL Context ·· 161
 6.2 Student Engagement with Teacher Feedback on Oral Presentations······ 165
   6.2.1 Interrelatedness of Affective, Cognitive,
     and Behavioral Engagement ····································· 165

  6.2.2 Multiple Factors Influencing Student Engagement with Teacher Feedback ········ 167
  6.2.3 Learner Agency and Engagement with Teacher Feedback ····· 170
 6.3 An Exploratory Conceptual Framework of Teacher Feedback on Task-Based Oral Presentation Performance ······················· 171
 6.4 Summary of Chapter ················· 174

Chapter 7 Conclusion ················· 175
 7.1 Summary of Main Research Findings ················· 175
 7.2 Significance of the Study ················· 177
 7.3 Limitations of the Study ················· 179
 7.4 Pedagogical Implications ················· 180
 7.5 Suggestions for Future Research ················· 183
 7.6 Summary of Chapter ················· 184

Appendices ················· 186
 Appendix A Informed Consent Form for Teacher Participants ········· 186
 Appendix B Informed Consent Form for Student Participants ········· 189
 Appendix C Sample Verbatim Transcripts of Student Speech in Oral Presentations ················· 192
 Appendix D Sample Verbatim Transcripts of Teacher Oral Feedback ··· 194
 Appendix E Teacher Semi-Structured Interview Guide ················· 198
 Appendix F Sample Verbatim Transcripts of Teacher Semi-Structured Interview ················· 200
 Appendix G Student Semi-Structured Interview Guide ················· 205
 Appendix H Sample Verbatim Transcripts of Student Semi-Structured Interview ················· 207
 Appendix I Prompts of Stimulated Recall with Teachers and Students ···· 210
 Appendix J Sample Verbatim Transcripts of Stimulated Recall with Teacher ················· 211
 Appendix K Sample Verbatim Transcripts of Stimulated Recall with Student ················· 214
 Appendix L Prompt of Reflective Account and Sample ················· 218

Appendix M	Scripts of Sample Ready-Made PowerPoint Slides Used to Teach Oral Presentations	220
Appendix N	Course Information for *An Introduction to Intercultural Communication*	225
Appendix O	Course Information for *Communicative English*（Ⅱ）	226
Appendix P	Abbreviations	227
Appendix Q	Author's Scholarship in Relation to This Book	228

References ·· 229

List of Tables and Figures

Table 2.1　Ellis's (2003) task-based language teaching framework ············16
Table 2.2　Bitchener, Basturkmen, and East's (2010) focus of supervisory written feedback ··31
Table 2.3　Example of linguistic targets of oral CF studies ·····················33
Table 2.4　Kumar and Stracke's (2007, p. 464) categorization of feedback according to speech functions ··34
Table 2.5　A classification of oral CF strategies according to Lyster and Saito (2010) ··36
Table 3.1　Demographic information of teacher participants in this study········66
Table 3.2　Demographic information of student participants from Amelia's class·····68
Table 3.3　Demographic information of student participants from Gwen's class 68
Table 3.4　Time frame of data collection ··78
Table 3.5　An overview of the alignment between research questions and data collection ··79
Table 3.6　Coding scheme of feedback focus ··81
Table 3.7　Coding scheme of feedback function··81
Table 3.8　Coding scheme of feedback strategy ··82
Table 3.9　Coding scheme of cognitive engagement with teacher feedback······83
Table 3.10　Coding scheme of behavioral engagement with teacher feedback···84
Table 3.11　Coding scheme of affective engagement with teacher feedback·····85
Table 4.1　Focus of teacher feedback provided by Amelia ·····························89
Table 4.2　Linguistic targets of learner errors addressed by Amelia ··············93
Table 4.3　Function of teacher feedback provided by Amelia ·······················94
Table 4.4　Distribution of CF types in Amelia's class ··97
Table 4.5　Focus of teacher feedback provided by Gwen ·······················101

Table 4.6　Linguistic targets of learner errors addressed by Gwen ············· 103
Table 4.7　Function of teacher feedback provided by Gwen ····················· 105
Table 4.8　Distribution of CF types in Gwen's class ······························ 108
Table 5.1　Wang's revision operations induced by teacher feedback ············ 127
Table 5.2　Li's revision operations induced by teacher feedback ················ 135
Table 5.3　Wu's revision operations induced by teacher feedback ··············· 141
Table 5.4　Chen's revision operations induced by teacher feedback ············· 146
Table 5.5　Han's revision operations induced by teacher feedback ·············· 151

Figure 2.1　Hattie and Timperley's (2007, p. 87) model of feedback to enhance learning ·· 27
Figure 2.2　Ellis's (2010a, p. 337) componential framework for investigating CF ··· 43
Figure 2.3　A tentative conceptual framework of teacher feedback on EFL learning and task-based oral presentation performance ···························· 51
Figure 3.1　Jin and Cortazzi's (2006, p. 13) framework of student learning activity in Confucian heritages ··· 58
Figure 3.2　The procedure of data collection in this study ······················· 77
Figure 3.3　Data triangulation for investigating students' behavioral engagement with teacher feedback ·· 80
Figure 4.1　Excerpt of PPT slide—Han—Presentation 2 ························ 107
Figure 5.1　Excerpt of PPT slide—Wang—Presentation 2 ······················ 123
Figure 5.2　Excerpt of PPT slide—Wang—Presentation 3 ······················ 125
Figure 5.3　Excerpt of revised PPT slide —Wang— Presentation 3 ············ 128
Figure 5.4　Excerpt of PPT slide—Li—Presentation 3 ·························· 134
Figure 6.1　An exploratory conceptual framework of teacher feedback on EFL learning and task-based oral presentation performance ··························· 172

Chapter 1　　Introduction

This chapter starts by introducing how this study has been informed by the research and practical backgrounds and then proceeds to describe the problems that currently exist in teacher feedback research in the field of L2 education. It then presents the research purpose and research questions, which is followed by a delineation of the key terms that occur in the study. Finally, this chapter provides a general introduction to the research methods and elaborates the outline of this study.

1.1　Background of the Study

In recent years, the communicative language teaching (CLT) and task-based language teaching (TBLT) methodologies have become the mainstream approaches of second language (L2) teaching in both English as a second language (ESL) and English as a foreign language (EFL) contexts (Nunan, 1989, 2004; Richards & Rodgers, 2001). In many EFL contexts like China, the government's recent English education policies have focused on increasing students' communicative competence, which has paved the way for the CLT and TBLT approaches in these contexts (Ahmad & Rao, 2013; Hu, 2005). Recent English education reform in China has emphasized two major paradigm shifts: from teacher-directed to more student-centered approaches and from a focus on reading and grammar to an emphasis on effective communication in English (Zhou, 2015). This has created many challenges for teachers and students in relation to pedagogical views and educational practices. For instance, the level of student competence and the corresponding failure on the part of students to adjust to the learner-centered teaching context appear to be major problems (Koosha & Yakhabi, 2013). In particular, students need to develop communicative competence and non-language skills related to self-regulation to attain the purpose of moving from passive receiving to active participating in language classrooms (Benson, 2011). One possible way of dealing with this situation is for teachers to provide deliberate guidance and assistance. On the one hand, teachers can use a variety of task-based activities such as oral presentations that focus on meaning and language use; on the other hand, language learners can be advised in terms of teacher feedback because of a widely held belief in the importance of feedback to language learners' successful learning and task performance (Aljaafreh & Lantolf, 1994; Hattie & Timperley, 2007; Li, 2010; Zamel, 1981).

Research has revealed that teacher feedback is multi-faceted in nature (Ellis, 2010b; Nicol & Macfarlane-Dick, 2006). On the one hand, informed by the cognitive perspective in mainstream second language acquisition (SLA) research, teacher feedback facilitates learner acquisition of target L2 structures by directing learners' attention toward mismatches between language output and the target input. On the other hand, teacher feedback is also a teaching practice loaded with social meanings and situated in the sociocultural context (Goldstein, 2006; K. Hyland & F. Hyland, 2006a). Teacher provision of feedback is subject to not only individual factors such as linguistic background (Hyland & Anan, 2006), beliefs, knowledge, and experiences (Junqueira & Kim, 2013; Junqueira & Payant, 2015), but also sociocultural factors such as the cultural norms, institutional policies, and students' expectations (Lee, 2008a, 2009; McMartin-Miller, 2014). Likewise, students' views and perceptions of teacher feedback are also mediated by learners' motivation, L2 proficiency, teacher feedback types, and the interpersonal relationships between teachers and learners (Lee, 2008b; Hyland, 2013; Rassaei, 2013). Therefore, the full account of teacher feedback requires a combined theoretical perspective incorporating both the cognitive and social dimensions (Ellis, 2010b).

Chapter 1 Introduction

In the past two decades, there has been a sharp increase in teacher feedback studies in the field of L2 education (e.g., Bruton, 2009; Chandler, 2003; Ferris, 2010; Lee, Mak, & Burns, 2015; Lyster & Saito, 2010), with a majority of the feedback research focusing on one particular form of teacher feedback—corrective feedback. Corrective feedback (CF), also termed error correction (e.g., Truscott, 1996), grammar feedback (e.g., Ferris, 2002), or grammar correction (e.g., Ferris, 2004), is an extended form of feedback that aims to remedy particular linguistic errors in students' oral or written production (Sheen & Ellis, 2011). When addressing students' linguistic errors, teachers employ various feedback strategies in terms of when to provide CF, what linguistic errors to correct, and how to correct them, etc. Following this line, the bulk of research on teacher feedback has examined the impact of different CF strategies on learners' acquisition of specific L2 structures on the one hand (Lyster, Saito, & Sato, 2013), and the overall effectiveness of student text revisions on the other hand (Ferris, 2010). So far, these studies have improved our understanding of the role of CF in contributing to L2 learners' development of linguistic competence at best, because CF can help learners to notice the gap between their errors and target linguistic forms, conduct metalinguistic reflections, and restructure their interlanguage systems (Bitchener & Ferris, 2012; Ellis, 2010a, 2010b).

However, as previously noted, although CLT and TBLT approaches have been encouraged and promoted in EFL contexts like the mainland of China to help students achieve communicative competence rather than linguistic competence, CF is still commonly used in EFL classrooms at different educational levels such as Hong Kong secondary schools (e.g., Lee, 2004, 2008a, 2009) and Chinese universities (e.g., Yang & Gao, 2013; Yang & Lyster, 2010), where many EFL teachers play the role of error hunters and focus on linguistic form itself (i.e., grammar, phonology, and vocabulary) rather than on the expression and comprehension of meaning through language. Since the communicative approach entails both appropriateness and readiness on the part of language learners to use relevant strategies in coping with certain language situations for better communication, this excessive attention to error correction in the field of teacher feedback research runs the risk of "premising the need to develop linguistic skills as a prerequisite for the learning of communicative abilities" (Ellis, 2000, p. 196). In short, there seems to be a disjuncture between current teacher feedback practices and the tenets of CLT. Much remains to be known about the nature and role of teacher feedback in communicative and meaning-focused EFL contexts. Specifically, we know little regarding how teachers provide feedback on oral communicative tasks in authentic EFL classrooms, as well as why teachers provide such feedback (Wang, Teo, & Yu, 2017).

To date, the field of feedback research has also gone beyond the examination of teacher feedback *per se* and addressed student perspectives on teacher feedback. Most previous studies have focused on student preferences and expectations based on questionnaire surveys (e.g., Ferris & Roberts, 2001; Lee, 2008b; Zhang & Rahimi, 2014), and there have been few attempts to investigate students' multi-dimensional engagement with teacher feedback. Indeed, students tend to be viewed as mere recipients—when in fact they can be and should be active and proactive agents in the feedback process (Winstone, Nash, Parker, & Rowntree, 2017). Without understanding how students engage with feedback, it is impossible to know how students improve their work and what factors may facilitate or inhibit their uses of teacher feedback. Therefore, teachers may run the risk of continually using feedback strategies that are counterproductive. Although Ellis (2010a) has proposed a multiple-dimensional theoretical framework of learner engagement with teacher CF that comprises a cognitive aspect, a behavioral aspect, and an affective aspect of engagement, very few empirical inquiries, such as Han and Hyland's (2015), Han's (2017), and Zheng and Yu's (2018) studies, have used and developed this framework with the aim of exploring and understanding learner engagement led by teacher CF on EFL students' writing drafts.

With regard to the research design of current teacher feedback research, most previous feedback studies were conducted either in experimental or quasi-experimental settings (e.g., Bitchener & Knoch, 2009; Ellis, Sheen, Murakami, & Takashima, 2008; Sheen, 2007). While these experimental and quasi-experimental studies that adopt a pretest-posttest-delayed posttest design have generated useful insights to the effectiveness of teacher feedback in L2 development, their findings are presented in a decontextualized fashion. We know little about the context surrounding the feedback. Indeed, feedback occurs between teachers and students in a multi-layered sociocultural, institutional, and interpersonal context, while student perspectives and engagement are also affected by different aspects of the context. Many researchers have called for expanding research to include naturalistic and qualitative studies to complement these quantitative studies for better interpretation of teacher feedback with reference to its embedded sociocultural and educational contexts (Ferris, 2010; Hyland, 2010; Storch, 2010; van Beuningen, 2010). Research design of qualitative case study has the advantage of capturing individual differences among study participants, as well as gaining a rich and holistic account of the phenomenon of teacher feedback in the context of real-life classrooms. Given the large number of EFL students in the mainland of China (Jiang, 2003; Jin & Cortazzi, 2011; Rao & Lei, 2014), investigating teacher feedback with this particular learner group is meaningful in terms of informing teachers' feedback practices in this particular pedagogical context and in other similar EFL contexts, as well as promoting EFL students' engagement with feedback processes and future EFL learning.

1.2 Purpose of the Study

The current study aims to obtain a holistic and in-depth understanding of teacher feedback on task-based oral presentations in the context of Chinese university-level EFL classrooms, using a qualitative, naturalistic, multiple-case study approach and involving multiple data sources. This study adopts an emic view of teacher feedback from the perspectives of those being studied, that is, from the perspectives of both university EFL teachers and EFL students. By conducting this study, the following objectives are expected to be met. The first objective is to explore the nature of university EFL teachers' feedback on students' task-based oral presentations as well as EFL students' engagement with teacher feedback at the cognitive, behavioral, and affective levels. The second objective is to reveal the reasons that underlie university EFL teachers' feedback practices in students' oral presentations and EFL students' engagement with teacher feedback. Overall, this study attempts to provide useful insights into the processes through which university EFL teachers can improve their feedback practices and EFL students can generate deep engagement with teacher feedback when they perform oral presentations.

1.3 Research Questions

With these research objectives in mind, the study seeks to answer the following four major research questions:

RQ1. What are the Chinese university EFL teachers' feedback practices in student oral presentations?

(1) What is the focus of teacher feedback on oral presentations?

(2) What is the function of teacher feedback on oral presentations?

(3) What strategies do the teachers employ when giving feedback on oral presentations?

RQ2. What factors might have influenced the Chinese university EFL teachers' feedback practices in student oral presentations?

RQ3. How do university EFL students engage with teacher feedback on their oral presentations?

(1) How do university EFL students engage cognitively with teacher feedback on oral presentations?

(2) How do university EFL students engage behaviorally with teacher feedback on oral presentations?

(3) How do university EFL students engage affectively with teacher feedback on oral presentations?

RQ4. What factors might have influenced university EFL students' engagement with teacher feedback on their oral presentations?

1.4 Definition of Key Terms

Task. A task can be defined as "an outcome-oriented instructional segment or as a behavioral framework for research or classroom learning" (Oxford, 2006, p. 97). Since the focus of task-based language teaching is primarily on meaning and communication, tasks are described as "activities that call for primarily meaning-focused language use" (Ellis, 2003, p. 3). Generally, language tasks can be grouped into different types according to the four macro-language skills: listening, speaking, reading, and writing.

Oral presentation. Oral presentation in this study refers to one type of oral task in EFL classrooms, which requires adequate planning and thorough preparation in using one's voice, body language, and visual aids such as slideshows to present and illustrate the points more effectively and to achieve the desired results. It requires "the combination of knowledge, skills, and attitudes needed to speak in public in order to inform, self-express, to relate and to persuade" (De Grez, 2009, p. 5).

Teacher feedback. Teacher feedback in this study is operationally defined as any information (given verbally, in written, or other nonverbal forms) provided by a language teacher, pertaining to a learner's language learning, task-based oral presentation performance as well as the anticipated proper criteria, in order to inform learners of the gap therebetween and to elicit improved language learning and oral presentation performance from the learner.

Corrective feedback (CF). Corrective feedback is an extended form of feedback intended to remedy particular problems in student learning. Sheen and Ellis (2011) referred to it as "the feedback that learners receive on the linguistic errors they make in their oral and written production in a second language" (p. 593).

Learner engagement. Learner engagement in this study is conceptualized as being composed of three dimensions: cognitive, behavioral, and affective engagement (Ellis, 2010a). Cognitive engagement deals with learners' processing, noticing, and understanding of teacher feedback they receive;

behavioral engagement involves learners' use of teacher feedback manifested at the action- and observable level; affective engagement concerns itself with learners' emotional and attitudinal responses to teacher feedback.

English as a Foreign Language (EFL). EFL is a term to refer to English teaching and learning in countries, such as China, Japan, South Korea and Thailand where the majority does not speak English as a means of communication. In these countries, students often study English as a subject and have a good command of the linguistic knowledge but do not get enough exposure to conditions where people converse only in English.

English as a Second Language (ESL). ESL is a term to refer to English teaching and learning in countries, such as Canada, France, Australia, etc. where English is spoken and used for communication. In these countries, the students mainly studied English in order to achieve proficiency in English to meet the requirements in the field of education and employment.

1.5 Methodological Considerations

This study adopted the methodological approach of qualitative multiple-case study. Specifically, this study took place in two naturalistic EFL classrooms of a university in the mainland of China. Two EFL teachers and six Year-2 English-majored undergraduates were selected through the purposive sampling strategy and recruited based on their backgrounds and willingness to participate.

The data collection lasted for 18 weeks during which no intervention was made by the researcher. Over this period, multiple sources of data were gathered. All of the six students' in-class oral presentations, together with teacher oral feedback, were video-recorded. Classroom observation was carried out to understand the institutional and instructional contexts, as well as the interactions and interpersonal relationships between teachers and students. The two teacher participants and six student participants were interviewed individually at the beginning and end of the research period. After each oral presentation, stimulated recalls were conducted individually with both the teacher and student presenter shortly after class. Furthermore, at the end of the semester, each student participant was asked to write a reflective account of his or her experience of receiving and using teacher feedback, as well as making revisions, if any, to their PPT slides. Additionally, field notes were written on a continual basis and relevant class documents (such as the teaching syllabus, students' PPT slides, and other written documents) were collected to triangulate other data sources.

All the data collected were fully transcribed and analysed qualitatively (Miles & Huberman, 1994). Text analysis dealt with transcripts of teacher oral feedback in terms of focus and function of feedback, as well as feedback strategies. Besides, the transcripts of other sources of data (i.e., semi-structured interviews, stimulated recalls, students' reflective accounts, as well as field notes) were recursively and carefully read line by line. The analytic process began with open coding during which open codes were assigned to the data. Then, through axial coding and selective coding, themes pertaining to the research questions gradually emerged.

1.6 Outline of the Study

The structure of the present study is as follows: Chapter 2 conducts a detailed review of both theoretical and empirical studies on task-based language teaching and teacher feedback in the field of L2 education. The research gaps and a tentative conceptual framework are put forward at the end of Chapter 2. Chapter 3 addresses the methodological issues, including the multi-layered research context, the methods of data collection and data analysis, as well as research ethics and trustworthiness. Chapter 4 and Chapter 5 present the research findings of this multiple-case study in the form of case narratives: Chapter 4 focuses on the two Chinese EFL teachers' feedback practices in students' oral presentations and Chapter 5 focuses on the six EFL students' engagement processes with teacher feedback. Chapter 6 compares the findings with the previous research literature and proposes an exploratory conceptual framework to account for the overall picture of Chinese EFL teachers' feedback on task-based oral presentations. The concluding Chapter 7 summarizes the research findings, highlights the significance of this study, acknowledges the limitations, and provides implications for teacher feedback practices and future research.

Chapter 2　Literature Review

This chapter first provides a brief review of task-based language teaching （TBLT） to develop a better understanding of what tasks are involved in language teaching and to shed light on the current investigation of teacher feedback provided in the post-task phase of language tasks of oral presentations. Following this overview is a detailed review of the cognitive, sociocognitive, and social constructive learning theories which constitute the theoretical perspectives adopted in the current study to understand teacher feedback. A systematic review of empirical studies on various aspects pertaining to teacher feedback in L2 education is then conducted to identify the research gaps and propose a tentative conceptual framework of teacher feedback on EFL learning and task-based oral presentations.

2.1　Task-Based Language Teaching

The past few decades have witnessed an enormous growth of interest in task-based research and pedagogy. This surge of interest has been motivated by the fact that a task is viewed as a construct of great importance to SLA researchers, frontline language teachers, and curriculum developers （Ellis, 2000）. On the one hand, a task can elicit samples of learner language for purpose of research （Corder, 1980）; on the other hand, it forms the basis for organizing daily and long-term lesson plans （Prabhu, 1987）. Such an approach based on the use of tasks as the central unit of organization and instruction in language teaching is referred to as task-based language teaching （TBLT） （Richards & Rodgers, 2001）. TBLT has slowly emerged since the 1980s to challenge the traditional form-based language teaching methodology. This approach can promote learners' competence in using the language to do what they need to do. It offers a change from the traditional teaching routines through which many learners had previously failed to communicate with lessons.

2.1.1 Definitions of Task

There are numerous definitions of task and these definitions focus on different aspects of what constitutes a task. For example, one frequently quoted definition is proposed by Long (1985), who referred to a task as:

> a piece of work undertaken for oneself or for others, freely or for some reward. Thus, examples of tasks include painting a fence, dressing a child, filling out a form, buying a pair of shoes… In other words, by 'task' is meant the hundred and one things people do in everyday life, at work, at play, and in between. (p. 89)

Obviously, Long's (1985) definition describes the real-world tasks by emphasizing the usage of language in the world beyond the classroom. When they are transformed from the real world to the classroom, tasks become pedagogical in nature. Nunan (1989) defined a pedagogical task as "a piece of classroom work which involves learners in comprehending, manipulating, producing or interacting in the target language while their attention is principally focused on meaning rather than on form" (p. 10). He stated that pedagogical tasks are intended to bridge the gap between the classroom and the real world because they serve to prepare language learners for real-life language use. Drawing on works of other researchers, Skehan (1998, p. 147) summarized five key characteristics of a task activity:

> (1) meaning is primary;
> (2) learners are not given other people's meanings to regurgitate;
> (3) there is some sort of relationship to comparable real-world

activities;

(4) task completion has a priority; and

(5) the assessment of tasks is done in terms of outcome.

This perspective of viewing a task as an outcome-oriented instructional segment is also acknowledged by Breen (1987), who indicated that language tasks can be viewed as a range of work plans, from simple to complex, with the overall purpose of facilitating language learning. More recently, Oxford (2006) conducted an exhaustive review of previous literature and produced a definition of task in L2 teaching and learning as "an outcome-oriented instructional segment or as a behavioral framework for research or classroom learning" (p. 97).

2.1.2 Procedure and Principles for Task Design

It is acknowledged that task performance derives interlanguage changes by causing learners to attend to and retain information about the target language as they use it (Ellis, 2001). Accordingly, teachers can carefully choose task designs to guide a learner's focus of attention to particular aspects of the target language (Tavakoli & Foster, 2008). Nunan (2004) proposed a three-phase procedure to be followed in designing tasks. To begin with, the teacher clarifies the goals and specific objectives of given tasks, interprets them in accordance with curriculum guidelines, and modifies these goals and objectives when necessary. Secondly, the teacher selects and creates students with authentic and comprehensible input through which students are provided with optimal learning opportunities. Thirdly, the teacher decides on which activities to adopt in accordance with the task rationale and settings, as well as the respective roles that teachers and students are likely to play. Meanwhile, Nunan (2004) summarized a total of seven principles for designing tasks in language instruction, which laid the foundation for effective TBLT practices.

Scaffolding. Scaffolding is the dialogic process by which one speaker assists another to perform a new function (Wood, Bruner, & Ross, 1976). In the case of TBLT, lessons and teaching materials are supposed to provide supporting frameworks within which language learning occurs. At the beginning stage, language learners should not be expected to produce certain language that has never been introduced explicitly or implicitly. Nunan (2004) stated that the art of TBLT is "knowing when to remove the scaffolding" (p. 35). If it is removed prematurely, language learners may not be able to complete the task properly, but if it is kept too long, learners will not develop autonomy to use the target language.

Task dependency. This principle deals with "how each task exploits and builds on the next one that has gone before" (Nunan, 2004, p. 35). Tasks should be designed in such a way that language learners are guided step-by-step to the final task in the instructional sequence. For instance, according to the receptive-to-productive principle, tasks can be developed in such a sequence that language learners spend a greater amount of time engaging in receptive (listening and reading) tasks than in productive (speaking and writing) tasks at the beginning of the learning process.

Recycling. Tasks should be designed to maximize opportunities for learning via recycling language. It is believed that if learners are unable to achieve total mastery when they encounter a linguistic item for the first time, they probably need to be reintroduced to that item again and again over a period of time. This recycling design allows students to confront target language in a range of different environments, and accordingly, they are able to see how a particular item functions in other situations.

Active learning. Tasks should be designed to provide learners with opportunities to learn best by actively using the target language. What underlies this principle is the concept that "learners learn best through doing" (Nunan, 2004, p. 36) and that knowledge is constructed by language learners themselves rather than transmitted from the teacher to learners. Accordingly, learner-focused work should dominate class time.

Integration. According to this principle, tasks should be designed to enable students to be taught in ways that clarify the relationships between linguistic form, communicative function, and semantic meaning. The communicative function should not be broken from its relationships with linguistic form and semantic meaning, as students must still master grammar and words for effective communication. In fact, meaning and form are highly interrelated in such a way that grammatical knowledge enables learners to express meanings and achieve communicative purposes.

Reproduction to creation. According to Nunan (2004), learners reproduce "language models provided by the teacher, the textbook or the tape" (p. 37) in reproductive tasks through which learners acquire linguistic forms, communicative functions, and semantic meanings. Furthermore, the design of reproductive tasks should provide a basis for creative tasks in which language learners are encouraged to recombine familiar items in creative ways.

Reflection. When designing tasks, language teachers should give learners opportunities to reflect on what they have learned as well as how they are doing and how to improve their task performance. Such reflection helps learners to focus on the process of language learning.

2.1.3 Task-Based Teaching Frameworks

Ever since the 1990s, language pedagogists have proposed a great number of teaching frameworks for task-based instruction. Willis (1996) proposed a three-phase model of task-based instruction framework of pre-task, task cycle, and language focus. The pre-task phase serves to introduce the topic and task. The task cycle involves three essential subphases of task, planning, and report. Students are assigned tasks, then prepare for those tasks, and finally present and report their tasks to the whole class. In the language focus phase, teachers oversee the practice of new words and phrases, while students discuss issues related to linguistic forms and ask questions about language features. Ellis (2003) argued that this instruction framework is in essence composed of three phases (i.e., pre-task, during task, and post-task); accordingly, he developed a task-based teaching framework composed of pre-task, main task, and post-task. Table 2.1 presents a brief summary of the strategies in each phase.

Table 2.1   Ellis's (2003) task-based language teaching framework

Phase	Goal	Typical strategies
Pre-task	Prepare learners to perform a task and promote language acquisition	Doing a similar task Providing a model Assigning non-task preparation activities Strategic planning
Main task	Complete task	Task-performance strategies Task-process strategies
Post-task	Repeat task performance Evaluate task performance Focus on form	Review of learner errors Consciousness-raising tasks Production practice activities Noticing activities

At the pre-task phase, Ellis (2003) suggested that teachers design a similar task to scaffold learners' performance in the main task. An alternative choice is to provide a model (e.g., oral and written texts) of how the task can be performed without actual performance. This strategy is helpful in reducing learners' cognitive load before they perform the main task. Some non-task preparation activities can also be organized to reduce the linguistic demand on the part of learners, which include introducing background information and activating topic language. It is also suggested that strategic planning should allow learners to consider the linguistic forms they may require to execute the work plan for the main task.

During the main task phase, two basic types of strategies are available to teachers: task-performance strategies (i.e., how the task is to be undertaken prior to the actual performance) and task-process strategies (i.e., how to perform the task as it is being undertaken). According to Ellis (2003), teachers need to decide whether or not to require learners to complete the task in a given time, to allow learners have access to the input data, or to introduce certain surprise elements like punishment into the task.

Finally, as Ellis (2003) pointed out, the post-task phase aims to provide learners with opportunities to repeat the task, which may promote language complexity and fluency. More importantly, task-based instruction emphasizes performance which is measured based on whether or to what extent learners can successfully perform the task. Receiving feedback on task performance is endorsed as a crucial characteristic of this post-task phase. Teachers seek to address errors or gaps in learners' L2 knowledge and their task performance, such as what and how many errors to correct, as well as how to correct learner errors, which entails learners focusing on linguistic forms once the task is completed. A range of options is available to teachers, including reviewing learner errors and using consciousness-raising tasks, production practice activities, and noticing activities to direct learners' attention to specific linguistic forms that they have used incorrectly in the main task. In order to maximize interactivity between learners, peer assessment and self-assessment can also be effectively adopted in the post-task. For example, learners can be encouraged to reflect on their task performance. They can also be invited to comment on which aspects of language use they focus on and why, as well as how they can improve their task performance.

2.1.4 A Task-Based Framework of Oral Presentations

Oral presentation is one of many options exemplifying a meaningful task-based activity in university EFL and ESL classrooms. As Morita (2000) observed, an oral presentation is a frequent, highly routinized part of classroom life in higher education settings. This section aims at rationalizing the selection of oral presentation as the task type investigated in the study by locating this classroom activity within the broad framework of TBLT.

First and foremost, as mentioned earlier, TBLT embraces a learner-centered educational philosophy; in this sense, oral presentations are essentially student-centered language tasks and have been shown to be beneficial to learner development of L2 and related personal skills (Girard, Pinar, & Trapp, 2011; King, 2002). In most cases, when students are asked to make oral presentations in class, they can choose what they want to address in their presentations, as well as how they present their topics to the audience (e.g., peers and teachers). Consider the group presentation as an example. Students are often engaged in a process-oriented learning in which they work together to prepare for their oral presentations. In some classroom settings, oral presentations also involve follow-up phases where students who present are asked to answer unanticipated questions. Both the planned and unplanned language output is potentially helpful for students to develop proficiency in English (Bunch, 2009).

Another benefit of oral presentations is that students can use the four English skills (i.e., listening, speaking, reading, and writing) in an integrated way (Brooks & Wilson, 2014; King, 2002). The spoken component of oral presentations is more often recognized because students are required to speak while presenting. Meanwhile, the communicative nature of oral presentations allows students as the audience to practice listening skills in such a way that they are able to interact with the presenters. When preparing for oral presentations, students need to conduct extensive English readings to find supporting materials for presentation topics and then write the contents of their PPT slides. In a nutshell, the use of oral presentations helps bridge "the gap between language study and language use" (King, 2002, p. 402). Oral presentations have far more advantages than simply promoting English proficiency. Preparing and performing presentations is a synthesis of different language and non-language skills and knowledge areas (e.g., vocabulary, discussion, research, note-taking, confidence building, fluency, and body language) (Cox, 2007). Oral presentations serve as effective means of teaching lifelong skills that can extend beyond the educational setting into a professional context after graduation since many future employers attach great importance to communication skills and the ability to give formal presentations (Pittinger, Miller, & Mott, 2004).

TBLT is also featured by its emphasis on a process-oriented learning cycle of preparation (pre-task), performance (task), and feedback (post-task). In the pre-task phase, language teachers can set up pedagogical objectives as broad as developing learners' communicative competence through more specific goals such as developing a fifteen-minute oral presentation to be evaluated by teachers or student peers. These goals should take into account learner needs and interests in order to stimulate motivation for using the target language of English. Moreover, language teachers can provide some guidelines on how to prepare and structure a presentation. For example, verbal elements can incorporate writing a PPT presentation script and nonverbal elements in the form of visual aids (Jeon

& Hahn, 2006). In the main task phase, language teachers act as facilitators of this activity by providing a classroom setting where learners become engaged in collaborative learning. For example, teachers can decide that oral presentations are to be delivered in pair, small group, or whole class modes to encourage interactive use of English language. The structure of the collaboration also takes the form of continuous teacher feedback (and possible peer feedback and self-feedback) in the post-task phase. In most cases, the post-task phase involves two-way interaction, such as "question and answer" time or other discussions between student presenters and audience in order to obtain a real picture of the learners' task performance and English learning. The audience may also be asked to give assessment rubic scores to student presenters.

To briefly summarize, this study specifically concerns the source of teacher feedback as one assessment strategy provided in the post-task phase of students' oral presentations. Oral presentations were selected as the major activities in EFL classroom instruction in this study because they emphasize English learning as a developmental process dependent upon communication and social interaction, rather than a mere learning product acquired by practicing language items like grammar and lexis. More importantly, oral presentations improve students' interaction and communication skills, encourage students' intrinsic learning motivation, and create a classroom culture of cooperative learning.

2.2 A Multi-Dimensional Theoretical Perspective on Teacher Feedback

L2 researchers have adopted various theoretical approaches to studying teacher feedback. In this section, the researcher first provides the operational definition of teacher feedback in this study and presents a brief history of teacher feedback research, after which three major orientations, i.e., the cognitive, sociocognitive, and social constructive understandings of teacher feedback are reviewed.

2.2.1 Defining Teacher Feedback

There have been numerous attempts to define the concept of feedback. According to an early definition provided by Ramaprasad (1983), feedback is "information about the gap between the actual level and the reference level of a system parameter which is used to alter the gap in some way" (p. 4). However, Ramaprasad's (1983) definition is derived from the discipline of business management and may not be appropriate to contextualize research that is conducted in educational settings. In the field of education, a well-known definition of feedback is proposed by Hattie and Timperley (2007), who defined feedback as "information provided by an agent (e.g., teacher, peer, book, parent, self, experience) regarding aspects of one's performance or understanding" (p. 81). This simple definition clarifies the multiple sources of feedback information as well as the targets at which feedback is aimed (i.e., learner performance and understanding). Hattie and Timperley (2007) further claimed that quality feedback can "reduce discrepancies between current understandings or performance and a desired goal" (p. 87). In other words, it seems clear that feedback, if provided effectively, can fill gaps in learning and understanding (Sadler, 1989). More recently, Boud and Molloy's (2013) definition informed not only the gap in learning but also how to address that gap. They defined feedback as "a process whereby learners obtain information about their work in order to appreciate the similarities and differences between the appropriate standards for any given work, and the qualities of the work itself, in order to generate improved work" (p. 205). Their definition puts emphasis on the significant role of learner agency in reducing gaps between the expected standard and current work.

All the definitions above have their own merits and drawbacks in conceptualizing what feedback comprises in general education research. One drawback concerns the lack of specification in concrete research contexts. Therefore, an operational definition of teacher feedback in this study is essential and necessary. In EFL classrooms, teacher feedback takes a variety of forms. Perhaps the most common teacher feedback practice is correcting learners' linguistic errors, which is referred to as error correction or corrective feedback (CF). There are nevertheless shades of meaning between feedback and CF. Precisely speaking, CF is an extended form of feedback encompassing feedback and additional demonstrations or explanations intended to remedy particular problems in student learning. Teachers can also give grades, scores, or lengthy comments as forms of feedback on students' writing or oral performance. In addition, teachers can use paralanguage in tandem with their oral feedback, such as a nodding head, a thumbs-up, a raised pitch, etc. Teacher feedback in this study is operationally defined as follows:

> Teacher feedback is any information (given verbally, in written, or other nonverbal forms) provided by a language teacher, pertaining to a learner's language learning, task-based oral presentation performance as well as the anticipated proper criteria, in order to inform learners of the gap therebetween and to elicit improved language learning and oral presentation performance from the learner.

2.2.2 A Brief History of Teacher Feedback Research

In reviewing the history of the social sciences, it is apparent that early theoretical views and studies on teacher feedback arise out of behaviorism psychology (Kluger & DeNisi, 1996; Kulhavy, 1977) and are influenced by the law of effect (Thorndike, 1913). Behaviorists conceive of feedback as stemming from reinforcers (positive feedback) or avoidance of punishment (negative feedback). Feedback, either positive or negative, could improve learning and performance because both reinforcement and punishment could contribute to learning. The former reinforces a learner's correct behaviors while the latter punishes one's incorrect behaviors (Kluger & DeNisi, 1996).

The concept of feedback is later brought into the specific field of L2 education where the potential role of teacher feedback is often associated with language instruction and perceived differently by teachers employing different language teaching approaches (Polio, Gass, & Chapin, 2006). For example, since the traditional grammar-translation method has its philosophical roots in structuralism and behaviorism, a grammar-translation teacher typically devotes a great deal of attention to students' accuracy in L2 and emphasizes the role of teacher feedback as correcting linguistic errors produced by language learners (Lyster & Saito, 2010). As mentioned in the previous section 2.2.1, this type of teacher feedback with its main corrective function is referred to as teacher CF and becomes an important topic in second and foreign language educational research. According to Ellis (2009a), the high place of CF is probably due to its potential role as an instructional tool for language acquisition. Furthermore, the focus on error correction is influenced by the fact that "the meticulous standards of accuracy…was a prerequisite for passing the increasing number of formal written examinations that grew up during the century" (Howatt, 1984, p. 132), which is still the reality in most EFL learning contexts. With regard to the interactional teaching approach, high priority is also attached to teacher feedback due to its interactional nature as a driving force to facilitate learner SLA, especially learner oral performance (Long, 1996; Mackey, Gass, & McDonough, 2000).

2.2.3 Teacher Feedback: Cognitive Perspective

Cognitivism emphasizes human information processing (Shuell, 1986) and in accordance with this theoretical position, SLA is referred to as a computational model that treats language acquisition as the end-product of processing language input and output (Lantolf, 1996). This indicates that the learning process is linear and teacher feedback activity begins with the act of teachers sending feedback information, followed by the learner receiving and decoding that information and finalizing it in learning outcomes.

The cognitive accounts of teacher feedback in L2 learning rest on relevant SLA theories, in particular the Interaction Hypothesis (Long, 1983, 1996), the Noticing Hypothesis (Schmidt, 1990, 2001), and the Output Hypothesis (Swain, 1995). This cognitive strand of research has offered important insights regarding the significant role of teacher feedback on learners' erroneous utterances during the interaction. Such feedback allows L2 learners to understand that their utterances were problematic (van Beuningen, 2010). Teacher feedback delivered during negotiated interaction can help direct L2 learners' attention toward the mismatches between what they produce (i.e., interlanguage forms) and what native speakers produce (i.e., target input). Furthermore, L2 learners must consciously notice input so that input can be converted into the intake. This process is referred to as noticing the gap in Schmidt's Noticing Hypothesis (Schmidt, 1990, 2001). Gass and Varonis (1994) argued that noticing a gap may lead to grammar construction, thus facilitating the development of L2. Another interactional process that can result from teacher CF is known as modified output which was argued by Swain (1995) for being helpful in L2 learning. Learners' output production has the ability to push learners to notice the gaps and problems in their interlanguage forms and reformulate the original utterances to the more target-like ones. To sum up, input, output, and interaction cannot be separated in L2 teaching and learning. On the one hand, learners make progress by producing language output; on the other hand, teacher feedback as a means of interaction provides the opportunity for negotiated interaction and becomes comprehensible input to facilitate the development of L2.

However, teacher feedback research using the cognitive perspective has been increasingly criticized for its limited research scope and depth, which concerns establishing a taxonomy of CF strategies and using (quasi-) experiments to examine the effectiveness of different teacher CF strategies (Goldstein, 2006; Lee, 2014). Such findings of cognitive-oriented research are also criticized for their remoteness from real classroom practices and may not lend themselves well to authentic pedagogical contexts where there is a host of contextual, social, and individual factors interacting with each other (Storch, 2010). Therefore, there is a need to investigate the complexity of teacher feedback by integrating cognitive and social factors.

2.2.4 Teacher Feedback: Sociocognitive Perspective

As argued by Ellis (2010b), teacher feedback is multifaceted and its full account requires "a sociocognitive orientation that combines the cognitive, social, and psychological dimensions" (p. 152). In this study, the sociocognitive perspective is conceptualized as a broad theoretical lens that jointly integrates the cognitive and the social. This section attempts to capture the interplay between the cognitive and contextual aspects of teacher feedback. On the one hand, language teachers' cognitions about providing feedback can stand alone but are mediated by specific contexts. On the other hand, language learners' cognitive engagement with teacher feedback can be not only analyzed separately from the behavioral and affective engagement, but also viewed as being embodied and embedded in multi-layered contexts and interacting with characteristics of individual language learners. The remainder of this section proceeds to review one specific theoretical conceptualization (i.e., Vygotsky's sociocultural theory) within the broad sociocognitive perspective on L2 learning.

The sociocultural theory (SCT) has its origins in the works of the Russian psychologist L.S. Vygotsky and the tradition of Russian cultural-historical psychology. Unlike traditional cognitive approaches to learning, SCT highlighted that "the social dimension of consciousness (i.e., all mental processes) is primary in time and fact. The individual dimension of consciousness is derivative and secondary" (Vygotsky, 1979, p. 30). Vygotsky proposed that by employing cultural artifacts (e.g., language, logic, and literacy), humans can take voluntary control over their consciousness. The role of these artifacts is to mediate between an individual and the environment (Lantolf & Thorne, 2007). Although not originally intended as a theory of L2 learning, SCT has inspired applied linguistics research and enriched the understanding of SLA and L2 education in important ways. One of the major claims of SCT is that language learning occurs not through interaction but during interaction and participation, which combines the social context and individual language acquisition (Ellis, 2000). In other words, learning itself is manifest in social interaction with others rather than in an individual learner's mind. From this SCT perspective, teacher feedback is viewed as a form of social interaction believed to facilitate or mediate the language learning process.

In this study, several SCT concepts (e.g., zone of proximal development, scaffolding, and mediation) are of particular relevance to our understanding of teacher feedback in the field of L2 education. Many SLA researchers have investigated language learners' linguistic development in the zone of proximal development (ZPD), probably the most-known Vygotskian concept. It refers to "the distance between the actual developmental level determined by independent problem-solving and the higher level of potential development determined through problem solving in collaboration with more capable peers or seniors" (Vygotsky, 1978, p. 86); that is, learning causes a variety of internal developmental functions that can only be activated when the language learner is interacting with his or her language teacher and/or peers in the environment. For example, developmental process can occur as the outcome of the language learner's participation in specific linguistic and cultural settings such as getting involved in interactions within language classrooms, peer activities, collaboration tasks, etc. This internalization process is referred to as an appropriation in SCT and later becomes "part of the learner's independent developmental achievement" (Vygotsky, 1978, p. 90).

From this perspective, a language teacher's feedback has the potential to achieve the transition from interpsychological functions (i.e., between the learner and teacher) to intrapsychological functions (i.e., inside the learner) and help language learners to move from stages of other regulation to self-regulation when they are engaged in certain language tasks. Since the major pedagogical implications of ZPD are its stress on scaffolding and social interaction, teacher feedback is important for providing learners with the choices central to new language and literacy skills and assisting learners in progressing toward the more advanced level of language learning and task performance within their ZPD.

The SCT also views learning as a mediated social practice and stresses the importance of sociocultural contexts in interpreting human learning behaviors. Accordingly, teacher feedback is a form of social action designed to accomplish educational goals, and like other acts of human communication, it occurs in particular sociocultural, interpersonal, and institutional contexts (K. Hyland & F. Hyland, 2006a). They defined context as "a frame that surrounds feedback and provides resources for its appropriate interpretation" (p. 10). It is necessary to go beyond the act of teacher feedback *per se* and to consider the contextual factors that may influence teachers' feedback options and student reactions. Specifically, the SCT perspective suggests that we should take into account the wider sociocultural context (e.g., the Chinese EFL context in this study), the immediate context of giving feedback (e.g., the delivery mode and focus of teacher feedback), and the interpersonal context (e.g., teacher-student relationships in the situated process of giving and receiving feedback).

2.2.5 Teacher Feedback: Social Constructive Perspective

Another theoretical perspective that adopts the social orientation is referred to as social constructivism. Unlike the SCT which emphasizes "the interdependence of the social and individual processes in the co-construction of knowledge" (Palincsar, 1998, p. 348), social constructivism focuses on how learners are actively engaged in constructing their knowledge (Jonassen, 1991). This perspective indicates that prior knowledge is the starting point for learning. Learning occurs by studying multiple examples, during which teachers guide this process and student peers are involved in the learning through collaboration. Accordingly, the feedback process starts with learners at a beginning stage in which multiple peers and teachers give feedback. Then, because the learning is continuous, learners move to another stage which becomes a new beginning stage.

Hattie and Timperley (2007) synthesized a model of feedback that is reasoned from social constructivism. Figure 2.1 (cited form Hattie & Timperley, 2007, p. 87) presents the model in which feedback can be conceptualized. According to this model, feedback is provided to close the learning gap between the current level of understanding and performance and a desired learning goal. This model recognizes the active role of learners in the feedback process. Teacher feedback, although provided by teachers directly, can also be sought by the learners on purpose. As stated by Brookhart (2008), feedback together with learners' self-regulation helps learners to decide on future learning goals, and to devise and employ specific strategies to reach those goals. There are many possible ways for students to eliminate the gap, including increasing their learning efforts, developing effective error detection skills, or simply abandoning the learning goals. There are also multiple ways in which teachers can assist in reducing the gap between actual performance and desired goal attainment. These include providing and clarifying learning goals, assisting students to reach these goals through the delivery of feedback, or creating a learning environment in which students develop self-regulation and error detection skills.

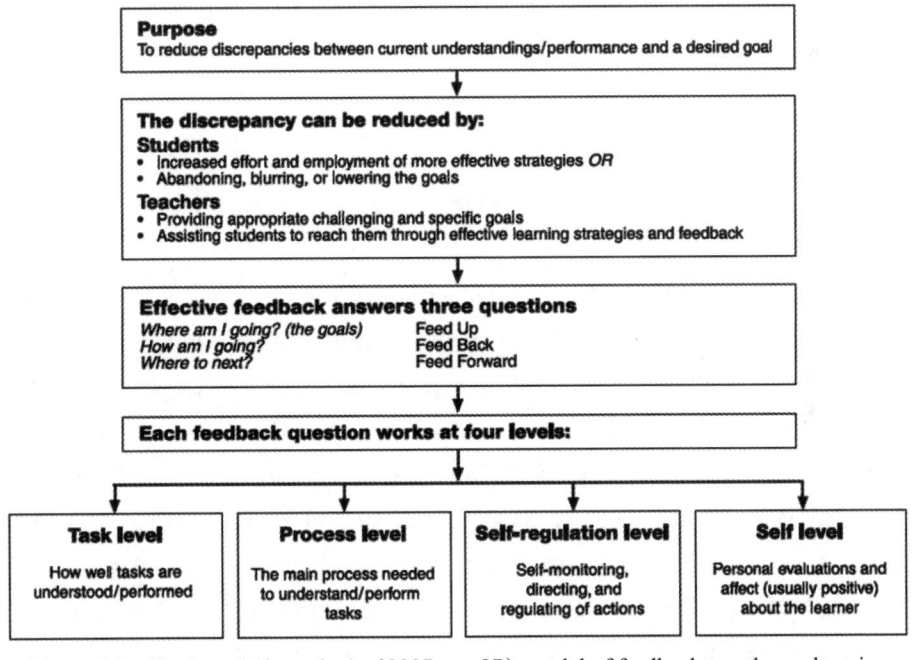

```
┌─────────────────────────────────────────────────────────────────────┐
│ Purpose                                                             │
│ To reduce discrepancies between current understandings/performance  │
│ and a desired goal                                                  │
└─────────────────────────────────────────────────────────────────────┘
                                    ↓
┌─────────────────────────────────────────────────────────────────────┐
│ The discrepancy can be reduced by:                                  │
│ Students                                                            │
│  • Increased effort and employment of more effective strategies OR  │
│  • Abandoning, blurring, or lowering the goals                      │
│ Teachers                                                            │
│  • Providing appropriate challenging and specific goals             │
│  • Assisting students to reach them through effective learning      │
│    strategies and feedback                                          │
└─────────────────────────────────────────────────────────────────────┘
                                    ↓
┌─────────────────────────────────────────────────────────────────────┐
│ Effective feedback answers three questions                          │
│ Where am I going? (the goals)     Feed Up                           │
│ How am I going?                   Feed Back                         │
│ Where to next?                    Feed Forward                      │
└─────────────────────────────────────────────────────────────────────┘
                                    ↓
┌─────────────────────────────────────────────────────────────────────┐
│ Each feedback question works at four levels:                        │
└─────────────────────────────────────────────────────────────────────┘
         ↓             ↓                   ↓                  ↓
┌─────────────┐ ┌─────────────┐ ┌───────────────────┐ ┌──────────────┐
│ Task level  │ │Process level│ │Self-regulation    │ │ Self level   │
│             │ │             │ │level              │ │              │
│How well     │ │The main     │ │Self-monitoring,   │ │Personal      │
│tasks are    │ │process      │ │directing, and     │ │evaluations   │
│understood/  │ │needed to    │ │regulating of      │ │and affect    │
│performed    │ │understand/  │ │actions            │ │(usually      │
│             │ │perform tasks│ │                   │ │positive)     │
│             │ │             │ │                   │ │about the     │
│             │ │             │ │                   │ │learner       │
└─────────────┘ └─────────────┘ └───────────────────┘ └──────────────┘
```

Figure 2.1 Hattie and Timperley's (2007, p. 87) model of feedback to enhance learning

To conclude, this study adopts a multi-dimensional theoretical perspective in understanding teacher feedback, L2 learning and task-based oral presentation performance. In order to further understand the theoretical perspectives used in this study, the researcher illustrates the role played by one particular form of teacher feedback, i.e., teacher CF in L2 learning and task performance. Based on a cognitive view, L2 learning is conceived of as something occurring inside the learner's head, and teacher CF facilitates learner acquisition of L2 by activating internal mental mechanisms (e.g., attention and rehearsal) which make the acquisition possible. Through a SCT lens, L2 learning is not perceived as an individual-based process but one shared between the learner and his/her teacher, and CF is given by the teacher to guide the learner to the next developmental stage (i.e., ZPD) in which learning outcomes are achieved. Ellis (2009, p. 13) illustrated this process with an example:

> S: oh my God, it is too expensive, I pay only 10 dollars
> T: I pay?
> S2: okay let's go
> T: I pay or I'LL pay? I will pay. I'll
> S: I'll. I'll pay only 10 dollars.

In the CF episode above, the student failed to use the future tense *I'll* and the teacher attempted to draw the student's attention by repeating his/her error (i.e., I pay) with a rising tone. Although another student, S2, carried on the conversation with attention paid to meaning, the teacher still focused on the linguistic form and used an explicit CF strategy — directly providing the student with correct verb tense (i.e., I'll pay). The student then successfully repaired his/her error by producing a correct version of the original sentence. According to Ellis (2009), this teacher CF episode "lasted only a few seconds but within this brief period the teacher was able to fine-tune her feedback to the learner's ZPD" (p. 13).

From the social constructive perspective, particularly Hattie and Timperley's (2007) model of feedback, teacher CF concerns "correctness, neatness, behavior, or some other criterion related to task accomplishment" (p. 91). If CF is related to the process level and/or self-regulation level, it can be powerful in enhancing learning of new skills or tasks because in this case CF contains information about progress or the next step. In contrast, if CF failed to result in a reduction in the discrepancy between current understanding and learning goal, it is least effective because students may claim "various attributions that reduce effort and engagement" (p. 89).

As illustrated above, the three theoretical stances complement each other and inform the current study by investigating both the cognitive and social aspects of L2 learning and discussing the relationship between individuals and contexts. The insights from cognitive theories of language learning highlight the mental mechanisms involved in internalizing teacher feedback information. The sociocognitive perspective highlights the importance of attuning scaffolding (by means of teacher feedback) to learners' developmental levels so as to continuously extend their ZPD. The social constructive perspective provides insights regarding a language teacher's mediational role in successful language learning by providing feedback, as well as the significant role of learner agency in explaining and reducing gaps between the current and expected levels of learning.

2.3 Empirical Studies on Teacher Feedback in L2 Education

In this section, this study presents a critical synthesis of the findings produced by empirical work to provide a comprehensive understanding of teacher feedback in the field of L2 education. Empirical findings are reported in respect of the following: teacher feedback practices, teacher cognitions about feedback provision, student perspectives on teacher feedback, student engagement with teacher feedback, effects of teacher feedback, context and teacher feedback, and teacher feedback on oral tasks.

2.3.1 Teacher Feedback Practices: Focus, Function, and Strategies

2.3.1.1 The Focus of Teacher Feedback

The focus of teacher feedback—whether on linguistic forms (e.g., grammar and spelling), contents (e.g., ideas and organization), or both has received considerable attention in L2 educational research. When it comes to L2 writing, some earlier studies of teacher feedback showed that teachers tended to focus heavily on surface-level features such as grammatical errors over contents in L2 writing classrooms (e.g., Kepner, 1991; Zamel, 1985). Although L2 learners do need to pay attention to the problematic aspects of their writing output, as supported by the Noticing Hypothesis (Schmidt, 1990), this feedback practice regards writing as an end-product and teachers tend to see themselves as language editors rather than writing instructors. With the advent of the process approach to L2 writing instruction, research evidence has suggested that teachers have begun to shift their feedback focus from linguistic forms to other issues like organization and ideas (e.g., Ferris, 1997; Ferris, Pezone, Tade, & Tinti, 1997; Saito, 1994). This is particularly the case of ESL/EFL academic writing which requires students whose first language is not English to possess not only language proficiency but also relevant genre knowledge and writing skills. Bitchener, Basturkmen, and East (2010) conducted an exploratory study to investigate the focus of supervisor feedback to thesis/dissertation students. They argued for a sociocultural perspective to supervisor feedback as it helps students organize their theses/dissertations with the consistency and balance required by academic communities and become independent researchers and writers. Based on self-report data, they conducted interviews and issued questionnaires to 35 supervisors at six New Zealand universities and found that feedback was given on five aspects (see Table 2.2) of student thesis writing. It can be seen that supervisors did not merely perceive themselves as "error hunters or correctors" to enhance students' linguistic proficiency; instead they intended to be "knowledge builders" who provide "discourse feedback at the paragraph level, and feedback on what is expected and required for the different part-genres of a thesis" (Bitchener, Basturkmen, & East, 2010, p. 95). In their subsequent study, Basturkmen, East, and Bitchener (2014) reported similar research findings by conducting a direct textual analysis of supervisory written feedback. It was found that supervisors across all three disciplinary areas (i.e., Humanities, Sciences/Mathematics and Commerce) provided written feedback on the same aspects of writing: content, requirements, cohesion/coherence and linguistic accuracy.

Table 2.2   Bitchener, Basturkmen, and East's (2010) focus of supervisory written feedback

Main category	Sub-category	Example
Content knowledge	the accuracy, completeness and relevance of content presented	gaps in literature, significance of study, justification or explanation of arguments
Genre knowledge	the functions of different parts of an academic thesis	structure and organization of and within part-genres, part/whole balance
Rhetorical structure and organization	the organization of content within chapters and sections	argument construction such as logic in students' building of arguments, linking of ideas, using bullet points and hedging
Argument development	writing coherence and cohesion	sectional links such as using initial markers and meta-texts
Linguistic accuracy and appropriateness	accuracy in lexis and syntax, appropriateness of vocabulary choice	grammatical and lexical errors, academic style, voice and stance

With regard to students' oral communication, a great many of oral feedback studies in SLA literature have generated meaningful insights about two issues: (i) whether oral CF should be unfocused or focused and (ii) what oral linguistic errors should be focused on during correction. Dealing with the first issue, both language teachers and SLA researchers are challenged by the selection of errors to be treated in error correction. Focused oral CF describes a common practice where a limited number of pre-selected linguistic forms are corrected in students' oral production, whereas unfocused oral CF entails a comprehensive or extensive approach to addressing all or most of errors students commit while speaking (Ellis, 2009). It is argued that oral CF given on one or a limited number of errors, namely the focused approach, is easy to implement in practice, because language teachers in classroom instruction often do not have time to ascertain and treat all of students' problematic forms in speech (Harmer, 1983) and SLA researchers in experimental studies need to pre-select several error categories to target so as to design appropriate testing instruments (Lyster, 2004).

Addressing the second issue, both (quasi-) experimental studies in laboratory settings and classroom-based observational studies have extensively investigated the types of learner errors that teacher oral CF generally target. For example, case studies such as Basturkmen, Loewen, and Ellis (2004) described three ESL teachers' oral CF in the whole class setting of intermediate-level communicative lessons; the results suggested that teachers prioritized oral errors related to vocabulary and grammar. In another study on ESL teachers' oral CF, Junqueira and Kim (2013) compared the practices of a novice and an experienced teacher and found that the latter's oral CF was more balanced in terms of linguistic target, i.e., pronunciation (40%), followed closely by grammar (32.5%) and vocabulary (25%). On the other hand, the novice teacher's oral CF focused mainly on phonological errors (72.8%), followed by grammatical and lexical errors (21.8% and 1.8% respectively). To be more specific, Table 2.3 shows examples of the linguistic targets that teacher oral CF research mostly focused on. While the research findings above have generated insights into what kinds of oral errors (grammar, vocabulary, or pronunciation) L2 teachers focus on in teacher-fronted and form-focused speaking activities, relatively little is known about how teachers formulate their feedback in terms of its focus on student-centered and meaning-based EFL oral presectations. It is worth noting that oral presentations are by no means like other oral production tasks (such as grammatical judgment tasks and narrative-retelling tasks) which are pedagogically designed to assess students' knowledge of the target L2. As aforementioned in section 1.4, EFL tasks of oral presentations address the interrelatedness of knowledge, skills, and attitudes of both English language and subject content, and therefore which aspect (s) of oral presentations focused on in EFL teachers' feedback have been called into question.

Table 2.3　　　　　　　　Example of linguistic targets of oral CF studies

Linguistic targets	Target forms	Key studies
Grammatical targets	question forms	Mackey & Philp (1998), Mackey & Oliver (2002), Loewen & Nabei (2007), Yang & Lyster (2010)
	past tense -*ed* and irregular past tense	Adams (2007), Ellis (2007), Mackey (2006)
	passive forms	Algarawi (2010)
	comparative -*er*	Ellis (2007)
	articles *a*, *an*, *the*	Sheen (2007)
	possessive determiners	Ammar & Spada (2006)
	plurals	Mackey (2006)
Lexical targets	New lexical items	Ellis & He (1999), Dilans (2010)
Phonological targets	the alveolar /ɹ/	Saito & Lyster (2012a)
	the low front vowel /ae/	Saito & Lyster (2012b)
Pragmatic targets	speech act of requests	Takimoto (2006) Koike & Pearson (2005)
	speech act of refusals	Nipaspong & Chinokul (2010)

2.3.1.2　The Function of Teacher Feedback

Apart from making decisions upon what to focus on, teachers also seek to establish relationships with students by means of giving feedback. Through the SCT lens, researchers have paid attention to the interactive aspects of teacher feedback and focused on the roles of the pragmatic and interpersonal in constructing teacher feedback. A number of studies have demonstrated that teacher feedback can be categorized based on its varying pedagogical, pragmatic, and interpersonal functions in classroom instruction. In Ferris et al.'s (1997) text analysis of ESL teacher written commentary, they summarized three main types of teacher comments based on their pragmatic functions, including "directives (i.e., ask for information, make suggestion/request and give information), grammar/mechanics, and positive comments" (p. 163). Along the same line, Kumar and Stracke (2007) and Stracke and Kumar (2010) regarded feedback giving and receiving as realizing three fundamental functions of speech between human interaction and they classified doctoral supervisory feedback into three main categories based on an analysis of pragmatic functions: referential, directive, and expressive functions. Table 2.4 (cited from Kumar & Stracke, 2007, p. 464) specifies these three functions with regard to collected data of written feedback on a PhD thesis. Data analysis of 289 in-text feedback and overall feedback revealed that the referential function (45%) was predominant in the feedback, which was followed by the directive (27.7%) and expressive (27.3%) functions. However, Kumar and Stracke (2007) stated that it was the expressive function (criticism and opinion in particular) that provided most opportunities for a self-regulated learning experience and further development during the doctoral journey. They thought that negative comments (criticism) were in fact constructive on the part of teachers because criticism could lead to substantial text revisions.

Table 2.4   Kumar and Stracke's (2007, p. 464) categorization of feedback according to speech functions

Main category	Sub-category	Example
Referential	Editorial Organization Content	*Please get rid of spaces.* *This does not belong in the literature review.* *Are you sure you can make such a claim?*
Directive	Suggestion Question Instruction	*Maybe this is not necessary.* *Whose term is this?* *Please clarify.*
Expressive	Praise Criticism Opinion	*Good, nice example.* *This table…does not add to the text.* *I would be interested to explore what triggered this.*

Similar reflections were also made by F. Hyland and K. Hyland (2001), who pointed out that some of the categories identified in Ferris et al.'s (1997) study (e.g., providing information, making a request, and making grammar/mechanics comments) were "essentially means of praising, criticizing and suggesting" (p. 191). They argued for the positive-negative feedback valence and considered teacher feedback in terms of three functions as praise, criticism, and suggestion. Specifically, praise acknowledges students' work by identifying their learning strengths, reinforces their behaviors, and builds a close and supportive teacher-student relationship, whereas criticism negatively expresses dissatisfaction about students' work and thus undermines their motivation and self-confidence. Suggestion (also called constructive criticism), unlike blunt criticism, is more positive-oriented and usually entails a proposal for future learning improvement. In their case study with two ESL teachers, F. Hyland and K. Hyland (2001) found that praise (44%) was the most frequently adopted function in teachers' feedback practices, but this was often used to mitigate the force of criticism rather than simply responding to good work. Overall, the selection of praise, criticism, and suggestion as the main functions of teacher feedback in this study is in line with the informational, pedagogic, and interpersonal roles of feedback suggested by the pertinent educational literature (e.g., Burnett, 2002; Hyland, 2000).

2.3.1.3 The Strategies of Teacher Feedback

Strategies are always present in classrooms, and it is often teachers who determine the direction toward which students are headed by choosing a strategy they assume to provide the best learning outcome. Many classroom observational studies have investigated teacher strategy use in correcting L2 students' oral and written errors (e.g., Ellis, 2009b; Lightbown & Spada, 1999; Lyster & Ranta, 1997). Based on these studies, Lyster and Saito (2010) presented a well-known classification of oral CF strategies: explicit correction, recasts, and prompts (i.e., elicitation, metalinguistic clue, clarification request, and repetition). On the one hand, explicit correction and recasts both provide students with target-like reformulations of their erroneous utterances. On the other hand, prompts include the use of various signals to push students to conduct self-correction. Table 2.5 presents these oral CF strategies with examples cited from Lightbown and Spada (1999, p. 104-105). One particular type of oral CF strategies merits our attention, namely recasts. Lyster and Ranta (1997) observed that L2 teachers sometimes translated the target L2 forms into their counterparts in first language (L1) when giving recasts to students. Similar observations about the use of L1 in oral CF during L2 classroom instruction have been made by Uddin (2021). He reported that teachers extensively used the strategy of accompanying L2-recasts with L1-metalinguistic clues and this practice led to the most learner uptake.

Table 2.5   A classification of oral CF strategies according to Lyster and Saito (2010)

Feedback strategy	Description	Example
Explicit correction	The teacher explicitly indicates that the student's utterance was incorrect, and meanwhile provides the correct form.	S: The dog run fastly. T: 'Fastly' doesn't exist. *'Fast' does not take –ly*. That's why I picked 'quickly.'
Recast	The teacher implicitly reformulates all or part of the student's utterance, minus the error.	S: Why you don't like Marc? T: Why *don't you like* Marc?
Elicitation	The teacher directly elicits a reformulation from the student by asking questions such as "*How do we say X in English*"? or by pausing to allow the student to fill in the blank such as "*It's a …*", or by asking the student to reformulate his or her utterance.	S: My father cleans the plate. T: *Excuse me, he cleans the ???*
Metalinguistic clue	The teacher poses questions or provides comments related to the well-formedness of the student's utterance, generally by means of providing metalanguage about the nature of errors.	S: We look at the people yesterday. T: *What's the ending we put on verbs when we talk about the past?*
Clarification request	The teacher uses phrases like "*Pardon me*" and "*I don't understand*", which follow the learner's errors to indicate the ill-formedness of the learner utterance; and meanwhile a reformulation is required on the learner's part.	T: How often do you wash the dishes? S: Fourteen. T: *Excuse me?*
Repetition	The teacher repeats the student's erroneous utterance with a rising intonation to highlight the error in most cases.	S: We is… T: *We is?* But it's two people, right?

Apart from the well-defined strategies employed by L2 teachers when correcting learners' oral errors, empirical evidence has demonstrated that L2 teachers provided other cues that may benefit learner uptake of feedback information. Brookhart (2008) proposed that teacher feedback strategies can also vary in four broad dimensions: timing, amount, audience, and mode. Regarding the timing, teachers can immediately respond to students' oral production or give delayed feedback until later. A fine-grained category for the timing of oral CF was developed by Rahimi and Zhang (2015, p. 118): (i) "immediately after errors occur even if it interrupts oral production", (ii) "right at the end of students' oral production", (iii) "after the activities end", and (iv) "at the conclusion of class". Considering the amount, teachers can provide feedback on selected or important learning targets or give comprehensive feedback covering all aspects of student performance. As for the audience, feedback can be addressed to either the individual student about the specifics of his or her performance, or the group (and even the whole class) for saving time and demonstration purposes.

With regard to the mode of oral feedback, teachers can accompany their verbal feedback with a range of nonverbal behaviors (such as facial expressions and body postures) which are acknowledged to be equally important for human communication (Goldin-Meadow, 1999). Being co-expressive with speech, nonverbal behavior either parallels speech (when it expresses the same meaning) or complements speech (when it conveys information in the speaker's mind not in his or her speech), as stated by Stam (2006). Only a few L2 studies have examined the nonverbal components of teacher feedback. Two earlier small-scale studies by Davies (2006) and Faraco and Kida (2008) only focused on the roles of gesture and gaze during feedback and classroom interaction. More recently, Wang and Loewen (2016) analyzed eight ESL teachers' nonverbal behaviors based on classroom observations and found that nonverbal behaviors took up 60.2% of the time in the teachers' oral CF, in which head movements like head nodding and shaking, and gestures of pointing at an artifact or a person most frequently occurred.

2.3.2 Teacher Cognitions about Feedback Provision

Following Borg (2006), language teacher cognition in this study is conceptualized as what teachers think, know, and believe, which has traditionally been described by such theoretical constructs as teacher belief, perception, knowledge, decision-making, attitude, and rationale. The particular term "teacher cognition" is selected in this study because it serves as an umbrella term that is able to, according to Borg (2006), "embrace the complexity of teachers' mental lives" (p. 50). For the purpose of this study, two particular points are important. First, teacher cognition can powerfully dispose and guide L2 teachers' thinking and behaviors in classroom practices. Second, teacher cognition is viewed as a sociocultural tool of mind mediating activity, which is interrelated with the contexts and experiences of L2 teachers (Barcelos, 2003). Understanding L2 teachers' cognitions about feedback practices is thus subject to the influence of sociocultural and contextual factors.

A handful of studies have focused on the specific CF beliefs and attitudes held by language teachers (e.g., Mori, 2011; Roothooft, 2014). For example, informed by prior language learning and teaching experiences as well as the knowledge of the Japanese context of schooling, the two EFL teachers in Mori's (2011) case study held teaching beliefs about developing university-level students' self-confidence, independence, and oral communicative abilities. Consequently, their feedback practices were characterized by implicitness; in other words, the teachers did not attempt to make overt verbal error correction. Several comparative studies were also conducted to examine the differences in novice and experienced teachers' cognitions and yielded contrasting findings on teachers' CF beliefs. For example, Junqueira and Kim (2013) found that both novice and experienced teachers shared similar oral CF beliefs in focusing on pronunciation and grammar, as well as the communication action of engaging in conversations with students. However, different perceptions were reported between two groups of novice and veteran teachers who were surveyed about the necessity, types of CF, and its timing when they taught English oral communication (Rahimi & Zhang, 2015). The results showed that experienced teachers drew on classroom teaching experience and perceived that there was no fit-for-all approach to error correction, whereas novice teachers believed that oral CF at the end of classroom activities was the most effective, regardless of the diversity of contextual variables such as error types, task types, etc. Overall, there is a general tendency for EFL teachers not to error correct durning the oral interaction for fear of interrupting flow of communication and damaging students' emotional well-being.

Meanwhile, there is also research indicating that teachers' stated beliefs are an unreliable guide to their actual feedback practices (Hattie & Yates, 2014). Basturkmen (2012) explained that this is due to the fact that teacher feedback, particularly oral CF, is an unplanned aspect of classroom instruction, for which teachers tend to depend on "automatic and generally unexamined behaviors" (p. 291). Moreover, an important factor accounting for such discrepancies is the conflict between language teachers' wish to promote EFL students' linguistic competence and the desire to enhance their confidence in speaking (Mori, 2011). Other studies highlighted a variety of learner variables and contextual constraints in creating inconsistencies between teachers' stated feedback beliefs and actual practices, including learners' cognitive styles and personalities (Mori, 2002; Yoshida, 2008), attitudes toward performance assessment (Lee, Leong, & Song, 2017), linguistic knowledge and communicative abilities (Mori, 2002, 2011), instructional foci, time constraints, and institutional requirements (Lee, 2009; Lee, Leong, & Song, 2017; Roothooft, 2014). To sum up, it appears that L2 teachers' cognitions are central to determining their actual feedback practices to students and yet subject to the interaction and mediation between a host of the teacher, student, and contextual factors.

2.3.3 Student Perspectives on Teacher Feedback

L2 students' perspectives on teacher feedback have been widely researched. Earlier survey studies indicated that ESL students expected, welcomed, and showed a preference for teacher written CF over other forms of feedback like peer feedback and self-evaluation (e.g., Leki, 1991; Ferris & Roberts, 2001; Saito, 1994). Similar results were also reported in Zhang and Rahimi's (2014) study on EFL learners who, regardless of anxiety level, favored receiving frequent teacher oral CF when they were made aware of the purpose, significance, and types of oral CF. However, students' specific preferences with regard to CF strategies are influenced by their beliefs and previous learning experience, as well as the surrounding context. For example, although Hong Kong EFL secondary students preferred direct written CF (Lee, 2008b), some ESL university students in Chandler's (2003) study favored indirect written CF which was found to be more fulfilling by allowing them to take control and explore the correct answers by themselves.

Empirical findings have also shown that students' attitudinal responses toward teacher feedback are mixed and vary across individuals. For example, many high school ESL and foreign language students in Jean and Simard's (2011) questionnaire study regarded grammar feedback (both oral and written) to be necessary but boring. Apart from negative attitudes, there are also some encouraging results. Although the experiences of disappointment were mostly reported among Hong Kong secondary school students, some students also indicated feelings of happiness (Lee, 2004, 2008b). Since the student participants of the questionnaire studies above differed in age, background, proficiency level, etc., and studied in different educational contexts, learner and contextual factors may play a role in influencing students' perspectives on teacher feedback. Case studies have the advantage of demonstrating the complexities of individual student's perceptions of and emotional responses to teacher feedback. For instance, some case studies have demonstrated that individual students may feel anxious (Hyland, 1998), self-confident (Storch & Wigglesworth, 2010), or even indifferent (Lee, 2011) when teachers correct their linguistic errors.

2.3.4 Effects of Teacher Feedback

There is a great number of empirical studies focusing on the effects of teacher feedback, particularly teacher oral CF on the acquisition of L2 structures and written CF on text revisions of L2 writing. SLA researchers are primarily concerned with the effects that teacher oral CF strategies have on learner acquisition of particular linguistic features by using experimental or quasi-experimental research designs (Lyster, Saito, & Sato, 2013). For instance, in a Japanese EFL context, Loewen and Nabei (2007) compared three patterns of teacher oral CF (i.e., recasts, clarification requests, and metalinguistic feedback) provided during L2 question formation and found that all treatment groups significantly outperformed the control group. Similarly, the acquisitional value of oral CF has also been found on other grammatical, lexical, and phonological features such as regular and irregular past tense forms (Yang & Lyster, 2010), English articles (Sheen, 2007), and the English phoneme /ɹ/ (Saito & Lyster, 2012a).

In the field of L2 writing, much research is concerned with how teacher written CF can help students improve the overall effectiveness of their composition writing. This body of work usually follows a response-revision study design and examines the effects of written CF in the contexts of single- and multiple-draft classrooms, that is, on the same paper and new pieces of writing (Ferris, 2010). Another strand of L2 writing research relates to investigating the influence of teacher written comments, as one form of feedback on student multiple-drafts. For instance, Ferris (1997) examined and compared over 1600 teacher comments on 47 ESL university students' first and second drafts of papers, and found that text-end comments on grammar and marginal comments requesting information appeared to contribute to the most substantive revisions. Less influential were question or statement comment types that provided information to students. Using Hattie and Timperley's (2007) classification of feedback focus mentioned in section 2.2.5, Arts, Jaspers, and Brinke (2016) suggested that written comments formulated on the process level or self-regulation level appeared more difficult for the students to repair than comments at the task level. These studies showed that most teacher comments appeared to be used by students for revision of their writing, but the characteristics of written comments can influence the extent to which students make revisions.

2.3.5 Student Engagement with Teacher Feedback

Ellis (2010a) defined engagement as "how learners respond to the feedback they receive" (p. 342). In his componential framework for investigating CF (see Figure 2.2, cited from Ellis, 2010a, p. 337), Ellis (2010a) identified the variables and aspects that CF research has addressed and investigated. In his own words, this framework is "intended not so much as a theory of CF but as a heuristic that can inform research" (Ellis, 2010a, p. 337). There are mainly four components which can become the object of investigation. In the first place, a substantial amount of both oral and written CF research has examined the strategies that can be used to correct L2 errors (e.g., the different types of CF and CF timing) and their effectiveness on learner acquisition of target L2 linguistic structures. Moreover, a great number of studies have also explored the learner factors (e.g., learner age and L2 proficiency) and contextual factors (e.g., immersion and L2 classroom settings), as well as the mediating effects that these factors exert on learning outcomes in terms of learner interlanguage development. As illustrated in Figure 2.2, although the choice of how CF is implemented and the impact of learner and contextual factors as mediating variables are significant in determining the effects of CF, neither of these two components seems to be as critical as learner engagement with CF. Ellis (2010a) explained this was because if learners failed to notice and use the CF, it will have limited impact on their acquisition of the target L2 structures. In other words, learner engagement plays an important role in the CF mechanism by connecting the provision of teacher CF with learning outcomes. He further suggested that the investigation of learner engagement can be approached from three perspectives: the cognitive, behavioral, and affective perspectives. The cognitive perspective relates to "how learners attend to the CF they receive" (Ellis, 2010a, p. 342); the behavioral perspective focuses on learners' uptake after oral corrections or revisions of their written texts; the affective perspective pertains to learners' emotional and attitudinal responses (e.g., dislike and anxiety) to the CF.

  Very few empirical studies have been undertaken to explore the three perspectives of learner engagement with teacher feedback in the above. Han and Hyland (2015) reported on a naturalistic case study involving four Chinese university EFL students to explore how they cognitively, behaviorally, and affectively engaged with teacher written CF. In this study, the analysis of multiple sources of data (including interviews, stimulated recalls, written texts, and teacher-student conferences) showed that the four EFL students implemented different cognitive operations in the processing stage, used external resources to generate revision operations (e.g., dictionaries), and expressed both positive and negative feelings toward error correction. This study also demonstrated the complexity of learner engagement with written CF, which is mediated by individual learners' learning goals, beliefs, and experiences about written CF and L2 writing, as well as the interactional context in which feedback is fine-tuned. Subsequently, in her doctoral dissertation, Han (2016) further investigated this phenomenon by expanding the number of student participants from four to six.

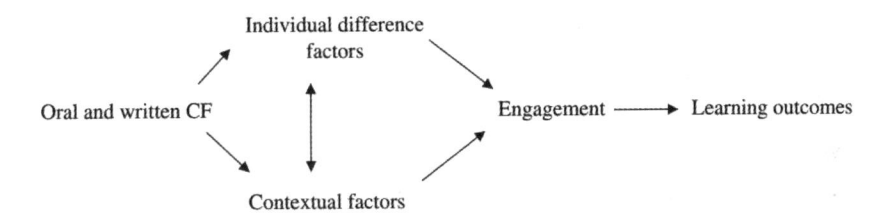

Figure 2.2 Ellis's (2010a, p. 337) componential framework for investigating CF

Another study in a Chinese EFL context was conducted by Zhang (2017), who reported a single-case study on student engagement with computer-generated feedback, known as automated writing evaluation (AWE) feedback. Specifically, the student's behavioral engagement was investigated by the number of draft submissions and the time spent on each writing draft. Affectively, the student indicated disappointment at low grades and showed excitement about high scores. With reference to cognitive engagement, the student was able to notice most of the errors in her writing and monitor the whole revision process with certain metacognitive operations. The findings from this study suggest that the three aspects of engagement are dynamically interconnected, as affective engagement with AWE feedback is often in line with action-taking and prompted by a mental process. More recently, Zheng and Yu (2018) extended the investigatory territory to Chinese lower-proficiency EFL students' engagement with teacher written CF and found that lower L2 proficiency can prevent students from extensive cognitive and behavioral engagement with teacher written CF.

To briefly sum up, learner engagement with teacher written CF consists of three dimensions: cognitive engagement, behavioral engagement, and affective engagement. Given the paucity of empirical studies (i) embracing a multi-dimensional theoretical perspective on learner engagement with feedback, and (ii) on engagement with teacher feedback beyond students' writing tasks, the depth and scope of the current L2 feedback research need to be expanded.

2.3.6 Context and Teacher Feedback

Teacher feedback as an important instructional tool is not provided and used in the void, but is embedded in complex sociocultural and educational contexts (Goldstein, 2006; K. Hyland & F. Hyland, 2006a, 2006b). The role of contextual factors in mediating teacher feedback has been recognized not only in cognitive-oriented research (Bitchener & Knoch, 2008; Ellis, 2010a; Ferris, 2010) but also in social-oriented research (K. Hyland & F. Hyland, 2006b; Lee, 2014; Storch, 2010). Since this present study incorporates both the cognitive and social aspects of teacher feedback and particularly the interaction between these two, it is important to view teacher practices of giving feedback and learner engagement with teacher feedback as being contextualized and situated in authentic classrooms. Put differently, the richness and complexity of the context should be taken into good account in the current investigation.

In general, context refers to "a frame that surrounds feedback and provides resources for its appropriate interpretation" (K. Hyland & F. Hyland, 2006a, p. 10). On the one hand, studies adopting a cognitive orientation toward teacher feedback have categorized context into two levels: the macro-level, that is, "the larger world that has an impact on participants' behaviors" (K. Hyland & F. Hyland, 2006a, p. 10), and the micro-level, that is, "the immediate interaction which they take place" (K. Hyland & F. Hyland, 2006a, p. 10). The macro-level context concerns the particular classroom setting and is often characterized as "immersion, foreign language (FL) and L2 settings" (Ellis, 2010a, p. 340). The micro-level context relates to the nature of the language activities and tasks in which the learners are participating when they receive teacher feedback, such as the characteristics of language tasks and pedagogical instruction (Bitchener, 2012).

On the other hand, feedback research that adopts the social orientation has provided a more fine-grained classification of context, which can provide better resources about the interpretation of teacher feedback within seemingly similar research settings. For example, although ESL and EFL settings differ in terms of students' learning motivations, goals, and available resources (Hedgcock & Lefkowitz, 1994), this distinction may fail to reflect the complexity and richness of a specific local classroom context, as EFL classroom contexts are not homogenous across countries and regions (e.g., Butler, 2015; Hu & McKay, 2012). In this study, context was conceptualized as a multi-layered one at the sociocultural, institutional, instructional, and interpersonal levels, in which teacher feedback is embedded and situated.

Sociocultural and institutional level of context. The influences of sociocultural and institutional contexts are extensively explored in Lee's (2008a, 2008b, 2015) feedback studies in the context of Hong Kong secondary schools which share many similarities to schools in the mainland of China, particularly in terms of their examination and assessment-oriented culture. Lee described the institutional context of Hong Kong schools as focusing on the learning product and test scores, which may possibly shape language learners' perspectives on teacher feedback.

Instructional level of context. The instructional context concerns how teacher feedback as a teaching and learning tool is embedded in specific ESL and EFL classrooms. For example, the approaches and ways in which teachers design form-and-accuracy or meaning-and-fluency tasks and organize pair-work or teacher-fronted activities can influence teachers' decision-making with regard to giving feedback as well as learners' processing and use of that feedback (Oliver, 2000).

Interactional and interpersonal level of context. The interactional and interpersonal layer of context refers to "the relationships that participants construct, confront, and deal with as they engage in the situated processes of giving feedback" (K. Hyland & F. Hyland, 2006a, p. 14). As reviewed in section 2.2.4, the SCT conceptualizes teacher feedback as a form of teacher scaffolding that helps learners internalize more advanced-level mental activities (Aljaafreh & Lantolf, 1994). Accordingly, effective feedback needs to be provided within an individual learner's ZPD. For example, Goldstein (2006) found that distant teacher-learner interpersonal relationships may result in misinterpretation of each other's personalities and intentions, which further influence teacher feedback and corresponding learner revisions.

To summarize, teacher feedback is not delivered in a vacuum but situated and embedded in a multi-layered context which encompasses sociocultural impacts, institutional requirements, teachers' specific instruction in relation to feedback, as well as teacher-student interactions and interpersonal relationships. This categorization is not intended to be definite, but it can serve as a heuristic in engendering a more thorough understanding of the complexity of teacher feedback in real-life EFL classrooms.

2.3.7 Teacher Feedback on Oral Tasks

Before embarking on the discussion in this section, it is worth restating that although a robust amount of research has examined L2 teachers' oral CF (e.g., Lyster & Ranta, 1997; Lyster, Saito, & Sato, 2013; Sheen, 2004, 2006), these studies mostly focused on L2 linguistic structures targeted by teacher CF provided during grammar drills and exercises. It is inescapably clear that grammar instruction is more teacher-controlled and emphasizes linguistic forms; by contrast, tasks are more student-centered and focus on meanings (Ellis, 2000). Thus, it merits our attention to conduct a critical review of teacher feedback solely given on oral "tasks" instead of "exercises".

Only a handful of quantitative studies have examined and compared the differential effectiveness of teacher, peer, and self-assessments of L2 tasks of oral presentations (e.g., Cheng & Warren, 1999, 2005; Saito, 2008; Saito & Fujita, 2009; Shimura, 2006). For example, in Shimura's (2006) study of Japanese EFL students and teacher assessment of oral presentations, upper intermediate students assessed in a way that was most similar to the language instructor, compared to their counterparts in lower intermediate and advanced levels. Gestures and eye contact were the common items mentioned in student assessment that most closely correlated with the instructor's ratings.

A key feature of these studies is that the feedback that teachers provided to EFL students remained predominantly outcome-based, with grades and scores being their habitual practices. Specifically, the teachers pre-established certain assessment criteria in their scoring rubrics and grade sheets, including language use in oral presentations and non-language criteria like "preparation and content", "quality of delivery", "organization", and "layout and presentation" (Cheng & Warren, 2005, p. 117). While these studies offered valuable insights into teacher feedback on EFL oral tasks, other forms of teacher feedback can also be provided to students, such as teacher comments indicating learning strengths and weaknesses or provision of guidance for learning improvement (Muñoz & Álvarez, 2010). Nevertheless, it remains unclear whether these comments may be differentiated from score reporting in terms of their foci and functions. Furthermore, these studies mainly drew on quantitative data by using a number of statistical tests to establish the levels of difference and relationship between peer, self, and teacher assessment. This runs the risk of leading to a decontextualized understanding of the complexity involved in teachers' decision-making in giving feedback as well as students' engagement with teacher feedback.

To date, classroom-based qualitative research has paid little attention to the provision of feedback on EFL students' task-based oral presentations. The study by Wang, Teo, and Yu (2017) used a single-case study design to investigate a teacher's practice of giving feedback on student oral presentations in EFL classrooms. Based on data from semi-structured interviews, the study found that the teacher gave oral comments mainly on pronunciation, content, and logical thinking, and focused on PPT design in his written commentary; he also used the specific pattern of praise-criticism-suggestion to comment on the students' oral presentations. However, this was a single-case study which could lead to an insufficient understanding of the phenomenon investigated. This paucity of understanding further justifies an in-depth investigation of teacher feedback on task-based oral presentations with multiple cases in authentic EFL classrooms.

2.4 Research Gaps

The reviewed literature has shown that the predominant focus of research has been on the topic of teacher CF, with benefits concerning learner acquisition of oral linguistic competence and grammatical accuracy in L2 writing (Bruton, 2009). There is much yet to explore in terms of L2 learners' development of academic literacy in relation to task-based oral performance facilitated by teacher feedback (not limited to oral or written CF). Though there does exist quantitative research that examines the provision of teacher feedback on students' oral task performance, such as EFL students' oral reports and presentations (e.g., Cheng & Warren, 2005; Shimura, 2006), these studies are as yet few and far between, and mostly focus on teacher provision of outcome-based feedback (such as scores and grades) to student task-based oral performance in somewhat controlled settings. Furthermore, quantitative findings that are drawn from such studies may hide individual variance and remain insufficient to inform us what teacher, learner, and contextual factors are involved in and related to the teacher feedback provided on these oral presentations. Therefore, more knowledge is needed regarding teachers' practices of giving feedback on students' oral presentations in authentic EFL classrooms, as well as the factors influencing such teacher feedback practices.

Another knowledge gap emerging from previous studies is the insufficient research on learner engagement with teacher feedback. A number of studies have attempted to understand L2 learners' perspectives on teacher feedback, particularly teacher CF (e.g., Jean & Simard, 2011; Zhang & Rahimi, 2014), or the impact of teacher CF on learner acquisition of L2 structures and overall effectiveness of text revisions (e.g., Ferris, 2010; Saito & Lyster, 2012a; Yang & Lyster, 2010). However, none of these studies has used learner engagement as the theoretical construct that mediates teacher feedback and L2 learning outcomes, involving the cognitive, behavioral, and affective aspects of learner engagement (Ellis, 2010a). There are only a handful of studies, such as Han and Hyland (2015), Han (2016), Zhang (2017), and Zheng and Yu (2018), which made empirical investigations into this multi-faceted construct. Yet, these studies have specifically focused on EFL learners' engagement with teacher written CF or computer-generated feedback provided on student writing tasks. On the one hand, written CF is only one form of teacher feedback intended to remedy particular problems in student writing; on the other hand, oral language tasks tend to differ from written ones in terms of instructional focus. Despite its importance, learner engagement with teacher feedback on oral communicative tasks has not been carefully explored in previous studies. Therefore, while Ellis's (2010a) conceptualization of learner engagement forms the basis of the current study, it may need to be adjusted to account for the particularity of the teacher feedback provided on oral language tasks. Moreover, due to the paucity of research that adopts a contextualized perspective to investigate teacher feedback in real-life EFL classrooms, further research is also warranted to enrich our understanding of the role of individual learner and contextual factors in learner engagement with teacher feedback.

To address these issues arising in the concurrent research on teacher feedback, the present study, which followed a naturalistic case study approach involving multiple cases in the context of Chinese university EFL classrooms, set out to answer four research questions which have been stated in section 1.3.

2.5 A Tentative Conceptual Framework

According to Maxwell (1996), conceptual framework in qualitative research refers to "a visual display of your current working theory — a picture of what you think is going on with the phenomenon you are studying" (p. 37). The conceptual framework (see Figure 2.3) developed tentatively for this study is based on two sources: existing cognitive, sociocognitive, and social constructive learning theories, as well as prior empirical research findings of teacher feedback. This framework helps contextualize the phenomenon of teacher feedback on student task-based oral presentation performance in the Chinese EFL context.

As revealed in section 2.2, language learning not only occurs in an individual learner's mind, but also is mediated through social interactions with the language teacher as well as being co-constructed by student peers. The dotted arrows in this tentative conceptual framework represent the multi-dimensional theoretical perspective on teacher feedback. Cognitively, teacher feedback is viewed as a student's individualized mental process: teacher feedback first serves as the negotiated interaction between a teacher and a student and then becomes comprehensible input to promote the student's output of language learning and oral presentation performance. The SCT perspective highlights the mediational role of teacher feedback as one type of scaffolding that can move a student along his or her ZPD when the student learns English and performs the task of oral presentation. The social constructive perspective focuses on the role played by a student who was not a passive feedback information-taker but an active participant seeking to engage with teacher feedback.

In addition, previous studies have shown that teachers tend to be informed and influenced by a multitude of teacher, learner, and contextual factors when they give feedback to students (e.g., Lee, 2009; Mori, 2011; Roothooft, 2014). Likewise, students might engage differently with teacher feedback under the influence of individual difference and teacher-student interactions in specific contexts (Han & Hyland, 2015; Han, 2016). Accordingly, as indicated by the solid lines in Figure 2.3, three types of factors (i.e., teacher, learner, and contextual factors) play a role in a language teacher's cognitions about providing feedback on student oral presentation performance, as well as a language learner's engagement with teacher feedback. Put another way, the language teacher takes into account relevant contextual factors and makes choices in giving feedback concerning its focus, function, and strategy to cater to learner needs. Similarly, learner factors and contextual factors closely interact with each other, determining the individual learner's engagement with and gains from teacher feedback.

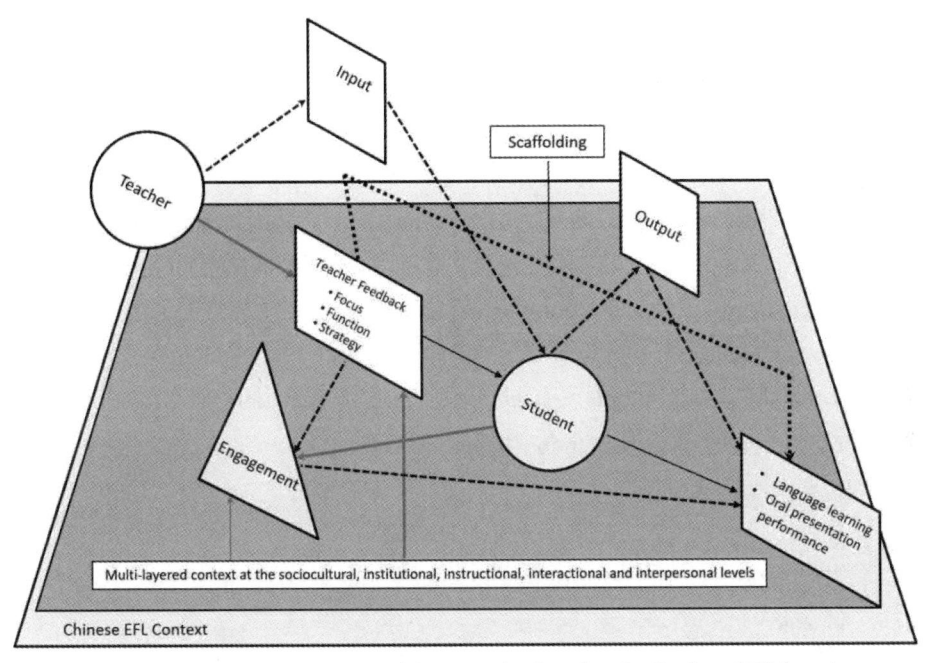

Figure 2.3 A tentative conceptual framework of teacher feedback on EFL learning and task-based oral presentation performance

This conceptual framework also helps to identify the research questions proposed in this study. Specifically, the parallelogram in the center deals with the first research question of the university EFL teachers' feedback practices in students' oral presentations in terms of feedback focus, function, and strategy. The triangle deals with the third research question of how EFL students engage with their teachers' feedback. The solid arrows in blue addresses the second and fourth research questions of potential factors influencing teacher feedback practices in oral presentations as well as student engagement with teacher feedback.

2.6 Next Step for Teacher Feedback Research and Practice

Although previous research has yielded rich insights into teacher feedback and inspired this study, many issues remain to be addressed, particularly regarding the nature and role of teacher feedback in facilitating EFL students' development of oral communicative competence through task-based oral presentations, as well as the processes by which EFL students engage with teacher feedback on such oral tasks. Also, given that current efforts to investigate teacher feedback on EFL oral presentations were mostly positivist quantitative studies that examined the differential effectiveness of teacher, peer, and self-assessment, it is warranted for qualitative, contextualized, and holistic case studies that focus on individual teachers and learners in authentic EFL classrooms to achieve conceptual advancement of teacher feedback. Guided by the research questions and the tentative conceptual framework, this study adopts a qualitative research paradigm and uses multiple data sources, which is presented in Chapter 3.

Chapter 3 Methodology

This chapter introduces the research methods of this study. It first justifies the qualitative multiple-case study approach used in the study. It then describes the research context from the broad sociocultural level, that is, university English teaching and learning in the mainland of China, the specific institutional and instructional levels, such as the English major undergraduate programme and assignment of in-class oral presentation as part of class coursework at LYU (a pseudonym) where the present study took place. The specific methods of data collection and data analysis of this study are further explained in the remainder of this chapter, which follows discussion of the trustworthiness and ethical issues considered in the study.

3.1 Qualitative Case Study

3.1.1 Qualitative Research Paradigm

Language educational research falls into two broad methodological approaches: quantitative and qualitative research (Mackey & Gass, 2005; Merriam, 2001). There appears to be a crude differentiation that qualitative research relies on textual data while quantitative research relies on numerical data. However, the differences between these two methodologies are deeply rooted in researchers' school of thoughts and use of research paradigms. Quantitative research is rooted in the positivism and the logical empiricism which believes that knowledge can be verified through replicable experiments and emphasizes statistical results measured by numbers. By contrast, the anti-positivist qualitative research takes phenomenology and symbolic interactionism as its philosophical roots. Yin (2011, p. 7–8) summarizes five features of qualitative research:

(1) studying the meaning of people's lives, under real-world conditions;
(2) representing the views and perspectives of the people in a study;
(3) covering the contextual conditions within which people live;
(4) contributing insights into existing or emerging concepts that may help to explain human social behavior; and
(5) striving to use multiple sources of evidence rather than relying on a single source alone.

The study was conducted within the research paradigm of qualitative methodology, which follows a naturalistic and interpretative approach to deal with the research questions. This research design is considered appropriate for the present study for the following reasons. First, the qualitative research paradigm focuses on "how the participants experience and interact with a phenomenon at a given point in time and in a particular context, and the multiple meanings it has for them" (Croker, 2009, p. 7). This position coincides with the underlying tenets of the sociocognitive perspective used in the study. As explained in section 2.2.4, the SCT conceptualizes human learning as being embedded and situated in specific contexts, rather than solely occurring within the human mind in isolation from the surrounding social and cultural environments (Vygotsky, 1978). Accordingly, how individual study participants perceive teacher feedback must be understood within the context in which teachers give feedback and students receive, process, and use that feedback. To this end, qualitative research was considered the optimal paradigm to gain an in-depth understanding of the complexity of teacher feedback by concentrating on the subjectively constructed relationships between study participants and context.

Other characteristics of qualitative research also make it relevant to this study. Regarding insider meanings in relation to specific contexts, which are manifest in individual participants' educational experiences, feelings, and views (e.g., Lincoln & Guba, 1985; Merriam, 2001), the adoption of qualitative research methods allows this study to adopt the emic perspective and investigate individual teachers' and students' indigenous perspectives, experiences, attitudes, and beliefs, as well as how these opinions emerge and change in terms of local environments. Furthermore, in order to investigate the phenomena of interest as they occur naturally without intervention, qualitative researchers need to immerse themselves in the research sites in order to observe, document, and analyze details of contemporary experiences (Denzin & Lincoln, 2000; Dörnyei, 2007). Following this approach, the researcher in this study remained fully engaged in the research setting and collected data without interfering in the teacher participants' feedback practices and student participants' engagement with teacher feedback for approximately one full academic semester. Additionally, multiple data sources and pertinent interpretative analyses make it possible to paint a vividly and richly descriptive picture of teacher feedback on student task-based oral presentation performance.

3.1.2 Case Study Approach

Within the qualitative research paradigm, the specific approach of case study was chosen for the current study. It is defined as "an empirical inquiry that investigates a contemporary phenomenon within its real-life context, especially when the boundaries and contexts are not clearly evident" (Yin, 2003, p. 13). On one hand, case study attempts to obtain a thick description of a single unit, or as Feagin, Orum and Sjoberg (1991, p. 2) stated, to provide "an in-depth multi-faceted investigation" of the phenomenon bounded by time and place. On the other hand, as noted by Pole and Morrison (2003), case study can be thought of as an ethnographic research which is "based on the first-hand experience of social action within a discrete location, in which the objective is to collect data which will convey the subjective reality of the lived experience of those who inhabit that location" (p. 16). Therefore, case study is frequently used to develop new hypotheses and understandings about a complex phenomenon.

In a word, case study emphasizes an in-depth description and situated understanding of a bounded system. The bounded system consists of "an individual (or institution) and a site", along with "the contextual features that inform the relationship between the two" (Hood, 2009, p. 68). Often, the boundaries of the case are determined by a researcher's interest. In this study, the researcher was interested in individual teachers' feedback on student oral presentation performance and students' engagement with teacher feedback in the context of Chinese university EFL classrooms; therefore, the case was seen as the bounded system composed of individual teacher/student, and the EFL classrooms in which teacher feedback and learner engagement occurred. Furthermore, the methodological choice of case study, as noted by van Lier (2005), has "become a key method for researching changes in complex phenomenon over time" (p. 195). To this end, the qualitative case study method was helpful to investigate the phenomenon of teacher feedback in a systematic and meticulous way and to present a rich and contextualized description of its particular happening. Moreover, given that case study is favorable in investigating "how" or "why" questions posed by researchers who exert little control over events (Yin, 2003), it is considered both appropriate and crucial to answer RQ2 (which investigated the factors influencing teacher feedback practices), RQ3 and RQ4 (which investigated how students engage with teacher feedback and the factors influencing such engagement).

Specifically, this qualitative research adopted a multiple-case study design, as it attempted to capture a wide range of variations across individual participants in terms of teacher practices of giving feedback and student engagement with teacher feedback. Another practical reason for covering multiple cases was to minimize the risk of attrition of research participants (Dörnyei, 2007). The study as a whole incorporated several teacher and student cases and will "lead to a better understanding, and perhaps better theorizing, about a still larger collection of cases" (Stake, 2005, p. 446). Each teacher or student participant was the subject of an individual case study, and each worked in different contexts. Moreover, information was collected about each participant, with each case serving a specific purpose within the overall scope of inquiry. As such, this study

Chapter 3 Methodology

created the potential for cross-case analysis and ensured some diversity in its research findings (Merriam, 2009).

3.2 Research Context

The study was conducted in the context of university-level EFL classrooms in the mainland of China. Since contextual conditions are highly pertinent to the phenomenon of study in qualitative inquiry, it is crucial to be fully aware of the characteristics of the multi-layered context to which participants belong. This section starts with the Chinese cultures of learning to draw attention to the socio-cultural aspects of teacher feedback. It then presents a portrayal of the role of English in the education system in the mainland of China and offers a brief overview of the English curriculum reforms undertaken in Chinese tertiary EFL teaching, followed by a specific description of Chinese College English teaching for English majors. This section also introduces English teaching and learning at LYU where the case study was conducted.

3.2.1 Chinese Cultures of Learning

Cortazzi and Jin (1996) proposed the notion of culture of learning to depict expectations, attitudes, values and beliefs, both of teachers and students, in classroom instruction as well as educational discourse system. While Chinese peoples embrace 56 officially recognized ethnic groups, they share a relatively homogenous linguistic and cultural heritage, that is, Confucianism. Education in China has a historical basis in the Confucian heritage that merits five Chinese traditional values of *ren* (humaneness), *yi* (justice), *li* (propriety), *zhi* (knowledge), and *xin* (integrity). The purpose of education is, therefore, to promote "cultural transmission, service to society, and moral transformation" (Jin & Cortazzi, 2006, p. 12). A Confucian model of student learning (see Figure 3.1) was proposed by Jin and Cortazzi (2006, p. 13) to describe features of Confucian-influenced learning from a student perspective. In this model, students are urged to make continuous and self-motivated efforts to learn: (i) they could learn from teachers and textbooks, both of which emerged as extremely powerful authorities; (ii) they could learn by following models like imitating and reciting sentences and paragraphs for practices; (iii) their practices are both rote learning (memorization and repetition) and reflection (reading, questioning, understanding and internalizing); and (iv) their practices intend to achieve extrinsic outcomes like passing exams and securing employment as well as intrinsic outcomes like self-cultivation and cultivation of moral principle.

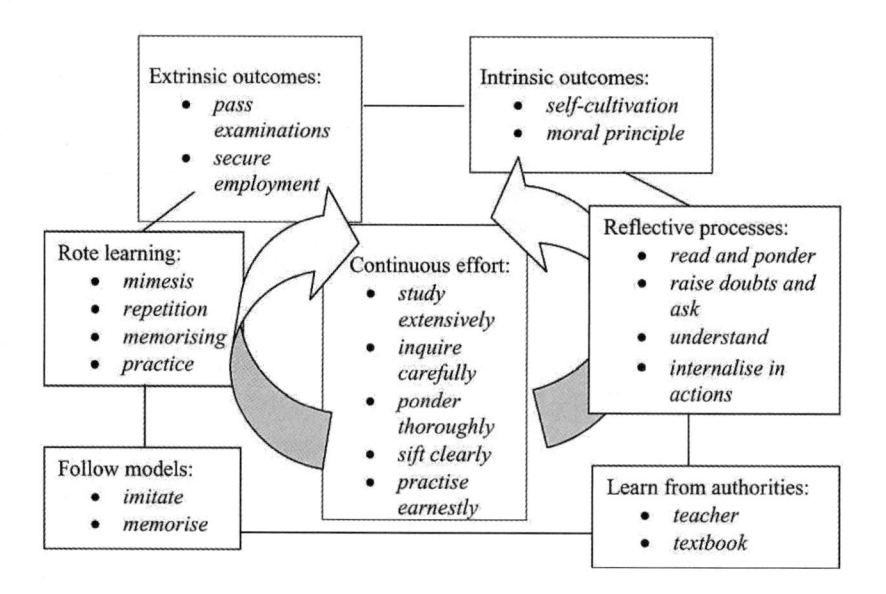

Figure 3.1 Jin and Cortazzi's (2006, p. 13) framework of student learning activity in Confucian heritages

Therefore, in view of English learning, Chinese students often show strong motivation and coordinated efforts for the purposes of not only passing exams in English and/or entering and graduating from university, but also finding employment since English plays gate-keeping roles for their educational, professional and social advancement. Jin and Cortazzi (2006) observed that although Chinese students still "memorize long lists of English vocabulary items or exemplary textbook paragraphs in preparation for the crucial College English Test exams" (p. 11), they are also engaged in informal learning and self-study in their practices of English learning. In contrast with the conventional western stereotypes of Chinese education as a rigid and dogmatic system with students lacking critical thinking abilities, the changing practices of Chinese cultures of learning emphasize "deep learning that goes beyond memorizing or recitation to practical application, through reflective study and high-achievement motivation with disciplined effort, in a continuing tension between outcomes of exam success or employment and the more intrinsic cultivation of the person" (Jin & Cortazzi, 2006, p. 14).

3.2.2 The Chinese EFL Context

The prominent role of English in the mainland of China has been promoted and recognized since China joined the World Trade Organization in 2001. In order to communicate with the rest of the world and succeed in a competitive social context, both the nation and individual Chinese people attach great importance to the learning of English. English is valued as an important instrument to help gain access to professional promotion and personal development (Jin & Cortazzi, 2002). This rationale is manifest in China's mainland education system which gives priority to English in comparison with other foreign languages, as well as launching huge governmental investment in English language education from elementary schools all the way up to universities (Gao, 2009). English is taught in almost every school at various educational levels and success in English examinations is often an essential precondition for entry into higher education settings. English is now offered as a compulsory subject from grade three at primary school all the way to high school, while in some eastern coastal cities such as Shanghai and Guangdong, English is actually taught to first-grade primary school students (Hu, 2002).

Generally speaking, students in the mainland of China can be admitted into tertiary institutions through the *Gao Kao* (i.e., National Tertiary Matriculation Examination) after they have graduated from upper secondary schools where they get intensive studies of English. Here it is necessary to say a few words about the Chinese College Entrance Examination of which English is only one dominant subject. The other two dominant subjects are Chinese and Mathematics. The English test of *Gao Kao* mainly emphasizes students' grammar and reading and pays less attention to productive language skills such as English speaking. Therefore, many young learners of English in Chinese primary and secondary schools attach less importance to the meaningful use of English in real-life situations and have a low level of intrinsic motivation to orally communicate in English (Zheng, 2012). They have to do thousands of grammar drills and pages of reading comprehension and engage in rote learning of more than 3000 words. Coupled with the gate-keeping role of English in a variety of assessments, English is no longer recognized as a mere tool of communication. In most cases, English is viewed as a compulsory school subject to study rather than a meaningful language in which students express ideas and communicate with others.

For this study, the specific research context relates to English language education at Chinese university level. Different from primary and secondary English language education, college English language education shows an increasing diversity in terms of teaching and learning methods, materials and course offerings. One can find college students getting together to talk in English at English Corners (which are actually open-air places) and gaining access to language learning materials like English newspapers, music, movies and TV shows. Colleges of foreign languages have different groups of undergraduate students to educate: English majors (relatively small in number) and non-English majors (much larger in number). Compared to non-English major undergraduates who commonly take compulsory English courses during their first and second years of study, English-majored undergraduates enroll for four-year study programmes and are conferred bachelor's degrees in English Language and Literature after graduation. The goal of the English major undergraduate programme at Chinese universities is not only developing students' English language skills and enhancing their language proficiency, but also promoting humanistic values among students. As commented by Zhou and Zha (2020):

English major programme as an academic subject should be considered a valid part of Humanities education. Consequently, the curriculum, syllabi, learning outcomes and resources should be designed, arranged and implemented base on the fundamental premise that the study of English language and literature, culture, philosophy etc. are not intended merely for the purpose of acquiring English language skills, but for the development of the critical and speculative capabilities necessary to study human society and culture. (p. 25)

The teaching for English-majored undergraduates operates at three interrelated levels. The top level is composed of national policy-makers, teaching syllabus designers, and developers of the Test for English Majors (TEM), who jointly decide how English education policies should be managed and how teaching and testing syllabi should be developed. The second level includes university administrators who set the specific teaching aims and design curriculums, such as the English courses to be offered, the textbooks to be used, etc. Universities of different regions and types vary in terms of their English curriculums. For example, foreign language studies universities may place more emphasis on language and literature while technology universities may introduce more science-related English courses. The third level refers to classroom teachers and students who are responsible for the implementation of the teaching syllabus and curriculum. Accordingly, the teaching for English-majored undergraduates is supervised by a national curriculum, i.e., the National Curriculum for English as a Major in Chinese Tertiary Institutions (Advisory Board for the Education of English as a Specialty, 2020), which has set up the following learning targets for English-majored undergraduates: English majors are supposed to turn out "composite-type" graduates with a solid English foundation, a wide range of knowledge, and communicative competence to work proficiently as interpreters, translators, teachers, administrators and researchers in institutions of foreign affairs, education, trade, culture, military, etc.

The four-year undergraduate programme for English majors is divided into the elementary stage (Year 1 and Year 2) and the advanced stage (Year 3 and Year 4). Courses offered are further divided into three main categories: courses on language skills (phonetics, grammar, listening, speaking, writing, translation, oral interpretation, and so on), courses on general knowledge of English (linguistics, English literature, English culture, and so on), and courses on related knowledge (foreign affairs, economics and trade, law, and so on). According to the National Curriculum for English Majors, some core courses recommended for the elementary and advanced stages are as follows:

(1) Elementary stage: *Comprehensive English*, *English Grammar*, *Oral English*, *Audio-Visual-Oral English*, *English Reading*, *English Writing*, and *Introduction to English Literature*;

(2) Advanced stage: *English to Chinese (E-C) /Chinese to English (C-E) Translation*, *E-C/C-E Interpreting*, *Introduction to Chinese Culture*, *Cultures of English-Speaking Countries*, and *Research Methods and Academic writing*.

3.2.3 The Institutional and Instructional Contexts

The study was conducted at LYU in the mainland of China. LYU is an elite university with multiple disciplines in a coastal city in East China, and it recruits about 5,000 undergraduates each year, who are mostly from the local province. This university was chosen for two main reasons. Firstly, oral presentations are commonly assigned as part of class coursework for English majors and regarded as a significant teaching tool at LYU. Secondly, the researcher studied at this university for her postgraduate programme and became very familiar with the environment, curriculum, faculty, and student body, which can enhance the feasibility of the study and bring an insider's view to it.

In accordance with the National Curriculum for English Majors, LYU has been vigorously devoted to the improvement of students' oral communicative competence. For example, the university makes constructive amendments to its curriculum, initiates and hosts quite a number of extracurricular activities (e.g., English public speaking and debating, and English Corners) in which students can communicate in English in real contexts. LYU also offers students abundant English learning resources, including software and digital intelligence laboratories to learn English, authentic books, and movies, as well as easy access to the internet on campus.

Specifically, the study focuses on LYU's department of English language and literature, which is responsible for teaching English-majored undergraduates. Approximately 70 to 80 undergraduates (20-23 students per class) are admitted into the English major programme each year. By the time the study began, English-majored undergraduates at LYU were required to obtain 160 credits before their graduation. Besides, the department of English language and literature actively collaborated with other departments (such as international trade, computer science, etc.) to launch joint study programmes. Students with double degrees had a heavy load of courses and needed to acquire approximately 210 credits during their undergraduate studies.

According to the department's English major programme handbook, the syllabus of each course is designed to fulfill distinct concrete pedagogical objectives, which differs from one another in light of their teaching plans, materials, and requirements. Despite serving as the guideline for the teaching process, the diversity of syllabi makes it viable that they only provide baselines for the planning of assignments, teaching schedules, teaching materials (adaptations allowed), and designing of tests, but by no means dictate or monopolize the teaching approaches so long as teachers center their instruction on the cultivation of students' English skills and communicative competence. This practice endows teachers with the opportunity and liberty for discussion of and cooperation in enriching teaching approaches. By and large, the requirements of courses put forward by teachers consist of class participation, oral and written assignments and projects, midterm written tests, and final oral and written tests, with adaptations and variations in response to course differences where necessary and appropriate. The diversity of such course requirements renders it a must for students to demonstrate adequate performance in a variety of assessment tasks in addition to good performance in the midterm or final tests if they aspire to achieve success in each course. In general, assignments and projects (including tasks of oral presentations), along with attendance and other performance in class accounted for 30% to 40%, and the final exam accounts for 70% to 60% in the hundred-mark system. In addition to course-level assessment, all students of the English-majored undergraduate programme are required to take oral English placement tests at the end of each academic year. The oral test is done separately in the form of International English Language Testing System (IELTS) speaking interview. Based on test scores, students are placed into three levels — Level A being the highest and Level C the lowest. Level A students are generally more proficient in oral English and motivated in English speaking, compared to their Level C counterparts, though diverse abilities may exist in each level. This practice facilitates the researcher's selection of student participants of different English proficiency levels in her study.

  The study took place in two Year-2 classes and focused on two core courses in the English-majored undergraduate programme (i.e., *An Introduction to Intercultural Communication* and *Communicative English II*) taught by Amelia and Gwen (pseudonyms), respectively. As already mentioned, the context of globalization requires Chinese English-majored undergraduates to be not only good at English language, but also gifted with the humanistic quality of intercultural exchange and communication. The course entitled *An Introduction to Intercultural Communication* was offered to help students adapt themselves to the environment of international business and cultural communication. Being practical was a great feature of this course. Seven thematic topics were covered as follows: (1) communication and culture, (2) cultural diversity, (3) culture and language, (4) culture and verbal communication, (5) culture and nonverbal communication, (6) cross-cultural understanding, and (7) cultural adaptation. The course instructor used the teaching methods like lead-in lecture and case study to guide students to understand the significance of intercultural exchanges and diverse cultural values. Besides, tasks of oral presentations were organized in order to allow students to compare

Chinese and Western cultures and to discuss effective ways of cultural adaptation.

Communicative English (II) was an integrated course centering on such language skills as listening, speaking, reading, writing, translating, etc. This course was run at two stages, with the first two academic years as the intermediate stage and the third as the advanced. Each stage featured a diversity of theme-related topics as the teaching materials, which aimed at cultivating students' productive skills of the language, especially their speaking skills. Each unit of this course was designed with miscellaneous oral communicative tasks which entailed students' active involvement to complete each assignment with the help of listening comprehension. The course instructor organized various oral tasks such as role playing, simulations, and group discussions, etc. among which in-class oral presentations were most frequently assigned to the students. There were no unified guidelines or requirements regarding the design of oral presentations and feedback, so the teachers decided their own practices which are described in detail in section 3.3.1 as well as Chapter 4.

3.3 Participants of the Study

3.3.1 Selection of Teacher Participants

In order to fully reveal patterns of teacher feedback provision, it was therefore decided to adopt a stratified purposive sampling strategy, aiming to recruit "multiple cases that exhibit the characteristics at predefined points of variation" (D. Gall, P. Gall, & Borg, 2003, p. 295). Since classroom experience has been found to significantly impact language teachers' beliefs about providing feedback (Mori, 2011; Rahimi & Zhang, 2015), teachers with different lengths of teaching experience have been recruited. The typicality of the case was also considered. Typicality refers to whether "cases exhibit the characteristics to an average or typical extent" (D. Gall, P. Gall, & Borg, 2003, p. 295). At LYU, EFL teachers' average years of experience exceeded ten. According to Tsui (2003), five years is a commonly accepted criterion in identifying experienced teachers. To this end, the potential teacher participants of this study included both novices as well as experienced teachers with different lengths of teaching experience. Other characteristics of a population of teacher participants may include gender, race, academic title, education background, etc. Most importantly, the study only focused on teachers who actually used oral presentations in their classroom instruction. Since teachers at LYU usually have a heavy workload, their interest and willingness to participate were also crucial when recurting participants. All EFL teachers in the department of English language and literature, who met the selection criteria above, were emailed to inform them of the study (see Appendix A). Four EFL teachers responded to the researcher's e-mails and ultimately two teachers were selected as the teacher cases of this study. The demographic information of the two cases is summarized in Table 3.1.

Table 3.1 Demographic information of teacher participants in this study

Participants	Gender	Teaching experience	Educational background	Academic Title	Course
Amelia	Female	Three	Ph.D. in applied linguistics	Lecturer	An Introduction to Intercultural Communication
Gwen	Male	Fourteen	Ph.D. in foreign linguistics and applied linguistics	Associate professor	Communicative English (II)

Amelia (female, a pseudonym) had obtained her Ph.D. in applied linguistics at a well-known British university. Although Amelia had accumulated three years' experience teaching tertiary English at the university, it was her first time teaching *An Introduction to Intercultural Communication* at the time of the study. Amelia decided to use oral presentations as in-class tasks to guide students to understand diverse cultural values. There were 22 students in her class, who were divided into small groups of approximately three students each. Although students were called upon to work as a group, each group had a regular presenter and needed to conduct three rounds of oral presentations on a self-selected topic in one academic semester. Specifically, the first presentation focused on Chinese culture, the second on Western culture, and the third on comparisions between Chinese and Western cultures. Each oral presentation lasted approximately five to seven minutes.

Gwen (male, a pseudonym) taught *Communicative English* (II) to another Year-2 class. According to the course syllabus, *Communicative English* was an integrated-language skill course, which aimed at cultivating students' communicative competence. Gwen had obtained his doctorate degree in foreign linguistics and applied linguistics at a Chinese university. As an experienced EFL teacher, he stated that he had persisted in assigning oral presentations in his classroom teaching. Like students from Amelia's class, the 18 students in Gwen's class also needed to complete three rounds of in-class oral presentations within one academic semester, but the presentation topics did not necessarily relate to one another. Unlike Amelia's group presentation with one regular student presenter, Gwen's pair presentation required both students in a pair to engage either in dialogues or monologues. That is to say, the two students in a pair can choose to exchange ideas in a conversation. Or, one student can go first and let the other continue in the half of the presentation. Presentation for one pair lasted ten minutes. It is worth mentioning that the selection of teacher participants teaching two different courses was in accordance with the purposive sampling strategy, which seeks to obtain the broadest range of information and perspectives on the subject of study and avoid biasing the study.

3.3.2 Selection of Student Participants

With regard to the selection of student participants, the purposive sampling strategy was also adopted to recruit diverse cases from each class of Amelia and Gwen. Specifically, divergent sampling was used to involve students of different levels of English proficiency, especially oral proficiency, so as to capture the diverse patterns of learner engagement and investigate the particularity of individual learner cases. As aforementioned in section 3.2.3, English-majored undergraduates at LYU were tested at the end of each academic year and then placed into three levels of oral English proficiency, with Level A representing high proficiency, Level B intermediate proficiency, and Level C lower proficiency.

Table 3.2 Demographic information of student participants from Amelia's class

	Deng	Wang	Li
Gender	Female	Female	Male
English learning experience	13 years	12 years	10 years
Group	Group 1	Group 4	Group 6
Oral proficiency ranking in class	1	12	20
Oral proficiency level	Level A	Level B	Level C

Table 3.3 Demographic information of student participants from Gwen's class

	Wu	Chen	Han
Gender	Female	Female	Male
English learning experience	14 years	12 years	12 years
Group	Pair 3	Pair 5	Pair 8
Oral proficiency ranking in class	1	10	16
Oral proficiency level	Level A	Level B	Level C

In order to avoid interfering with the two teachers' decision-making processes, the researcher began to recruit student participants after the teachers had decided upon the groupings. Of the seven student presenters in Amelia's class, three students (see Table 3.2) were selected based on their (i) oral English placement test grades in the previous academic year, (ii) in-class performance, especially their oral participation and performance observed by the researcher (from week one to week three in this academic year when formal data collection was not initiated), and (iii) the teacher's suggestions (for example, the researcher asked for Amelia's opinion to check whether the selected students' L2 proficiency reflect their real abilities in daily language learning). Likewise, three students (see Table 3.3) were accordingly selected from Gwen's class. The six students' background information is presented in Chapter 5 to better contextualize their engagement with teacher feedback. After informing these students of the purpose of the study, they all gave consent to participate (see Appendix B).

3.4 The Pilot Study

The pilot study took place in June 2016 at the same university (i.e., LYU) because (i) I could make a relatively easy access to the field through personal contact; (ii) I wanted to generate insights into the to-be-investigated phenomenon of teacher feedback on task-based oral presentations; and (iii) I wanted to deepen understanding of the institutional and instructional contexts.

This pilot study was exploratory in nature because no qualitative knowledge pre-existed about the phenomenon of Chinese EFL teachers' feedback on task-based oral presentations. I decided to focus on how EFL teachers commented on students' oral presentation performance and investigated the nature of their comments in terms of being feedback- and/or assessment-oriented. Compared to the final case study, the pilot study covered a shorter span of time (only four weeks), relied on one single data collection instrument (semi-structured interview), and involved a less heterogeneous sample of teacher participants (merely three experienced EFL teachers). The three teachers were recruited through both convenience and purposive sampling strategies and none of them participated in the main study. Their self-reported accounts of commentary experiences during the interviews were analyzed to examine the mode, function, focus, and nature of teacher comments. The data analysis showed that the three teachers mostly delivered their comments in the oral mode and sometimes provided hand-written and computer-mediated comments. The majority of their comments were positively formulated to achieve the functions of praise and suggestion, but criticism is perceived equally favorable for error correction. Regarding the focus of teacher comments, three aspects upon which teacher comments centered are: the aspect of oral presentation task performance (i.e., how well the task was performed by students), the aspect of process underlying an oral presentation task (i.e., how students performed the task), and the aspect of self-regulation (i.e., how students monitored, directed, and regulated actions). Instead of pedagogically assessing students' task performance through their vocalized comments, the teachers primarily provided feedback-focused comments on oral presentations. Further details about the pilot study are presented in Wang, Yu, and Teo (2018).

The findings of pilot study provided three implications for the main case study. First, as the teachers reported providing comments on the aspect of self-regulation, they intended to help students seek and act upon their comments. As exemplified by the following quotes in the pilot study (Wang, Yu, & Teo, 2018), "A student once made a presentation about the distribution of well-known German enterprises... I believed his topic did not adequately arouse other students' interest. I asked him why he chose this topic and whether there were other perspectives...after several days, the student reported again and his topic changed to the culture of well-known German enterprises. This time he was loudly applauded" (p. 79). It occurred to me that how students responded to teacher feedback was equally important, which led to the construct of learner engagement in the main study. In addition, teacher participants in the pilot study acknowledged that verbal comment was one form of feedback delivered to students, so the construct of teacher comment was modified into teacher feedback in the main study to embrace conceptual clarity. Second, as variations of teacher commentary practices were observed in the pilot study, I decided to resort to a stratified purposive sampling strategy so as to include both experienced and novice EFL teachers in the main study. Third, the pilot study drew on a single source of data (i.e., teachers' self-reports during semi-structured interviews) to investigate their commentary practices in students' oral presentations. These interview data are in fact secondary data in that a researcher's perceptions are, in Yin's (2011) words, "filtered by what others might have (self-) reported to you" (p. 143). To better conduct the main study, multiple sources of data should be derived from interviewing, observing, and collecting (materials, artifacts, etc.) in fieldwork.

3.5 Data Collection

As argued by Dörnyei (2011), the data elicitation of a given domain should not be prescribed to one single type; nor is there necessarily a correct or incorrect elicitation technique for data collection. Data for case study may come from multiple sources of evidence. In this study, a number of techniques have been employed, including classroom observations, video-recordings of teacher feedback and student oral presentations, semi-structured interviews, reflective accounts, field notes, and a variety of documents.

3.5.1 Data Sources

3.5.1.1 Classroom Observations

Observation is an essential mode of investigation when conducting qualitative case studies. Observational data are often useful in providing researchers with direct information about the topic of interest rather than the participants' self-report accounts. In Dörnyei's (2011) words, investigators can directly observe "what people do without having to rely on what they say they do" (p. 185). For example, during observations of language classrooms, researchers can learn how language is taught by teachers, how students react to their teachers and engage with their language learning, etc. Clearly, such observational data are invaluable aids for obtaining a more objective view of the classroom reality than second-hand verbal reports.

In this study, an observational protocol was developed as part of the case study protocol. Since the researcher was interested in the case teachers' feedback episodes during and/or after students' oral presentation performance, three main issues related to teacher feedback were observed: (i) students' delivery of oral presentations, which helped to increase her familiarity with student participants; (ii) teachers' provision of feedback on student performance, such as the delivery mode, focus, and function of teacher feedback; and (iii) the interaction between students and teachers regarding feedback, such as whether and how student presenters behaviorally approached the teachers' feedback and answered questions. The classroom observations lasted from the very beginning of the courses until the end of the semester, allowing the researcher to obtain a longitudinal and consistent view of teacher feedback and student engagement. After spending an extensive period of time in class, it was hoped that the researcher could be considered a natural and integral part of the classroom, with few possibilities of changed behaviors and attitudes on the part of the teachers or students.

However, observational evidence has its own limitations and drawbacks. For instance, the presence of a researcher in authentic classrooms may impact how teachers and students behave (Merriam, 2001). The researcher in this study used two strategies to reduce this negative influence. Firstly, the researcher served as the teaching assistant and this position benefited her in conducting data collection and fieldwork less obtrusively. Specifically, the researcher sat at the back of the classroom to avoid interrupting classroom routines and activities, which also made it convenient to observe how the teachers and students behaved and interacted with each other. Secondly, observations are less useful in probing into study participants' mental processes (such as motivational beliefs and decision-making) responsible for their behaviors and actions (Mackey & Gass, 2005). In order to mitigate this weakness, other data elicitation methods, including semi-structured interviews, stimulated recalls, etc. were used to procure a comprehensive understanding of teacher feedback.

3.5.1.2 Video Recordings

Videos provide valuable opportunities for qualitative researchers to conduct fine-grained analyses of social institution practices, culture, and communication (Heath, Hindmarsh, & Luff, 2010). In educational research, there are a number of ways to use videos and their use is increasingly considered as a data collection tool for researchers who are interested in multifaceted social interactions, like the phenomenon of teacher feedback in language instruction. In this case study, the researcher used a video camera placed on a tripod and positioned at the back of the classroom to minimize researcher presence and interaction. Only the students' oral presentations and teachers' oral feedback that occurred during and after student performance were video-recorded. The video data were transferred to smaller dimension flv-style videos, and then transcribed and coded by the researcher. The use of videos in this study had the advantages of validating and cross-checking the researcher's own interpretations as well as the study participants' self-report accounts in semi-structured interviews. Meanwhile, data elicitation using videos can be used to prompt stimulated recalls for better participant reflection (Roth, 2009).

3.5.1.3 Semi-Structured Interviews

Interviewing serves as a basic mode of qualitative inquiry. It enables researchers to understand what meaning participants make of their behavior as it provides "access to the context of people's behavior" (Seidman, 2006, p. 10). Three types of interviews can be used when conducting empirical research: highly structured interviews, semi-structured interviews, or unstructured interviews (Merriam, 2001). In this study, semi-structured interviews were adopted to investigate teachers' beliefs and perceptions of feedback practices as well as students' perceptions, understanding, and use of teacher feedback, along with their psychological reactions to teacher feedback. This interview format is generally considered conducive to balancing between controlling the interview and letting participants build on their responses (Dörnyei, 2007).

The interview questions were carefully developed and piloted (see Appendix E and Appendix G). Based on the implementation of the interviews in the pilot study, the interview questions moved from the general to the specific, and guiding questions or yes/no questions were minimized. Each study participant was interviewed twice. The first interview occurred before student first oral presentation to gather information regarding previous experience in English teaching, learning, and oral presentations, as well as other pertinent issues. The final interview was conducted after the completion of student third oral presentation to (i) gather teacher participants' opinions and views on teacher feedback and the rationales underlying actual teacher feedback, (ii) observe student participants' understanding and use of, as well as attitudes toward teacher feedback, and (iii) help study participants to reflect on teachers' feedback practices and students' engagement with teacher feedback. Each interview was audio-recorded with the participants' informed consent, and the researcher also took notes during interviews. To build a rapport with participants and ease the cognitive load in producing responses, the interviews were conducted in Chinese as the main medium for interviewing (but English was also used when necessary).

3.5.1.4 Stimulated Recalls

As one particular type of interview, stimulated recall is also called introspective interview and is used to gain further information about participants' mental processes responsible for their own behaviors (Gass & Mackey, 2000). Unlike traditional interviews in which the interviewees may have a short memory under certain circumstances, stimulated recall interviews can overcome the drawback of memory and explore the original motivations and strategies underlying certain interactions and practices. Put differently, what interviewees describe and think may not conform to what they actually held at the precise moment of the experience. Therefore, the method of using stimuli during interviews brings interviewees a step closer to the moment of their actual behaviors. It gives interviewees "the chance to listen or view themselves in action, jog memories, and give answers of 'I did', instead of 'I might have'" (Dempsey, 2010, p. 350).

In this study, the stimuli mainly comprised video-recorded student oral presentations and teacher oral feedback episodes. During the stimulated recall session, the researcher met the teachers and students one by one in a quiet tutorial room. For instance, a student participant and the researcher would watch the video recordings together, during which time the student was allowed to stop the recordings and report and recall his or her thoughts and feelings when cognitively processing teacher feedback. The same procedure of stimulated recall was also applied to the teacher participants, making it easier for the researcher to gain access to the teachers' decision-making at the very moment of providing feedback to students. The prompts of stimulated recalls with teachers and students are presented in Appendix I. Nevertheless, this technique has its own pitfalls. The participants may report what they are thinking at the moment of recall instead of the moment in which they acted. To deal with this potential problem, the stimulated recalls were conducted as soon as possible within 24 hours of students' oral presentations to help them better recall their feelings and thoughts at the original moment of their actions. All of the stimulated recall sessions were audio-recorded and conducted in Chinese (but English was also used when necessary).

3.5.1.5　Reflective Accounts

Reflective accounts can provide "a first-hand account of a language learning or teaching experience documented through regular candid entries" (Bailey, 1990, p. 215). In this study, student participants were asked to write reflective accounts of their cognitive, behavioral, and affective engagement with teacher feedback (see Appendix L). When writing reflective accounts, student participants were given opportunities to examine their own experiences of and feelings about teacher feedback, leading to more open and honest recordings of their engagement with teacher feedback on their oral presentations. These reflective accounts not only served as part of the data collected but also triangulated other data sources such as student semi-structured interviews and stimulated recalls. After completing their third oral presentations, the student participants were instructed to record their overall feelings, attitudes, perceptions, and opinions that had arisen when receiving, processing, and responding to teacher feedback throughout the study. Furthermore, students also included any factors that could have influenced their experiences and feelings. To mitigate any tension, the researcher made it clear to students that their reflective accounts, either in Chinese or in English, would not be graded and were gathered after the completion of their third oral presentations. This research design was made out of consideration for (i) undermining the researcher influence on student participants' willingness to engage with teacher feedback, and (ii) relieving the students' pressures caused by the collection of multiple sources of data.

3.5.1.6　Field Notes

Field notes refer to the production of written accounts that describe researchers' experiences and observations in research settings (Emerson, Fretz, & Shaw, 1995). Writing field note descriptions, therefore, is not only a matter of noting down what happened but also an active process of interpretation and sense-making on the part of researchers. Put differently, researchers who are engaged in fieldwork should get close to the day-to-day affairs over an extended period of time as well as make on-going interpretations and analyses of their experience.

During the one-semester fieldwork, the researcher in this study wrote field notes that focused on the teacher participants' practices of giving feedback and students' engagement with teacher feedback. For example, the researcher wrote down the interactional details throughout the sessions of student oral presentations and teacher feedback, including when and how teachers provided feedback, and other nonverbal clues given by both teachers and students. By attending to these interactional details, it is possible to see beyond static entities to grasp the meaning of social life (Emerson, Fretz, & Shaw, 1995). Moreover, the researcher also attempted to retain the indigenous meanings of study participants' voices rather than simply presenting an end-product of her own ultimate interpretation of their meanings.

3.5.1.7 Documents

Documentary information is of great value in qualitative case studies because it can "corroborate and augment evidence from other sources" (Yin, 2003, p. 87). Merriam (2001) referred to documentation as "a wide range of written, visual, and physical material relevant to the study at hand" (p. 112). For example, newspaper clippings, government policies, public records and materials created can all be considered as documents when conducting qualitative case studies.

This study involved various documents: the first type of documents comprised the transcripts of video-recorded students' speeches and teachers' oral feedback provided on presentations (see Appendix C and Appendix D), which were analyzed to shed light on teacher feedback practices, including the focus and function of teacher feedback as well as the feedback strategies used. The second type of documents comprised the teachers' lesson and course plans, the handbook of English major undergraduate programme at LYU, the National Curriculum, and other types of curriculum files (see Appendix M, Appendix N, and Appendix O). These documents were useful to contextualize this research in providing background information and shedding light on the underlying reasons for specific teacher feedback practices. The third type of documents comprised students' PPT slides and other written materials, which were helpful in data triangulation and cross-checking the correct spellings and names that students mentioned in their oral presentations, semi-structured interviews, and reflective accounts.

3.5.2 The Procedure of Data Collection

The data collection lasted for approximately one academic semester. Apart from classroom observations and video recordings that were carried out in class, the semi-structured interviews, stimulated recalls, and reflective accounts of students were all administered out of class to avoid interrupting regular classroom activities. Figure 3.2 and Table 3.4 show the data collection procedure and specific time frame of data collection, respectively.

```
┌─────────────────────────────────────────────────────────────┐
│   1st semi-structured interviews with teachers and students │
│              regular classroom observation                  │
└─────────────────────────────────────────────────────────────┘
                              ⇩
┌─────────────────────────────────────────────────────────────┐
│   1st oral presentation task and teachers provide feedback  │
│           classroom observation, video-recordings           │
└─────────────────────────────────────────────────────────────┘
                              ⇩
┌─────────────────────────────────────────────────────────────┐
│       Stimulated recalls with both teachers and students    │
└─────────────────────────────────────────────────────────────┘
                              ⇩
┌─────────────────────────────────────────────────────────────┐
│ 2nd and 3rd oral presentation tasks and teachers provide feedback │
│           Classroom observations, video-recordings          │
│       Stimulated recalls with both teachers and students    │
└─────────────────────────────────────────────────────────────┘
                              ⇩
┌─────────────────────────────────────────────────────────────┐
│                Reflective accounts of students              │
└─────────────────────────────────────────────────────────────┘
                              ⇩
┌─────────────────────────────────────────────────────────────┐
│   Final semi-structured interviews with teachers and students │
└─────────────────────────────────────────────────────────────┘
```

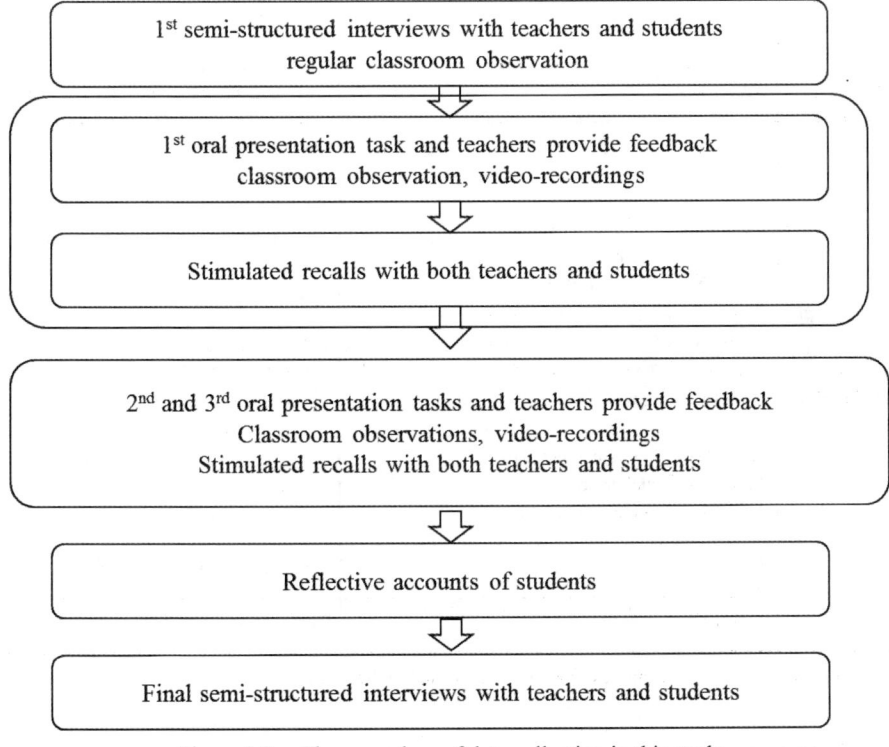

Figure 3.2　The procedure of data collection in this study

Table 3.4   Time frame of data collection

Class	Time	Major data source
Amelia's class on Monday	Week 1-3	Classroom observations First semi-structured interviews*
	Deng: Week 4 (1st oral presentation) Week 8 (2nd oral presentation) Week 12 (3rd oral presentation)	Video-recordings Stimulated recalls* Classroom observations
	Wang: Week 5 (1st oral presentation) Week 9 (2nd oral presentation) Week 13 (3rd oral presentation)	
	Li: Week 6 (1st oral presentation) Week 11 (2nd oral presentation) Week 15 (3rd oral presentation)	
	Week 16	Reflective accounts
	Week 17-18	Final semi-structured interviews*
Gwen's class on Thursday	Week 1-4	Classroom observations First semi-structured interviews*
	Wu: Week 5 (1st oral presentation) Week 9 (2nd oral presentation) Week 13 (3rd oral presentation)	Video-recordings Stimulated recalls* Classroom observations
	Chen: Week 6 (1st oral presentation) Week 10 (2nd oral presentation) Week 14 (3rd oral presentation)	
	Han: Week 7 (1st oral presentation) Week 11 (2nd oral presentation) Week 15 (3rd oral presentation)	
	Week 16	Reflective accounts
	Week 17-18	Final semi-structured interviews*

*represents that data were collected from both teacher and student participants.

Data from each source were collected and analyzed to answer the research questions. Table 3.5 illustrates the alignment between research questions and data collection.

Table 3.5   An overview of the alignment between research questions and data collection

Research question	Data collection
RQ1 What are the Chinese university EFL teachers' feedback practices in student oral presentations?	Video-recordings of teacher oral feedback; Classroom observations; Field notes; Documents like feedback sheets
RQ2 What factors might have influenced the Chinese university EFL teachers' feedback practices in student oral presentations?	Semi-structured interviews and stimulated recalls with teachers; Field notes
RQ3 How do university EFL students engage with teacher feedback on their oral presentations?	Semi-structured interviews and stimulated recalls with students; Reflective accounts; Video-recordings of oral presentations; Documents like PPT slides; Classroom observation; Field notes
RQ4 What factors might have influenced university EFL students' engagement with teacher feedback on their oral presentations?	Semi-structured interviews and stimulated recalls with students; Reflective accounts; Field notes

3.5.3 Data Triangulation

Triangulation is an important technique that can facilitate validation of collected data through cross-checking from two or more sources. The researcher carried out triangulation to corroborate empirical evidence. By using multiple data collection methods and sources, evidence supporting the research findings of each research question was identified and examined in order to eliminate the information drawn from single data collection method and source. When reporting teachers' feedback practices, data of video-recorded teacher oral feedback and classroom observation were mainly used and triangulated with teacher interviews. Likewise, this triangulation technique is used when the researcher captured students' multi-dimensional engagement patterns. Take students' behavioral engagement as an example. Student interviews, reflective accounts, classroom observation, and students' original PPT slides and revised ones were cross-checked against findings obtained through one data collection method to another. Figure 3.3 shows how data triangulation is adopted to corroborate the validity of research findings about students' behavioral engagement with teacher feedback.

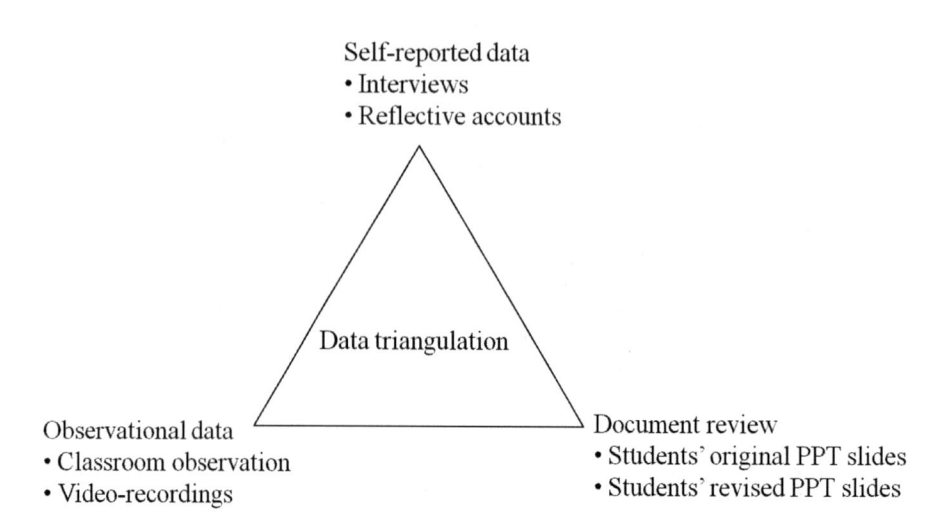

```
                    Self-reported data
                     • Interviews
                     • Reflective accounts

                           /\
                          /  \
                         /    \
                        / Data \
                       /triangu-\
                      /  lation  \
                     /_____\
Observational data                   Document review
 • Classroom observation             • Students' original PPT slides
 • Video-recordings                  • Students' revised PPT slides
```

Figure 3.3　Data triangulation for investigating students' behavioral engagement with teacher feedback

3.6　Data Analysis

Data analysis began by organizing all the data according to data sources and individual cases. All the video-recordings of teacher oral feedback, semi-structured interviews, and stimulated recalls were transcribed in the original language in which they occurred. Field notes and reflective accounts that were written on paper were then input into the computer for further analysis.

3.6.1　Analysis of Teacher Feedback

Text analysis dealt with the verbatim transcripts of teacher oral feedback (see Appendix D) which were parsed into meaningful T-units. A T-unit is "a minimal terminable unit into which the theme should be segmented" (Hunt, 1965, p. 21). Based on the review of literature in section 2.3.1, the coding schemes (see Table 3.6, Table 3.7, and Table 3.8) were developed to fit the feedback data and ascertain the teachers' feedback focus, function, and strategies.

Table 3.6   Coding scheme of feedback focus

Feedback focus	Description	Example
Language	Correct and proper use of L2 in students' speeches and written texts on PPT slides	Yeah, there is a grammatical mistake here, right? How to pronounce this word? So, do you think the word order is right?
Content	Accuracy, completeness, and relevance of content presented	I don't appreciate the poem here...Or, would you like to choose another literary work to replace this poem? Do you know something about the seating arrangement for people when they are having formal dinners with some important guys? I think this part should be contained in your presentation. Okay?
Organization	Argument construction, linking of ideas, transition of PPT slides	Also, I think you need a brief summary for today's presentation, right? Maybe you could illustrate your point, but think about it. Try to say more about it. Do the linking. Do the connection work. How do these two slides relate to each other?
Presentation aid	Font size, background and text color, layout and design of PPT slides	I am not so sure about the font size here. It is still small. Try to use a darker background with light text colors. This one is quite interesting. Use an animation to attract our attention.
Presentation delivery	Eye contact, speaking volume and rate, gesture, mode of delivery	It seems like you are trying to remember something or read something. You are always lowering your head like this. You should raise your voice. As for me, it's a little bit quick. I haven't finished reading the title and you immediately moved to the second slide.
Others	Overall impression of student performance, group collaboration, rehearsal before the task	I think you did a good job today. Did you make all the slides by yourself, or if anyone in your group helped you? You need to do a rehearsal because it helps you to gain confidence.

Table 3.7   Coding scheme of feedback function

Feedback function	Example
Praise	I think you did a good job today.
Criticism	Your intonation is just like um, um, um. So flat. Always goes like this.
Suggestion	I think you should put this English version on the same slide so we can read it and compare those sentences.

Table 3.8 Coding scheme of feedback strategy

Feedback strategy	Description	Example
CF strategy	Error correction technique employed by the teacher to correct a linguistic error	*Metalinguistic feedback*— Pay attention to the last syllable /ə/. You pronounced it incorrectly when you presented just now.
L1 use	Use of Chinese when providing teacher feedback	The teacher translated the previous sentence in English into its counterpart in Chinese. For example, 评价一下你所选的四个标题的词性，你觉得选的这个标题是一种平行结构吗？(Why did you choose the four words here? So, do you think they are in the parallel style?)
Use of nonverbal language	The teacher's use of paralanguage to accompany his or her oral feedback	As observed by the researcher, *the teacher sometimes hovered the computer mouse over the problematic areas on students' PPT slides*
Selective feedback	The teacher's pre-selection of a limited number of aspects of oral presentation on which to give feedback	The teacher did not correct all the linguistic errors in students' oral presentations.
Peer feedback/self-generated feedback	The teacher's eliciting comments from student peers or the presenter himself/herself	The teacher asked a student to comment on his or her own performance by saying "*How do you think of your presentation?*"

3.6.2 Analysis of Semi-Structured Interviews, Stimulated Recalls, Reflective Accounts, and Field Notes

Miles and Huberman's (1994) qualitative data analysis approach (involving data reduction, data display, and conclusion drawing) was adopted to inductively analyze the verbatim transcripts of semi-structured interviews (see Appendix F and Appendix H) and stimulated recalls (see Appendix J and Appendix K), reflective accounts (see Appendix L), and field notes. The within-case analysis was carried out first. The transcripts, relevant field notes, and some documents were organized on the basis of individual participants. Three types of coding were involved in this process of data analysis: open-coding, axial coding, and selective coding (Strauss & Corbin, 1990). In the open-coding phase, the researcher attempted to develop categories of information by reading line by line through pages of the transcripts and meanwhile writing words or short phrases that identified specific analytic dimensions. Such coding was written in the margin next to the transcripts. Once the initial sets of categories had been generated, the researcher began the axial coding process in which the original codes were related to each other through both deductive and inductive thinking. According to Creswell (2007), information from the axial coding phase is then "organized into a figure, a coding paradigm, that presents a theoretical model of the process under study" (p. 161), which is called selective coding. In other words, the researcher chose one category as the core category to which all other categories were related. In-process analytic memos were also written throughout the whole coding phase, which helped the researcher explore, identify, and refine the general patterns or themes related to the research questions.

Analytic generalization was achieved by constantly comparing each participant's data with those of another; that is, first within-case analyses and then between-case comparisons (Miles & Huberman, 1994). For example, intra- and inter-case analyses were conducted to show individual teacher participants' rationales for giving feedback and the shared patterns and differences between participants' decision-making in providing feedback. This process was helpful in refining the coding systems because the original coding might not have been mature and exhaustive before the cross-case analyses.

Some details about the development of codes and categories can be illustrated as follows. The coding schemes of students' cognitive, behavioral, and affective engagement are illustrated in Table 3.9, Table 3.10, and Table 3.11, respectively, which have been adapted from Han and Hyland (2015).

Table 3.9 Coding scheme of cognitive engagement with teacher feedback

Category	Description	Example
Oversight	The student did not pay attention to teacher feedback at all.	Deng: "At that time, I did not listen attentively to what the teacher said."
Noticing	The student attended to a feedback point and recognized the teacher's intention of providing feedback.	Li: "When I finished reading a passage or answering a question, the teacher would ask me 'how to say this word in English?' or 'Please read this word for us.' Usually this was the case where I mispronounced the word. It's the teacher's common CF practice."

continued table

Category	Description	Example
Complete understanding	The student provided accurate explanations for teacher feedback.	*On the other hand, it makes us be-embarrassed.* Wu: I remember my high school teacher said "make sb do sth" or "make sth+ adjective". The adjective serves as the complement of the word "make". The word "be" should be deleted.
Partial understanding	The student provided explanations for teacher feedback, but incorrectly.	Wang: "She said I need a specific illustration. Illustration? Does an illustration mean an example? But, I already used the poem as an example".
Misunderstanding	The student misinterpreted the meaning of teacher feedback.	T: How do you say 唐宋时期 in English? Chen: Tangsong Dynasty. Chen: "I thought the teacher did not hear me clearly while I was presenting, so he asked me to repeat it".
Cognitive operation	The student used a cognitive skill to process teacher feedback.	Reasoning: "When the teacher gave the explicit correction /ˈdezət/, I was comparing it with my own pronunciation /dɪˈzɜːt/. It turned out that I put the stress on the wrong syllable, and also the second letter 'e' was mispronounced as /i/".
Metacognitive operation	The student used a certain skill to regulate his or her own mental processes when processing feedback and generating revisions.	Planning: "There were two rounds of revisions… During the first round of revisions, I made a pause at the content and structural issues and then addressed them in the second round".

Table 3.10　Coding scheme of behavioral engagement with teacher feedback

Category	Description	Example
Revision operation	Problematic area in the students' speeches and PPT slides was addressed.	Correct repair/revision: *They don't date with unless they like each other.* → *They don't date unless they like each other.*
Action taken to apply feedback insights about presentation delivery to next presentation	The student used the teacher's suggestion about presentation delivery and made improvement in the next oral presentation.	Deng managed to slow down her speech during her second and third oral presentations.
Revision and learning strategy	Strategy reported by the student to make revisions, and/or to improve the presentation performance, even future L2 competence.	Li consulted his roommate when revising the conclusion of his second oral presentation.

Table 3.11 Coding scheme of affective engagement with teacher feedback

Category	Description	Example
Attitudinal response	The student's overall attitude toward teacher feedback throughout the research period.	Positive, negative, mixed
Emotional response	The student's emotional reaction to teacher feedback upon the receipt of feedback, and the change of emotional reaction during and after revisions.	Happiness, appreciation, upset, embarrassment, disappointment, etc.

3.7 Ensuring Trustworthiness

Lincoln and Guba (1985) proposed the concept of trustworthiness to establish the quality of empirical research, especially qualitative studies in naturalistic settings. Altogether, four criteria contribute to the trustworthiness of research findings in naturalistic studies: credibility, transferability, dependability, and confirmability. It is worth mentioning that these four criteria are interrelated with each other as a whole, rather than being separate from one another.

Credibility is seen as equivalent to internal validity for judging qualitative research. It involves establishing that the research findings are believable from the inner perspective of those being investigated since the purpose of qualitative research is to understand the phenomenon of interest through the participants' eyes. Two specific tactics for achieving the credibility of this study are identified as follows: long-term fieldwork and member checking. First, the researcher immersed herself in the research site for approximately one full academic semester, during which time she conducted continuous classroom observations and stimulated recalls after each observed session. These long-term interactions with the participants helped establish trust relationships with them and avoid any misinterpretations possible on the part of the researcher. Moreover, the interpretations and conclusions in case study reports were sent to the corresponding participants for member checking which is one of the most crucial techniques for ensuring credibility.

Transferability refers to the degree to which the findings of qualitative research are generalized or transferred to other contexts. From this perspective, transferability is the typical responsibility of the investigator who does the generalizing. However, there have been concerns among qualitative methodologists about using this standard for evaluating qualitative studies. The job of qualitative researchers is to make detailed depictions of research contexts and methods, whereas readers of research can have their own interpretations and conclusions "through personal engagement in life's affairs or by vicarious experience so well constructed that the person feels as if it happened to themselves" (Stake, 1995, p. 85). That is to say, transferability invites readers of research to decide whether or not the research findings can be applied to their specific contexts. To this end, the researcher in this study employed the tactic of providing a full account of the theoretical framework and specifying the details of the research contexts, the background information of the case study participants, the data collection and analysis procedures, and other information that is useful to contextualize this research. The measures above helped ensure the transferability of this study and made it convenient for readers to make connections to their own experiences and feelings.

Dependability deals with the extent to which the research results are consistent and can be replicable. It is close to the concept of reliability in quantitative studies. As argued by Lincoln and Guba (1985), dependability is crucial for qualitative inquiry since "there can be no credibility without dependability" (p. 316). Nevertheless, it appears impossible to obtain the same results when replicating a qualitative study because human behaviors are ever-changing (Merriam, 2001). To increase the dependability of this qualitative case study, several precautions were taken. The researcher followed proper case study protocols which made it convenient to guide the investigation and check the research findings. Furthermore, a thick description of the research design, settings, and methods made it possible for replication by other researchers who are interested in understanding teacher feedback on student task-based oral presentations in similar EFL contexts. Thirdly, the researcher conducted check-coding to increase the dependability of the study. For example, the researcher re-coded the first dozen pages of the interview transcripts on an uncoded copy several days after the initial coding. The code-recode agreement rate was 87.3% which is higher than 80%. After testing the initial intra-coder reliability, the researcher invited an extra coder to analyze the same interview transcripts and the inter-coder agreement was 85.1%. The majority of disagreement was resolved after negotiations of revising codes and refining categories, and the final inter-coder agreement rates reached 93.1%, thus ensuring data dependability (Miles & Huberman, 1994).

The final criterion of confirmability refers to the degree to which the research findings can be confirmed by others. It deals with the extent to which researcher subjectivity is involved in data analysis. Since qualitative studies tend to assume that researchers may bring their unique perspectives during the inquiry, it is important to avoid their "bias, assumptions, patterns of thinking, and knowledge gained from experience and reading" (Strauss & Corbin, 1990, p. 95). Two strategies were used to enhance confirmability in this study. Firstly, the researcher employed multiple methods of data collection for triangulation which was helpful for mitigating her subjective viewpoints. In addition, the researcher documented the specific data collection and analysis procedures for cross-checking the data throughout the study. Nevertheless, it is worth noting that the researcher in this study is fully aware as well as acknowledge that her going native inevitably brings subjectivity in terms of interpreting the data collected, since a researcher is the major instrument of a qualitative study (Lincoln & Guba, 1985).

3.8 Ethical Issues

Since educational research deals with human beings in the real world, it inevitably involves ethical issues. This is particularly true of research of a qualitative nature as researchers often irrupt into study participants' private lives. A range of measures were taken to meet the ethical requirements as well as the circumstances that emerged throughout this study.

The ethical frame in this study was largely drawn from the researcher's worldview and the established principles of fieldwork in literature (e.g., Dörnyei, 2011; Fetterman, 2010). At the outset, the researcher submitted the study to the Institutional Review Board (IRB) at her university and obtained approval to conduct the research. Upon approval, the researcher then sought the acceptance of the field-site university (i.e., LYU) to which the participants belonged. Formal letters of invitation were sent to all the study participants to negotiate their permission.

The consent forms were formulated in such a way that they clearly explained the research purpose of this study. Also included in the consent forms were the significance of this study and the procedure of data collection. Voluntary participation was also made clear and the specific time and place for each interview and stimulated recall were negotiated on the basis of the participants' schedules. The participants were free to contact the researcher if they had any questions. In order to maintain privacy and confidentiality, the researcher used pseudonyms to replace the participants' real names throughout the research process.

In this study, the researcher did not affect any professional decisions made by the teacher participants in their instructional contexts. They experienced the same case study protocol and had the right to review the transcripts of their individual video-recorded feedback episodes, semi-structured interviews, as well as stimulated recalls for accuracy and permission to publish the findings. Likewise, the researcher bought small gifts (e.g., notebooks) for each student participant, offered them useful suggestions concerning English learning websites, books, and expressed her gratitude for their participation in the study.

Chapter 4 Teacher Feedback Practices in Oral Presentations

This chapter presents the findings from the two teacher cases — Amelia and Gwen who provided contrasting teacher feedback on students' oral presentations. Two case narratives are reported to describe the focus, function, and strategies of teacher feedback, as well as to unveil the underlying factors that might have influenced the teachers' feedback practices.

4.1 Amelia's Feedback Practices

4.1.1 Feedback Focus: Comprehensive Feedback

Based on the results of feedback analysis, Amelia provided 27 feedback points to Deng, 39 to Wang, and 40 to Li, making 106 feedback points in total. As shown in Table 4.1, Amelia was relatively comprehensive in her feedback practices. She commented on language, content and organizational issues, presentation aids, and delivery. Nevertheless, it was found that Amelia mostly formulated her feedback on content (29.2%) and organizational (22.6%) matters in students' oral presentations.

Table 4.1   Focus of teacher feedback provided by Amelia

Focus	Percentage (Total=106)
Language	14.2% (15)
Content	29.2% (31)

continued table

Focus	Percentage (Total=106)
Organization	22.6% (24)
Presentation aid	16.0% (17)
Presentation delivery	12.3% (13)
Other	5.7% (6)

Amelia prioritized content feedback because she wanted to facilitate students' deep understanding of the course materials. When asked about her aim in providing feedback, Amelia expected that her feedback would help to guide students to understand diverse values in Chinese and Western cultures. As remarked by Amelia, "If student presenters have misconceptions about certain cultural issues in their oral presentations, I hope my feedback can alert the students and inform them of correct conceptions" (1st interview with Amelia).

In addition, Amelia's instructional beliefs which largely hinged upon the type of course she was teaching also led her to prioritize giving content feedback on students' oral presentations. For Amelia, the course (i.e., *An Introduction to Intercultural Communication*) was knowledge-based rather than language skill-oriented, and therefore she intended to use oral presentations to facilitate students' acquisition of content knowledge related to intercultural communication:

> I have read the course description which states that acquiring culture-related knowledge is a great feature of this course. I think students should first and foremost focus on learning content knowledge rather than language skills. For this reason, I divide the class into small groups and assign each group an oral presentation task to allow them to present different intercultural topics. This task design can stimulate students' interest in this course. We all know that culture is a broad concept. There are huge differences between different cultures.
>
> (1st interview with Amelia)

Chapter 4 Teacher Feedback Practices in Oral Presentations

It was found that Amelia often provided feedback on the accuracy and relevance of contents presented in students' oral presentations. The following excerpt illustrated Amelia's content feedback.

> I don't appreciate the poem here. Look at the expressions. Are they really straightforward? [...] Or, would you like to choose another literary work to replace this poem?
> (Amelia's feedback—To Wang—Presentation 2)

The excerpt above showed that Amelia commented on the appropriateness of the literature used by Wang in her second oral presentation. Interestingly, although Amelia expressed her dislike of the supporting literature used, she mitigated this force by using the euphemism ("would you like…"). As Amelia recalled, she simply wanted to respect Wang's revision choice by not being bossy.

With regard to feedback on organization, Amelia highlighted the importance of conclusion and rhetorical effectiveness in oral presentations. The classroom observations showed that the students did not have a clear conception of rhetorical structure when they made presentations. In Amelia's own words, "Either there was an absence of summary or they summarized their presentations inappropriately" (Final interview with Amelia). Below are some examples of Amelia's feedback on this organizational issue:

> I think you need a brief summary for today's presentation, right?
> (Amelia's feedback—To Deng—Presentation 1)
> Actually, for me, I perceive it as the conclusion for this presentation. You still need a general conclusion for all the three presentations.
> (Amelia's feedback—To Wang—Presentation 3)
> When you draw conclusions, just summarize what you have got. Never try to make new statements here…
> (Amelia's feedback—To Li—Presentation 2)

In another example, Amelia identified a fundamental flaw in Wang's argument construction which lacks logic and effectiveness.

> It's just a little bit far from this point — thinking pattern. [...] What's the relationship between thinking pattern illustrated by the two lines and the topic of love? [...] You haven't made it clear. Maybe you could illustrate your point. Try to say more about it. Do the linking. Okay? Do the connection work.
>
> (Amelia's feedback—To Wang—Presentation 2)

As exemplified in this feedback, creating a logical argument was Amelia's primary concern, as she remarked that although Wang had presented the underlying reasons for western attitudes towards love, she failed to integrate these reasons into her argument. Put simply, there was a poor linking of ideas in Wang's speech during her second oral presentation.

In contrast with her great concern about content and structural issues, Amelia attached less importance to the correct use of English language in students' oral presentations and argued that it would have been odd if she had conducted too much error correction in her feedback. When interviewed, Amelia said that she neither had a preference in terms of which specific errors were corrected, nor did she believe in the efficacy of oral CF, arguing that "even though I have pointed out the students' mispronunciations or ungrammatical structures, they probably forget the corrections because this (oral presentation) is a meaning-oriented activity not a grammar exercise" (Final interview with Amelia). Consequently, she only provided 15 points of CF focusing on non-target-like L2 structures, as shown in Table 4.1. The specific types of linguistic errors addressed are described in Table 4.2. Amelia's CF appeared to be more balanced regarding its linguistic target as she primarily provided CF on vocabulary (40.0%), followed closely by pronunciation (33.3%) and grammar (26.7%).

Chapter 4 Teacher Feedback Practices in Oral Presentations

Table 4.2   Linguistic targets of learner errors addressed by Amelia

Linguistic target	Percentage (Total=15)
Pronunciation	33.3% (5)
Grammar	26.7% (4)
Vocabulary	40.0% (6)

Another factor that may have helped shape Amelia's comprehensive feedback practices was the innate feature of oral presentation which is capable of conveying multimedia. Unlike conventional L2 writing tasks, communication in an oral presentation is a multi-directional process and does not merely depend on a student's abilities to articulate orally. This task feature of multimodal performance prompted Amelia to pay attention to the presentation aids and delivery of presentation. The data analysis showed that other foci of Amelia's feedback included the PPT slide design and format (e.g., suggestion about enlarging font size of text), volume and intonation of student speech (e.g., "you should raise your voice"), as well as the pacing of the PPT slide display (e.g., "we haven't finished reading this slide yet, and you already turned to the next slide"). As Amelia put it, "Other than content and language use, how students present their topics is also important. Poor delivery can undermine the effectiveness of an oral presentation" (Final interview with Amelia).

4.1.2 Feedback Function: Praise-Criticism and Criticism-Suggestion

Amelia made use of praise (34.0%), criticism (26.4%), and suggestion (39.6%) when commenting on the students' oral presentations (see Table 4.3). Overall, Amelia preferred to give positive-oriented feedback (i.e., praise and suggestion) to the students. When asked about this practice, Amelia remarked, "I do not want to demotivate my students. An appropriate amount of positive feedback motivates them to work harder" (Final interview with Amelia).

Table 4.3   Function of teacher feedback provided by Amelia

Function	Percentage (Total=106)
Praise	34.0% (36)
Criticism	26.4% (28)
Suggestion	39.6% (42)

A detailed text analysis revealed that praise was, on the one hand, manifested in Amelia's feedback when she responded globally to student performance, as illustrated in the following excerpt:

> I think you did a good job today. The topic is quite interesting. Through your presentation, I have acquired knowledge about how to use English to introduce dishes in the eight traditional Chinese cuisines.
> (Amelia's feedback—To Li—Presentation 1)

On the other hand, praise was presented to tone down the negative effects of critical comments. In the following two examples quoted from Amelia's feedback, one can observe that the full force of criticism is mitigated by placing it adjacent to the act of praise.

> I really like the style of your PPT slides. It's simple but clear to present your ideas. Except for the punctuation here. If there's no question mark, then that's much better.
> (Amelia's feedback—To Deng—Presentation 3)

> Maybe you are trying to summarize the reasons for this phenomenon, which is very good. But, I don't like the ideas here. Personal independence? Autonomy? No. Actually, in small restaurants in the western countries, people are usually sitting close to each other.
> (Amelia's feedback—To Li—Presentation 2)

Chapter 4 Teacher Feedback Practices in Oral Presentations

In the two excerpts above, one can easily perceive that Amelia identified and acknowledged the strengths of student task performance in the first half of her comments, while describing their weaknesses in the latter half of her comments. One plausible reason for such mitigation is that Amelia took students' personality traits and emotional wellness into account. When interviewed, Amelia said she particularly attended to students' feelings upon receiving her feedback.

> I know some students are very introverted, especially the female students. They care a great deal about the teacher's comments. If the comments are acute and negative in public, they feel blue or even embarrassed. So, I decided to first say something nice and then point out what was wrong with their performance.
> (Final interview with Amelia)

Criticisms of student performance were also accompanied by suggestions, i.e., criticism-suggestion. Once again, the critical force was thus undermined by the second part of this pair. For example:

> Look at those sentences and think about the connections and the logic behind those sentences. It does not work here actually. So, think about it. Next time, be cautious when you are trying to conclude your presentation. Do not introduce new ideas here in your conclusion.
> (Amelia's feedback—To Li—Presentation 2)

Amelia first criticized the student for his lack of logic among sentences in the conclusion of his second oral presentation. This blunt criticism (i.e., "it does not work here actually") was immediately expanded into a proposal for future task improvement. As Amelia recalled, "Just giving critical feedback without offering suggestions can only suppress learning opportunities" (Stimulated recall with Amelia).

Both of the two paired patterns above (i.e., praise-criticism and criticism-suggestion) had the potential to soften the negativity of comments and contributed to the supportive classroom climate and learning environment. Amelia claimed that Chinese EFL students sometimes lacked communicative confidence in public speaking and attributed her use of paired patterns to the overall context of Chinese cultures of learning, which stresses face-saving issue:

> I am Chinese. I grew up around people who are Chinese. I am familiar with so-called face-saving because Chinese often say "do not hurt another's face"... Face-saving holds true for providing critical comments to students, especially when these comments are verbally delivered in front of the whole class.
>
> (Final interview with Amelia)

Amelia's intent to mitigate the critical force of her feedback was also influenced by the teacher appraisal system at the university. As a novice teacher, she wishes to build a good rapport with her students because surveys are sent to students to evaluate their teachers' teaching skills and performance. Student assessment scores are considered in academic promotion and tenure. Hence, Amelia was reluctant to give extensive critical comments to students despite being dissatisfied with their poor performance.

> Although it may be inappropriate to say that students are nowadays like customers who pay for teachers' services, sometimes it's just the case. We are appraised not only by superiors and colleagues, but also by students. We call it student evaluation of teaching; that is, students rate our teaching performance based on their satisfaction. The score is one of the criteria for academic promotion. If a teacher does not get high scores in student evaluation, he or she may have few chances of getting promoted.
>
> (Final interview with Amelia)

As a result, it was unsurprising that Amelia was keen to maintain good teacher-

Chapter 4 Teacher Feedback Practices in Oral Presentations

student interpersonal relationships. Overall, the socio-affective factor of students' emotional states, as well as the macro-levels of the Chinese sociocultural context and institutional requirement jointly mediated Amelia's feedback functions.

4.1.3 Feedback Strategies: Input-Providing CF, Use of L1, and Non-verbal Feedback

A careful examination of the feedback data revealed that Amelia employed three broad types of strategies when providing feedback on oral presentations: CF strategies, use of L1, and nonverbal behaviors. First, based on Lyster and Saito's (2010) classification, five specific oral CF strategies were identified (see Table 4.4), among which explicit correction and metalinguistic feedback were the most frequently used error correction techniques. Examples of these two CF strategies are illustrated in the following excerpts.

Table 4.4   Distribution of CF types in Amelia's class

CF type	Percentage (Total=15)
Explicit correction	40% (6)
Recast	6.7% (1)
Clarification request	13.3% (2)
Elicitation	6.7% (1)
Metalinguistic feedback	33.3% (5)

Oral CF Episode 1

Amelia: There is a grammatical mistake here. Right? It should be "open ways" not "opening ways". [→explicit correction]

(Amelia's feedback—To Wang—Presentation 2)

In this oral CF, Amelia alerted the student to the error and pointed out its problematic nature. She then provided the correct form explicitly: "It should be open ways not opening ways." Obviously, this technique is an input-providing approach (Ellis & Sheen, 2011), which is immediate and quick, yet does not encourage the student to self-monitor. When prompted, Amelia remarked, "I thought it may be a spelling mistake. It did not involve complex metalinguistic knowledge. So, I just corrected it" (Stimulated recall with Amelia).

> Oral CF Episode 2
> Amelia: (The teacher is pointing to the word "manner" on the PPT slide) You had the wrong pronunciation just now. It should be /ˈmænɚ/ not /mainɚ/ [→explicit correction]. Right? Pay attention to the vowel sound. /æ/. Try to open your mouth widely as if you are smiling. Your jaw should be very low and your tongue should be very flat.[→metalinguistic clue]
> (Amelia's feedback—To Li—Presentation 2)

As shown above, Amelia not only provided the student with the correct pronunciation, but also explained her correction with the metalinguistic clue (i.e., vowel sound). What underlies this explicit input-providing approach is that Amelia's CF belief in explicit feedback which overtly draws the students' attention to linguistic errors and easily contributes to their noticing the gap between the target inputs and their interlanguage forms. In other words, explicit feedback provides students with opportunities to understand what specific errors are being corrected.

In this study, the use of L1 (i.e., Chinese) was also referred to as a strategy that mediated Amelia's provision of feedback. As Amelia explained:

> Chinese can be a great tool in facilitating students' understanding of my feedback, especially when I perceived that students did not respond to my feedback.
> (Final interview with Amelia)

The data analysis of teacher feedback showed that Amelia preferred to use Chinese for the sake of imparting subject knowledge about intercultural communication. According to Amelia, she depended on Chinese to explain sophisticated cultural

Chapter 4 Teacher Feedback Practices in Oral Presentations

concepts because she was afraid that students would not grasp her meanings if she used English. For instance, when commenting on the student's second oral presentation, Amelia used Chinese to provide further information about Chinese table manners, as exemplified in the following quote:

> 这个用中文和大家稍微说一点，我懂的也不是特别多，但是我明确知道的是在中国，最主要的宾客的位置，然后他旁边是陪客人的，主陪副陪，一边一个，然后接着交叉，二席，三席一直往下。中国陪宾客特别讲究的是这个样子，咱们现在比较随意，但是婚宴上仍然延续这个.
>
> （Amelia's feedback—To Li—Presentation 2）

In the stimulated recall, Amelia remarked that this knowledge was not covered in the student's oral presentation, so she consciously spoke in Chinese to help the student think profoundly. Although Amelia perceived that English should be the sole medium of instruction in class, she worried that lower L2 proficiency would prevent some students like Li from understanding her feedback, thus rendering Chinese a useful tool for communicating with her students. Supported by the sociocultural theory, this particular finding indicated that L1 use served as a mediational means in assisting students' internalization of feedback information.

Another feedback strategy used by Amelia was a series of nonverbal clues that accompanied her feedback. This strategy is closely related to her belief about nonverbal behavior as an important element of oral feedback. Amelia stated in the first interview:

> Giving oral feedback to students is the same as any other means of human communication during which nonverbal information is co-expressive with speech. Students may notice that the teacher is nodding his or her head, smiling, or using hand gestures. This information conveys meaning to students and facilitates their understanding of a spoken message.
>
> （1st interview with Amelia）

Specific nonverbal behaviors that were observed when Amelia commented on students' oral presentation performance were facial expressions, voices, and pointing at artifacts (i.e., students' PPT slides). A typical example was that Amelia corrected students in a gentle way with a pleasant voice and smiling face. In Amelia's words, "This manner helps students to accept error corrections more easily and can save their 'faces' (i.e., mianzi)" (Final interview with Amelia). However, it appeared that this practice was not appreciated by the two student participants (i.e., Wang and Li), because they still expressed feeling embarrassed upon receiving teacher CF.

It was also observed that Amelia often hovered the computer mouse over the problematic areas on students' PPT slides, which can be directly perceived through the computer screen. Although Amelia recalled that she did it unconsciously, this action helped the student to better interpret and make sense of the teacher's intentions. As Li recalled:

> Perhaps it would have taken more time for me to realize what exactly the teacher was talking about, if she had not used the computer mouse to point out the problems. For example, in my third presentation, the teacher criticized that the font size on some PPT slides was too small. Although I did not know the meaning of the word "font", I found the teacher was hovering the computer mouse over the written texts, so I guessed the teacher was suggesting that I use a larger font size.
>
> (Final interview with Li)

These particular findings indicate that nonverbal feedback plays a role in capturing students' attention as it engages more of the human senses and grounds the teacher's oral feedback in the physical context (Hostetter & Alibali, 2004). Indeed, nonverbal feedback particularly benefited the student participant, Li, who was able to figure out Amelia's intentions by connecting her nonverbal behaviors with oral feedback, as illustrated in section 5.1.3.2.

To sum up, Amelia took a comprehensive approach to commenting on students' oral presentations and yet attached greater importance to content issues than linguistic forms. Paired patterns of praise-criticism and criticism-suggestion were adopted by Amelia as a means of mitigating the force of negative feedback and enhancing teacher-student interpersonal relationships. Besides, Amelia used the CF techniques of providing input to students through explicit correction and metalinguistic feedback, as well as resorted to L1 of Chinese and other nonverbal strategies during her feedback practices.

4.2 Gwen's Feedback Practices

4.2.1 Feedback Focus: Language-Focused Feedback

The data analysis yielded a total of 110 feedback points provided by Gwen to the three students' oral presentations: 31 feedback points to Wu, 40 to Chen, and 39 to Han. The focus of Gwen's feedback is shown in Table 4.5, where he predominately emphasized language (40.9%). Unlike Amelia, Gwen showed less concern for the content and organizational issues in oral presentations — only 16.4% and 9.1% respectively.

Table 4.5   Focus of teacher feedback provided by Gwen

Focus	Percentage (Total=110)
Language	40.9% (45)
Content	16.4% (18)
Organization	9.1% (10)
Presentation aid	19.1% (21)
Presentation delivery	11.8% (13)
Other	2.7% (3)

This feedback practice appears to be in line with Gwen's belief that effective oral presentations mostly depend on students' oral language skills. Gwen explained that oral presentations were assigned as useful tools to further develop students' oral competence because the course he was teaching, i.e., *Communicative English*

(II), is a language skill-oriented course; therefore, "oral feedback should center on students' development of oral language proficiency and communication skills" (1st interview with Gwen).

Gwen's language form-focused approach in feedback is also attributed to his concern for students' L2 proficiency. When interviewed, Gwen said that he paid great attention to oral accuracy because the Year-2 students were still at the foundation stage of their undergraduate studies.

> The students in this class are sophomores in the English-majored undergraduate programme. I have taught them ever since they got accepted in the university. I find that they have too many errors in their spoken English and some of these errors are very simple pronunciation mistakes which are intolerable to me.
>
> (Final interview with Gwen)

However, Gwen added that it was not necessary to correct all linguistic errors. He saw merit in the focused oral CF approach because this practice was more manageable. As he said, "Perhaps selective correction was the best way to address the students' spoken errors. It saved me a lot of time. After all, there may not be enough time for me to fix all their errors in speech" (Final interview with Gwen). Gwen also acknowledged that he could not have remembered or noted down all of the students' errors even if he had wanted to. He said:

> It's nothing like an essay which you can read over and over again. Listening to an oral presentation is a one-time thing. I need to listen attentively to the contents as well as pay attention to the use of language. It's not just oral language. The written English on the PPT slides also directs my attention. Sometimes, I have to rely on my memory when giving feedback to students after their presentations.
>
> (Final interview with Gwen)

Chapter 4 Teacher Feedback Practices in Oral Presentations

One can see that giving oral feedback immediately after student performance was an arduous job for Gwen because it increased his cognitive load. This situation made Gwen realize that he needed to selectively attend to the problematic areas. When asked about his preferred choice of errors to be corrected, Gwen said:

> My principle is I only correct linguistic errors that impede my comprehension of students' oral presentations. Some grammatical errors are acceptable, such as wrong verb tenses. However, pronunciation errors can pose difficulties for me in understanding the students' speeches. This is also true with the lexical inappropriateness on their PPT slides.
>
> (1st interview with Gwen)

This CF belief corroborated his actual feedback practices. It was observed that Gwen left many errors untreated. The results of the feedback analysis (see Table 4.6) showed that the majority of Gwen's CF focused on pronunciation errors (47.5%), followed by CF on lexical errors (37.5%). Grammatical errors in particular were found to receive the least attention.

Table 4.6   Linguistic targets of learner errors addressed by Gwen

Linguistic target	Percentage (Total=40)
Pronunciation	47.5% (19)
Grammar	15% (6)
Vocabulary	37.5% (15)

Specifically, Gwen placed a great deal of emphasis on accuracy in terms of phonetic structure. For instance, all three student participants (i.e., Chen, Wu, and Han) in his class had trouble in accurately pronouncing the consonant /ð/. As Gwen commented, "Chinese EFL students always pronounce /ð/ incorrectly. They tend to pronounce it as /s/" (Final interview with Gwen). Other phonetic mispronunciations were also addressed by Gwen, such as /l/, /ae/,

/aʊ/, etc. With regard to lexical errors, it was found that these errors often appeared on students' PPT slides. Examples from the data are as follows. These results were hardly surprising given that "lexical and pronunciation aspects of L2 speech are relatively important for successful L2 communication" (Lyster, Saito, & Sato, 2013, p. 22).

> We should promote piece during Olympic Games. (→*peace*)
> Encouraged by the desire to win a price, one shall... (→*prize*)
> Nobody can casually succeed; it comes from the through self-management and perseverance. (→*thorough*)

Another possible reason why Gwen mainly provided form-focused feedback instead of content feedback was his lack of familiarity with the topics of the students' oral presentations. While Gwen claimed in the final interview that he was willing to give more content feedback, he met difficulties in evaluating whether the contents covered in the students' oral presentations were complete or not, arguing that the "topics were self-selected by the students, but it was a disadvantage to me because I often have limited knowledge about some unfamiliar topics" (Final interview with Gwen). For example, the topic of Wu's first oral presentation was "Constellation and Consumption". When prompted, Gwen remarked that he had limited knowledge of constellation and could barely understand what Wu had said; thus, he had provided form-focused feedback instead, as demonstrated in the excerpt below.

> I felt foggy for a while after the presentation. To be honest, I only knew she talked about the relationship between the twelve constellations and consumption habits. Since I am no expert in this aspect, I cannot tell whether the presentation was complete in terms of its contents. So, I mostly pointed out her pronunciation errors and poor delivery of presentation.
> (Stimulated recall with Gwen)

Chapter 4 Teacher Feedback Practices in Oral Presentations

Overall, it appeared that Gwen's decision to focus on linguistic forms was influenced by his beliefs about language teaching and error correction, which was further mediated by the limited time in class, the teacher's short-term working memory, and the students' presentation topics.

4.2.2 Feedback Function: Praise-Criticism-Suggestion

Unlike Amelia's practice, the three functions of praise, criticism, and suggestion in Gwen's feedback were fairly evenly distributed. The results (see Table 4.7) showed that 30.9% of Gwen's feedback was related to praise, 36.4% to criticism, and 32.7% to suggestion.

Table 4.7   Function of teacher feedback provided by Gwen

Function	Percentage (Total=110)
Praise	30.9% (34)
Criticism	36.4% (40)
Suggestion	32.7% (36)

It was evident that the majority of feedback provided by Gwen was also positive-oriented. In the first interview, Gwen showed awareness of the influences of positive feedback on EFL students' communicative confidence. He explained:

> Delivering an oral presentation is the same as other public speaking activities, which can be stressful. I know most of the students do not like this task. So, if I express explicit dissatisfaction about their weak performance, I am pretty sure the students will feel insecure and anxious. But, if I say something positive, at least the students will not lose confidence in public speaking.
> (1st interview with Gwen)

However, as an experienced teacher, Gwen avoided giving simple praise such as "Good" or "Well done". Instead, he often provided explanations for these compliments. The analysis of Gwen's feedback practices indicated that praise was mainly used to describe what was good in terms of student task performance. Two examples of this positive teacher feedback are presented as follows:

> Well, your PPT design in general is excellent, such as the selection of pictures and photos, the use of the animation, and especially the clear organization. I can see that the audience have been attracted to your presentation.
> Well, the structure is very clear and consistent. Also, you combine your own statements with supporting details. You use charts and tables. This is great because we can clearly know how you illustrate your argument.
> (Gwen's feedback—To Wu—Presentation 1)

With regard to the other two functions, it was found that they were often paired with praise. The most common pattern was the so-called feedback sandwich, i.e., praise-criticism-suggestion. However, unlike the conventional sandwich method characterized by the teacher's monologue, Gwen added a more interactional dimension by attempting to build a conversation between him and the student, as illustrated by Figure 4.1 and the excerpt below.

> Gwen: The slides are well made. Neat and tidy. [...] Now, you can refer to the first slide, the cover page, the title. There is no question mark at the end of this sentence. I wonder whether you are trying to, um, to ask a question or use the statement as your title.
> Han: Um, statement.
> Gwen: So, do you think the word order is correct?
> Han: (silence)
> Gwen: If you want to use a declarative sentence or statement, the word order is wrong. Try to change the word order and formulate it as a statement.
> (Gwen's feedback—To Han—Presentation 2)

Chapter 4 Teacher Feedback Practices in Oral Presentations

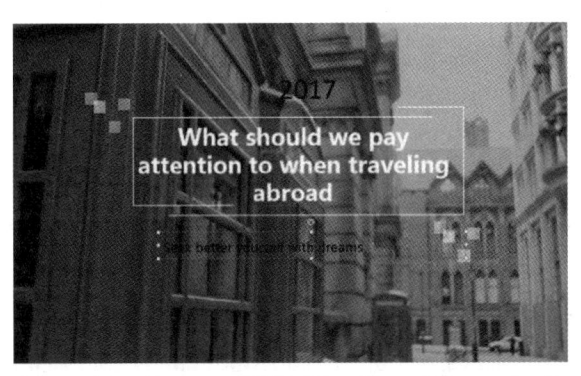

Figure 4.1 Excerpt of PPT slide—Han—Presentation 2

One can see that Gwen first acknowledged that the student's slides were well-made. He then followed the compliment with a criticism that was more implicitly expressed (i.e., there is no question mark at the end of this sentence). Meanwhile, he used a question to motivate the student to self-assess the title of his presentation. After failing to elicit responses from the student, Gwen explicitly pointed out the grammatical error (i.e., wrong word order) and suggested the correction accordingly.

Overall, both Amelia and Gwen in this study decided to mitigate their critical oral comments by using paired act patterns (praise-criticism, criticism-suggestion, and praise-criticism-suggestion). The reasons underlying their decisions are closely related to the traditional Chinese cultural concept of "face" (i.e., mianzi). The two Chinese EFL teachers, Amelia and Gwen, and all of their EFL students are in a homogeneous cultural group that is embedded in the macro-level Chinese sociocultural context. This cultural homogeneity may be an important factor in influencing the interpersonal functions of teacher feedback. According to Jin and Cortazzi (2002), the concept of "face" emphasizes interpersonal harmony and self-dignity in the Chinese sociocultural context; as a result, the Chinese prefer not to vocalize their criticisms in public. In this study, both Amelia's and Gwen's oral feedback was delivered through face-to-face teacher-student interactions, which particularly highlighted the necessity of maintaining a sense of indirectness to preserve the students' public self-image.

4.2.3 Feedback Strategies: Output-Prompting CF, Use of L1, and Peer/Self-Feedback

Three broad types of strategies were also identified when Gwen provided feedback on students' oral presentations: explicit output-prompting CF strategies, use of L1, and peer and self-generated feedback. In contrast with Amelia's input-providing CF, Gwen saw merit in the output-prompting approach manifested in his frequent practices of combining elicitations with clarification requests (see Table 4.8).

Table 4.8　　　　　Distribution of CF types in Gwen's class

CF type	Percentage (Total=40)
Explicit correction	7.5% (3)
Clarification request	35% (14)
Elicitation	37.5% (15)
Metalinguistic feedback	20% (8)

Below is a typical example of Gwen's output-prompting strategy.

Oral CF Episode 3

Gwen: How do you pronounce 肥胖的 [fat] in English? [→elicitation]

Wu: /fait/ [→uptake with no repair]

Gwen: Excuse me? [→clarification request]

Wu: (a brief silence) [→no further repair]

Gwen: Pay attention to the vowel sound. Put your tongue low and at the front of your mouth and stretch out. [→metalinguistic clue]

Wu: /fæt/ [→successful repair]

Gwen: Very good.

(Gwen's feedback—To Wu— Presentation 2)

Chapter 4 Teacher Feedback Practices in Oral Presentations

As shown, Gwen's elicitation and clarification request did not lead to the student's successful repair of the non-target-like pronunciation (/fait/), so he continued to provide metalinguistic clues which are followed by student uptake involving self-correction (/fæt/). This CF practice is in line with Gwen's CF belief that feedback should be motivating to encourage self-correction and situated in dynamic interactions. According to Gwen, oral error correction is best conducted during meaning-negotiation, given the dialogic nature of oral feedback in communicative language teaching. In Gwen's words, "Asking a student to clarify his or her meanings can help decide whether it's an ill-formed utterance or just a slip of the tongue" (Final interview with Gwen).

Like Amelia, Gwen also made strategic use of L1 (i.e., Chinese) when providing feedback on students' oral presentations. For example, he found that the students had great difficulty comfortably communicating in English during the question-answer phase after oral presentation, thus rendering the use of Chinese necessary to maintain social interactions with the students. In the excerpt below, Gwen initially used English to give feedback, and then translated the previous English utterance into Chinese as Chen did not respond to him.

> Gwen: So, my question for you is how you think of the title for each section, the sub-sections like, "replenish", "active", "strength", and "signal". Why do you choose the four words here? So, do you think they are in the parallel style?
>
> Chen: (a brief silence)
>
> Gwen: 评价一下你所选的四个标题的词性，你觉得选的这个标题是一种平行结构吗？
>
> Chen: No.
>
> (Gwen's feedback—To Chen— Presentation 3)

To Chen, the teacher's use of Chinese immediately led to her response of "No". When prompted, Chen remarked that she had highly appreciated the teach-

109

er's action: "It's really awkward. I did not know the meaning of the word 'parallel'. My heartfelt thanks went to the teacher's hint in Chinese" (2nd stimulated recall with Chen). This finding suggests that L1 use is at work in two aspects: cognitively, the teacher uses Chinese to facilitate students' interpretation of teacher feedback. Socially, L1 use is related to teacher-student interpersonal negotiations.

Finally, Gwen reported the strategic use of peer/self-feedback on students' oral presentations, and this use was repeatedly confirmed through the examination of feedback data. In his class, Gwen proposed a session of question-answer phase in the teacher-led feedback to elicit peer/self-feedback. For Gwen, effective communication with students was necessary during the feedback process. He explicitly mentioned that teacher oral feedback should be dialogic and collaborative in nature, as illustrated in the following quote:

> By providing oral feedback, I want to get the student presenter to respond to me. Um, the presenter may talk with me when he or she has trouble in understanding or using my feedback. I hope it can lead to rounds of conversations between me and the presenter or among the student themselves, which in turn can increase opportunities for the presenter to practice communication skills.
>
> (1st interview with Gwen)

Indeed, this feedback belief was found to be consistent with his actual feedback practices. For example:

> Gwen: Again, I am going to ask individual students for your reflections and thoughts on the presentation. Which aspects are good in your understanding of this oral presentation?
> S1: Clearly pronunciation.
> Gwen: Clear pronunciation. Clear is an adverb. Anything else?
> S2: They did not put a lot of texts on their PPT slides.

Gwen: Yeah. They had text-light presentation slides.

(Peer feedback—To Wu—Presentation 1)

In the excerpt above, Gwen encouraged the class to comment on the strengths of student performance; as a result, two students provided feedback accordingly. Gwen depicted this strategy as the "demonstration effect" in the stimulated recall:

I think peer feedback is quite beneficial. On the one hand, I can check whether the class have listened attentively to the presentation; on the other hand, peer feedback can encourage students to learn from each other.

(Stimulated recall with Gwen)

In addition to eliciting peer feedback, Gwen also emphasized the importance of self-generated feedback, arguing that "this self-led delivery of feedback gives students a sense of ownership. They have the right to evaluate and comment on their own work" (Final interview with Gwen). The data analysis showed that Gwen often used the following methods to generate student self-feedback.

How do you think of your presentation? For example, the use of background and the highlighting method in your presentation.

(Gwen's feedback—To Chen— Presentation 2)

How about your own reflections on this PPT slide? How do you think your design of this slide?

(Gwen's feedback—To Han— Presentation 1)

As indicated, Gwen invited student presenters to reflect on their own task performance. This finding highlighted the active role of language learners in the feedback processes: they need to generate feedback from multiple sources such as the teacher, peers, and themselves (Nicol, 2010).

To conclude, unlike Amelia, Gwen focused a great deal on students' use of language during oral presentations and used the sandwich method of praise-criticism-suggestion in his feedback. When correcting errors, Gwen liked the output-prompting strategy to facilitate students' self-correction. Using L1 and eliciting peer feedback and self-feedback were also two prominent strategies in Gwen's feedback practices.

4.3 Summary of Chapter

This chapter has reported on the two EFL teachers' (i.e., Amelia's and Gwen's) feedback practices in students' oral presentations, which were not only shaped by the teachers' beliefs about feedback and language teaching, but also mediated by students' emotional states and the multi-layered context (i.e., the Chinese cultures of learning, face-to-face classroom interaction, and teacher appraisal system). Analysis of the teacher feedback data revealed that Amelia mainly focused on the content and organization of oral presentation, whereas Gwen's predominant concern was students' language use while delivering oral presentations. It was also found that both Gwen and Amelia provided positive-oriented feedback, with praise and suggestion being the main functions. When providing feedback on students' oral presentations, Amelia chose to use input-providing CF techniques while Gwen preferred to correct linguistic errors through an output-prompting approach. Other than CF strategies, L1 use, nonverbal behaviors as well as self- and peer feedback were also used by the teachers.

Having examined the feedback practices of the two teachers, the lingering questions concerned whether the students responded to their teachers' feedback, and in what ways they perceived, interpreted, and used teacher feedback during the research period. Chapter 5 delves into these issues by investigating the six student participants' engagement with teacher feedback provided on their oral presentations.

Chapter 5 Student Engagement with Teacher Feedback on Oral Presentations

Having explored the two teacher participants — Amelia's and Gwen's different feedback practices in oral presentations, it is still unclear how teacher feedback is attended to, perceived and used by the six student participants. Hence, this chapter first presents the findings of how students in this study engaged with teacher feedback on oral presentations. Specifically, the three case narratives of Deng, Wang, and Li in Amelia's class are presented in section 5.1, which is followed by section 5.2 reporting another three case narratives of Wu, Chen, and Han from Gwen's class. This chapter ends with a discussion of multiple factors that can exert influence on student engagement with teacher feedback provided on their oral presentations.

5.1 Engagement with Teacher Feedback: Student Cases from Amelia's Class

5.1.1 Deng: A High-Proficiency Student's Engagement with Teacher Feedback

5.1.1.1 Deng's Background

Deng was a female sophomore majoring in English Language and Literature and minoring in International Trade. She was a high-proficiency student in Amelia's class and had ranked first in the oral English placement test in the previous academic year. Deng perceived the English language as a tool of communication. She lacked intrinsic interest in English language, but felt highly motivated to be proficient in English so as to become a qualified business interpreter in the future. Deng stated that one of her relatives owned a foreign trading company and she was expected to "pursue a master's degree in economics and make a living in the commercial world" (1st interview with Deng).

Deng gave high priority to oral English and believed that public speaking skills would be most frequently employed in her future career. Deng had participated in many English speech contests to improve her oral English in her first year of college study. As a result, she had gradually learned to overcome her speech anxiety and deal with stage fright. When asked what aspects of English oral presentations were most crucial, she seemed to prioritize oral competence over content and organization.

> If I am going to make an in-class presentation, I first need to pronounce the words correctly and use common English words. After all, the presentation is delivered in an oral mode. I will then try to make the contents attractive to the audience and organize my presentation clearly, which helps make everything easier to be understood.
>
> (1st interview with Deng)

Deng attached great importance to self-regulated learning. For instance, she had learned how to articulate her speech by repeatedly listening to TED talks since high school. She also watched American TV series, during which she tried to imitate the pronunciation and intonation.

During the research period, Deng was chosen as the regular presenter of her group. Their group presentations were related to the Chinese and Western education, in which they addressed basic concepts of education, school education, and family education in both China and western countries. Although students were supposed to collaborate in group presentations, Deng complained that she had done almost all the work by herself at the pre-task stage, including searching for supporting materials, making PPT slides, and preparing speeches. It seemed that there was a lack of group harmony due to the "free-rider" effect.

5.1.1.2　Deng's Engagement with Teacher Feedback

At the beginning of the research, Deng described herself as experiencing no mood swings when receiving feedback. She attempted to maintain an objective and fair attitude to both the teacher's positive and negative feedback, claiming:

> While I thought teacher feedback was important for learning improvement, I did not take it seriously. My point was that teacher feedback was simply the teacher's comment on my performance. I was certainly not overwhelmed by the teacher's compliments or criticisms. If I did a good job, I would be praised, and if not, I would be criticized and then I would work harder. I am a goal-oriented person.
>
> (1st stimulated recall with Deng)

Interestingly, however, Deng reported that she felt extremely happy when the teacher thought highly of her third oral presentation for its clear structure and effective organization. Deng said that it was because she has recently been preparing for a national English public speaking contest and her advisor criticized her lack of logic and clear structure. Deng invested all her efforts in learning how to create a unified structure for her speech. She repeatedly drafted and revised her speech and eventually made significant progress. On the one hand, it seemed that this incident of the English public speaking contest mediated Deng's affective engagement with Amelia's feedback. As Deng stated:

> When I reviewed the PPT slides, I felt very delighted because there was a grecd improvement on the organization of the third presentation. I subdivided the major ideas into smaller and more compact units to better hold the attention of the audience. I gave supporting evidence for my argument and also explained how that evidence was related to my argument.
>
> (Final interview with Deng)

On the other hand, this positive attitude toward teacher feedback resonated with Deng's changing belief about the importance of presentation organization. While Deng began by perceiving oral English skills as first and foremost when delivering oral presentations, she then moved on to prioritize organizational matters like argument development over oral competence.

> Researcher: How do you perceive the organization of an oral presentation now?
> Deng: Organization may perhaps be the most essential aspect of oral presentation. It resembles the bones of our body.
> Researcher: Can you further explain your point?
> Deng: A well-structured oral presentation ensures that different parts of the presentation contents fit together and helps the presenter to send a clear and concise message to the audience.
> (Final interview with Deng)

The textual analysis yielded a total of 27 feedback points to Deng, which mostly centered on the presentation delivery (i.e., speech rate and gesture) and content. The analysis indicated that Deng's cognitive engagement was surprisingly limited, probably because most of the teacher's feedback, in Deng's view, was not addressed to her but to the group or even the whole class. Out of the total 27 feedback points, only 11 feedback points were perceived by Deng as being concerned with herself. The excerpt below is an example in this regard.

> For most of you, could you tell me what's the main topic of her presentation? Which aspect of her presentation impressed you most? Okay, the first question, the main idea, the main topic or the theme of her presentation. Right? And the second question is which part of her presentation impressed you most. Okay, any volunteer?
> (Amelia's feedback—To Deng—Presentation 1)

Chapter 5 Student Engagement with Teacher Feedback on Oral Presentations

The teacher apparently attempted to use questions to invite the whole class to reflect on the theme of Deng's presentation. However, Deng paid no attention and thought less of this feedback, as she commented:

> I simply heard this feedback, but I thought it had nothing to do with my thoughts and ideas because the teacher did not ask for my opinion, right? Also, this feedback served as a summary of this presentation. I thought it was addressed to the group not to me. To be honest, whenever the teacher gives feedback, my first thought is whether the feedback deals with my problems or not. I care about the feedback on my own problems.
> (1st stimulated recall with Deng)

Deng's willful lack of care and attention prevented her from further cognitive responses to this feedback. Indeed, Deng clearly expressed her preference for the just-for-me nature of individual feedback because such feedback can give useful information about her own subsequent learning and performance. Deng even acknowledged that she did not listen to the teacher's feedback on other groups' oral presentations. This feedback preference may be in line with her attitude toward the teacher's decision to assign group tasks.

> Researcher: What do you think of the teacher's assignment of group presentations in this course?
> Deng: I don't like it. I prefer to pick up my own teammates rather than being assigned to a group by the teacher. It seems that I and group members are physically bound to each other.
> (Final interview with Deng)

Apart from intentional cognitive disengagement from teacher feedback, Deng attempted in vain to interpret one content feedback on her second oral presentation. The teacher said, "I think your group made a small mistake here, because you, kind of, mixing the different levels of education, such as higher education and education for pupils" (Amelia's feedback—To Deng—Presentation 2). While Deng acknowledged that she might have mixed different levels of education, she failed to understand why the teacher had mentioned pupils in her feedback.

> Researcher: Why were you confused with this feedback?
> Deng: The pupil thing.
> Researcher: How come you did not understand it?
> Deng: I did not use the word "pupil" in my presentation. I remember giving an example about one former classmate of mine, who was in middle school when he went to America for study. Middle school is lower secondary school, right? But, pupils are students in primary school. So, I thought the teacher did not follow what I said.
> (2nd stimulated recall with Deng)

The word "pupil" certainly did not occur in Deng's speech as observed through the video-recordings of her second oral presentation. It appeared that the teacher had misheard this word, which probably caused Deng's non-understanding in this regard.

Deng's cognitive engagement with teacher feedback was particularly manifested in her growing awareness of the audience's needs in terms of presentation delivery. For instance, it was suggested that Deng slow down a little when the teacher commented on her speech rate.

> Amelia: Could you all follow her? Yes? Could you show me your hands for those who followed her speech?
> (Some students put up their hands.)
> Amelia: All right. Not so many. For most of you, how do you feel? Is it a little bit quick or a little bit slow?
> (A student answered, "Quick.")
> Amelia: So next time, take your time.
> (Amelia's feedback—To Deng—Presentation 1)

Chapter 5　Student Engagement with Teacher Feedback on Oral Presentations

When receiving this feedback, Deng first responded defensively to the teacher's suggestion and argued that there was no problem with her speech rate: "Did I speak fast? I did not think so. This was my average conversation rate and nobody ever complained about it" (1st stimulated recall with Deng).

However, Deng quickly acknowledged that she might have spoken a bit too fast in her reflective account, as she recalled that some of her classmates had put up their hands in response to the teacher's question. Clearly, Deng used the cognitive operation of predicting based on the contextual clues to help her identify the problematic rate of delivery. Furthermore, Deng employed the cognitive operation of making connections to aid in her deep-processing of this feedback. Deng related her own speech rate with that of speakers in TED talks.

> I watched some of my favorite TED talks once again after class. When I was watching, I compared my speech with theirs. It appeared that they spoke at a pleasing rate. Not too fast and not too slow. My speech was perhaps fast and my thinking process was faster than the audience's auditory processing. Anyway, my audience were not native speakers of English.
>
> (Final interview with Deng)

In addition to the cognitive operations of predicting and making connections, Deng used visualization to understand why the teacher had criticized her frequent uses of gestures during presentations. Deng mentioned that she originally could not make sense of the teacher's criticism, and then she was able to process it by producing mental imagery of a speaker gesturing constantly throughout the presentation: "Too many and too big gestures look unnatural and can distract the audience's attention" (1st stimulated recall with Deng).

In terms of behavioral engagement, although there were three written errors on PPT slides treated by the teacher CF, no revision operations can be identified because Deng did not modify her PPT slides of the three oral presentations, which was totally unexpected. In the words of Deng, "It (oral presentation) is a one-time thing. I think our revisions are not mandated. They are optional and not strictly required by the teacher" (Final interview with Deng). Nevertheless, Deng argued that she had acted upon teacher feedback in terms of applying feedback insights to her subsequent oral presentations. An example of her behavioral engagement was that Deng converted her rapid speech rate into a more pleasing one in her second oral presentation. Her change of delivery rate was also observed and acknowledged by the teacher who commented, "Actually, it is quite good this time because you controlled the rhythm of your speech" (Amelia's feedback—To Deng—Presentation 2). When asked how she managed to slow down, Deng said, "I attempted to imagine punctuations, such as commas for pauses and periods for breaks. I also used pausing as the strategy to control my rates, such as pausing between one PPT slide and the next slide" (Final interview with Deng).

In addition, a mismatch was revealed between Deng's cognitive engagement and behavioral engagement. As mentioned earlier, Deng was fully aware that frequent gestures could distract the audience, but she still failed to control her gestures during her second and third oral presentations. This is probably because, in Deng's words, "it's not easy to break old habits" (Final interview with Deng).

To summarize, although Deng affectively engaged with most of teacher feedback with calm and rationality, her cognitive engagement was not as extensive as expected. The analysis showed that Deng opted to pay attention to the teacher's just-for-me feedback which she was able to process except for one feedback point. Specifically, Deng used three cognitive operations (i.e., predicting, making connections, and visualization) to make sense of the feedback received. In terms of behavioral engagement, although Deng did not revise her PPT slides of the three presentations, she managed to act upon the teacher's feedback on her speech rate during presentation delivery.

5.1.2 Wang: An Intermediate-Proficiency Student's Engagement with Teacher Feedback

5.1.2.1 Wang's Background

Wang was a female sophomore who chose the English Language and Literature as her major. She was an intermediate-proficiency student and had ranked twelfth in the oral English placement test in the first year of college. Like Deng, Wang was also highly motivated to learn English, but unlike Deng, she did not opt for any minors as she claimed, "I only care about learning English" (1st interview with Wang). Wang's intrinsic motivation to learn English was derived from her appreciation of the beauty of the English language. She liked experiencing new cultures and was especially fond of reading English poems, essays, and novels.

Wang described herself as a shy introvert. She was unwilling to take part in any student societies or associations. The classroom observation and field notes showed that Wang often blushed and avoided eye contact when she spoke in public. Moreover, Wang was an obedient and well-behaved student who, according to Amelia's comments, listened attentively to lectures and finished assignments on time.

Wang recalled her past experience of learning English in high school as being full of exam papers, tests, vocabulary, and grammar.

> Every day we were immersed in numerous grammar and vocabulary exercises. We needed to memorize new words and grammar rules. Actually, I don't remember having many listening exercises. Also, we did not take oral tests either.
>
> (1st interview with Wang)

Prior to her formal college study, Wang was already aware of her lack of listening and speaking proficiency, so she had read the words that should be mastered at the level of the Test for English Majors Band 4 (TEM4) in order to achieve accurate word pronunciation. However, Wang was still stunned by some of her classmates' excellent pronunciation and oral fluency, claiming, "I felt like all my efforts were in vain. While my pronunciation is fine, the intonation is not good and I cannot express myself in English in a very clear way" (1st interview with Wang).

Wang had mixed feelings about Amelia's assignment of group presentations. On the one hand, Wang was afraid that her inadequate competence in oral English led to her feeling nervous when speaking in front of her classmates. On the other hand, she was happy to have this opportunity to practice public speaking skills, because she did not have much experience in this regard. As indicated in the first interview, Wang perceived oral fluency as important as interesting content, as she said, "Both these two aspects can impress the audience and grab their attention and interest" (1st interview with Wang). Wang volunteered to be the regular presenter of her group presentations. The presentations focused on Chinese and Western attitudes towards love, in which they talked about the position of love in people' hearts and the manner of expressing love.

5.1.2.2　Wang's Engagement with Teacher Feedback

The data analysis showed that Wang's affective engagement was different from that of Deng. In contrast to Deng's rationality, Wang had mixed feelings upon the receipt of teacher feedback. Below is an example of the teacher's use of hedges when commenting on Wang's speaking volume.

> You should raise your voice. I don't know. How about those boys sitting at the back of the classroom? Could you hear her words or sentences? Could you hear her clearly? No, they are shaking their heads. So, you should pay attention to your voice.
>
> (Amelia's feedback—To Wang—Presentation 1)

Wang recalled that she was extremely nervous at first because she had always known that she had a weak voice and thought the teacher was going to bluntly criticize her. Then, the feeling of appreciation welled up in her when she realized that the teacher asked for a peer response which was, in Wang's opinion, "the act of protecting her public image" (1st stimulated recall with Wang).

Meanwhile, she also reported negative emotional experiences induced by teacher feedback. For instance, Wang felt embarrassed when the teacher pointed out grammatical and punctuation errors on her PPT slides, claiming "The mistakes were quite obvious. Anyone could detect them with a simple glance. I should have checked and double-checked the PPT slides before presentations began" (Wang's reflective account). The stimulated recalls also suggested Wang's anger and disappointment when the teacher questioned her about evidence and information provided

Chapter 5 Student Engagement with Teacher Feedback on Oral Presentations

in oral presentations: "Better find some supporting statements from academic writing or from some internet data. Find something more reliable" (Amelia's feedback—To Wang—Presentation 2). Upon hearing this, Wang was prompted to an outburst of anger and argued that they did find pertinent research materials from the Baidu's Online Library (Baidu is a Chinese search engine giant), claiming that "the teacher accused me unfairly" (2nd stimulated recall with Wang). One possible explanation for Wang's anger was that no references or URLs were found on Wang's PPT slides, which was met with the teacher's incredulity. Another emotional response was the lingering upset felt by Wang while revising the PPT slides. She reported that she was unable to incorporate some suggestions from the teacher and felt helpless during the revisions: "Strong feelings of anxiety welled up in me. I wish I knew how to make the suggested revisions" (Final interview with Wang).

Wang received a total of 39 teacher feedback points, predominantly on content and organizational issues. Nevertheless, the stimulated recalls showed that Wang's cognitive engagement was mostly manifested in her processing of language form-related feedback, as shown in the example below.

The teacher commented on this PPT slide (see Figure 5.1) by using the CF strategy of explicit correction (see oral CF episode 1 in section 4.1.3 for more details). While the teacher did not provide detailed metalinguistic explanations, Wang activated prior knowledge of what she had learned in another course of *Communicative English* and conducted a metalinguistic analysis to work out the semantic difference between the two words: "opening" and "open".

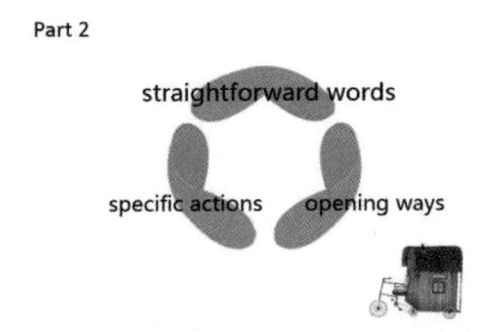

Figure 5.1 Excerpt of PPT slide—Wang—Presentation 2

Researcher: Did you understand this feedback?

Wang: Yes. The teacher said I should change "opening" into "open".

Researcher: Well, did you know why you should make such a revision?

Wang: Um. I remembered the *Communicative English* teacher explained to us that the word "open" meant being sincere in expression and the word "opening" meant the beginning of something. So, it should be "open" ways.

(2nd stimulated recall with Wang)

In addition, Wang was able to work out the teacher's intention despite not understanding some unfamiliar words in teacher feedback. Below is an example of Wang's use of multiple cognitive and metacognitive operations when processing teacher oral CF on her PPT slide (see Figure 5.2).

Oral CF Episode 4

Pay attention to the detail. It should be contents, the letter "s", because you cover more than one content, right? [→explicit correction] So, there should be a plural form of the word "content".

(Amelia's feedback—To Wang—Presentation 3)

Wang: I did not hear the word "plural", but I heard that the teacher said I had covered more than one content. She also repeated the letter "s".

Researcher: Did you know the meaning of the word "plural"?

Wang: Perhaps it meant more than one because the teacher said more than one in her feedback.

Researcher: So, did you understand why the title should be changed into "contents"?

Wang: Um... At that time, I was not really sure, but I think it's because I covered three parts in my presentation. You can see there are three bullet points (Wang is pointing to the PPT slide).

(3rd stimulated recall with Wang)

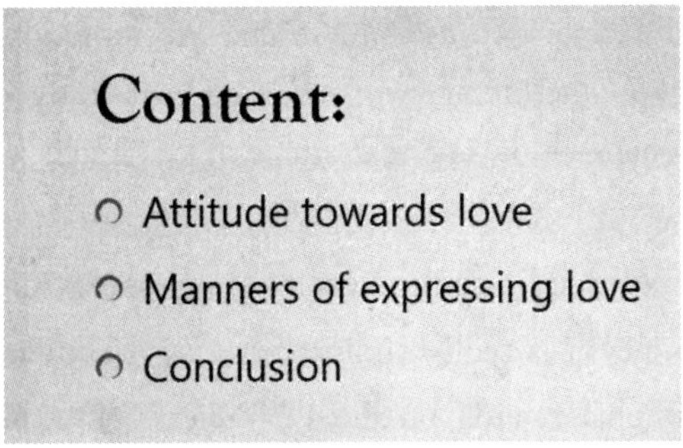

Chapter 5 Student Engagement with Teacher Feedback on Oral Presentations

> **Content:**
>
> ○ Attitude towards love
> ○ Manners of expressing love
> ○ Conclusion

Figure 5.2 Excerpt of PPT slide—Wang—Presentation 3

At the very moment of receiving this oral CF, Wang did not catch the word "plural", nor did she understand why the title "Content" should be modified into "Contents", as suggested by the teacher. Wang honed her attention by listening selectively to the linguistic marker "*s*", and made the connection between "more than one" and "plural" to work out the semantic meaning of "plural." Wang also used the contextual clue (i.e., three bullet points on this PPT slide) to predict the reason for the teacher's suggested revision.

Wang's cognitive engagement with teacher feedback was also manifested in her employment of a metacognitive operation (i.e., planning) in the revision processes. She first dealt with form-related feedback and then addressed feedback on presentation content and organization: "There were two rounds of revisions. The first round of revisions centered on correcting form-related problems pointed out, such as grammatical and lexical errors, inappropriate font size, and PPT layout. During the first round of revisions, I made a pause at the content and structural issues and then addressed them in the second round" (Wang's reflective account).

While Wang managed to process form-related teacher feedback, her engagement with feedback at the macro-level (e.g., feedback on content and organization of presentation) was superficial. There was one case where Wang's cognitive processing was constrained by her limited knowledge about the structural organization of oral presentation. In her three oral presentations, Wang used literary works (e.g., poetry and drama) as supporting materials to exhibit her topic (i.e., the attitude to love in Chinese and Western cultures). However, she did not explain how the literary works related back to the central argument of her speech. The feedback below is one example of this issue.

> There is no specific illustration. Just one poem here... Then, why do you think this poem is really straightforward? (The teacher is pointing to the word "straightforward" on the PPT slide) How is it related to your point? Think about it.
> (Amelia's feedback —To Wang—Presentation 2)

Researcher: Did you understand what the teacher said?

Wang: Um, I did not quite get it. She said I need a specific illustration. Illustration? Did an illustration mean an example? But, I already used the poem as an example. What else could I do? Shall I find a more appropriate poem to replace it? I had no idea what to do with it.
(2nd stimulated recall with Wang)

In the excerpt above, Wang had a partial understanding of the word "illustration", believing it meant "an example". When processing this feedback, she failed to make the connection between the teacher's intention and the teacher's paralanguage (i.e., pointing to the word "straightforward" on the PPT slide). In other words, Wang inaccurately connected the feedback to a content issue instead of a structural problem because she thought of replacing the original poem with another one.

Wang's behavioral engagement can be primarily examined from two aspects: the revisions to the PPT slides and the specific actions taken to apply feedback to improve oral presentation delivery. Since Wang did not revise the PPT slides of her first oral presentation, the analysis of the revision operations only included revisions made on PPT slides of her second and third oral presentations. Table 5.1 summarizes the revision operations induced by different types of teacher feedback.

Table 5.1   Wang's revision operations induced by teacher feedback

Focus of feedback	Language	Content	Organization	Presentation aid
Feedback point	5	4	7	4
Correction	5	1	2	3
No change	0	3	5	1
Feedback in total	20			
Total correction	11			
Revision rate	55%			

Note. The feedback excludes teacher compliments.

The analysis yielded 20 teacher feedback (excluding compliments) points. Wang only acted upon eleven feedback points (55%) in which she successfully corrected all the written grammatical and lexical errors on the PPT slides. Given Wang's deep cognitive engagement with form-related feedback, it is not surprising that she addressed linguistic accuracy and appropriateness effectively. However, Wang only managed to address three feedback points on presentation content and organization. For example, the teacher suggested that Wang summarize the main contents of her third presentation before reaching a final conclusion.

> This part could be a little bit confusing. Actually, for me, I regard it as the general conclusion of your three whole presentations. Okay. Next time, think about the layer of the presentation. You still need a brief summary of today's presentation, your third presentation.
> (Amelia's feedback—Wang—Presentation 3)

Although Wang believed that "there was no need to sum up what she said in her third presentation" (3rd stimulated recall with Wang), she did act upon this feedback by adding a slide titled "A Brief Summary" (see Figure 5.3) in her revisions to PPT slides. As an obedient student, Wang explained her revision, claiming that "I think the teacher is authoritative in this regard. So better do exactly what she tells me, although I do not agree with her" (Final interview with Wang).

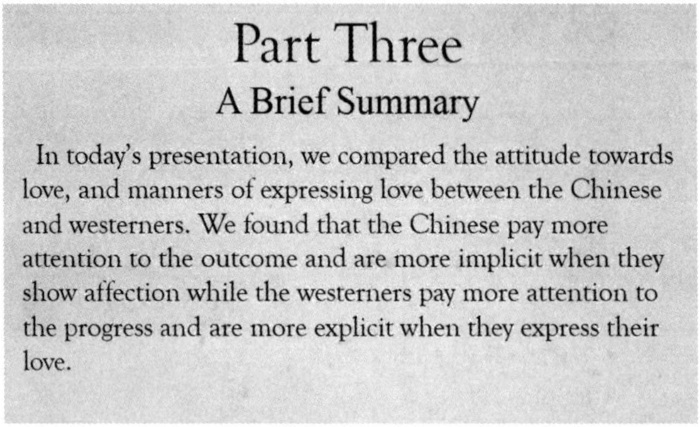

> **Part Three**
> **A Brief Summary**
> In today's presentation, we compared the attitude towards love, and manners of expressing love between the Chinese and westerners. We found that the Chinese pay more attention to the outcome and are more implicit when they show affection while the westerners pay more attention to the progress and are more explicit when they express their love.

Figure 5.3 Excerpt of revised PPT slide —Wang— Presentation 3

There were also two self-edited revisions after comparing Wang's original PPT slides and revised ones: Wang changed the PPT background and deformed fonts in the slides, which were originally in different styles, into a harmonized whole. In Wang's words, "The original slides looked like being made by different people because of the different font sizes and colors of PPT background. I think it looks much better now after my modification" (Wang's reflective account).

In addition, Wang's behavioral engagement was manifested in the aspect of presentation delivery, which can be observed in the video-recordings as well as verified by teacher feedback. After her first oral presentation, it was suggested that Wang pay attention to the volume of her voice and the appropriacy of her pauses: "As for me, it's a little bit quick. I haven't finished reading the title and you immediately moved to the second slide. Just take it easy. Take your time and slow down a little bit." (Amelia's feedback—To Wang—Presentation 1). Unlike Deng who resorted to external sources of TED talks, Wang acted upon this feedback by video-recording the rehearsal: "I used the cellphone to record my rehearsal. It turned out that I did not make any pauses when I went through the PPT slides. So, I performed it again and intentionally used pauses to slow down the pacing of my presentation" (Wang's reflective account). Wang's

Chapter 5 Student Engagement with Teacher Feedback on Oral Presentations

adoption of this suggestion was also acknowledged by the teacher who said after her second oral presentation: "This time the volume of the voice is fine and the speed and the rhythm is really good" (Amelia's feedback —To Wang— Presentation 2).

To sum up, Wang's multi-layered affective engagement was reflected in her varying emotional reactions to teacher feedback: anxiety, appreciation, anger, and upset. It appeared that her negative emotions impeded her immediate processing of teacher feedback and further revision operations. The stimulated recalls revealed that Wang cognitively engaged with the teacher's form-related feedback, whereas she disengaged from content- and organization-focused feedback. Specifically, Wang employed three cognitive operations (i.e., activating prior knowledge, making connections, and prediction) to figure out errors and reflect upon previous metalinguistic knowledge. Wang also used the metacognitive operation of planning to regulate her revision operations. In line with her cognitive engagement, Wang's revision operations were effective concerning linguistic accuracy but ineffective when it came to content and structural issues. Not only did she revise her PPT slides, she also used external resources of video-recordings to improve her presentation delivery.

5.1.3 Li: A Lower-Proficiency Student's Engagement with Teacher Feedback

5.1.3.1 Li's Background

Li was a male second-year English-majored undergraduate at the university. He was a lower-proficiency student and had ranked twentieth in the oral English placement test in the previous academic year. Li came from Gansu Province in the west of China, where the quality of primary and secondary English language teaching is still relatively low. Li neither liked studying English at high school, nor did he have opportunities to practice English speaking and listening at that time. He acknowledged that he was pushed to learn English by his father and had to cram for English exams. Li was not enrolled in the intended major of Chemical Engineering because of low grades at the College Entrance Examination. Therefore, he had to apply for a transfer to the English major. In the words of Li, "I felt lost. I did not choose to be an English major. I find it hard to follow what teachers said during the lectures. Most of the time I am absent-minded" (1st interview with Li). Amelia also commented that Li did not seem to be highly motivated to study English, as he always lowered his head and looked down at his cellphone in class.

In contrast to Deng and Wang, who more or less acknowledged the importance of speaking in English learning, Li had no ambitious goal and simply wanted to pass all the exams so that he could graduate. As an English major, Li did not take the initiative in self-regulated oral English practice. On the one hand, he perceived that limited vocabulary constrained his ability to carry out conversations with his peers; on the other hand, he was afraid that other students would not understand him if he spoke English.

> I seldom speak English or attempt to practice oral English after class. There was one time in my freshman year when I was dragged by my roommate to accompany him to the English Corner. It was a terrible experience for me. I opened my mouth to say something, but nothing except very simple English words and sentences came out.
>
> (1st interview with Li)

Although Li claimed that there was a small chance that he would be able to speak fluent English in the future, he expressed his wish to become an English sports reporter for the National Basketball Association (NBA) tournament.

Li's beliefs about the role of oral presentation in English learning evolved over the course of the research. He indicated in the first interview that he did not think highly of oral presentations because they could increase his learning pressure and academic burden and lead to nervousness. Like Deng, Li also complained of being the regular presenter of his group presentations. However, in his final interview, Li changed his attitude to oral presentations, stating that "making oral presentations actually helps improve my confidence and willingness to speak English" (Final interview with Li). The topic of Li's group presentations was die-

Chapter 5　Student Engagement with Teacher Feedback on Oral Presentations

tary cultures, in which food and eating patterns, cooking methods, and table manners in both China and Western countries were addressed.

5.1.3.2　Li's Engagement with Teacher Feedback

The stimulated recalls indicated that Li immediately experienced annoyance, embarrassment, and guilt when the teacher gave feedback on his poor task performance. However, unlike Wang who had been upset throughout the revision processes, Li was able to regulate these negative feelings because he placed full focus on working out the corrections and revisions: "I attempted to think hard about figuring out how to use the teacher's suggestions. All the bad moods seemed to disappear" (Li's reflective account). In fact, in the final interview, Li claimed that he was not at all anxious or upset about receiving negative feedback: "Now I tend to think criticism also demonstrates the teacher's concern because she wants to help me to improve my performance" (Final interview with Li).

Li's motivational trajectory was also one important aspect of his affective engagement with teacher feedback. In his reflective account, Li described how motivation played a part in his engagement with teacher feedback. For Li, the teacher's act of giving public feedback had a function of incentivizing him to make more revisions and perform better in future oral presentations.

> When I found that the teacher praised other groups' eye-catching delivery instead of ours, I also wanted her compliments. Therefore, in the second presentation I set some animations in the display of the PPT slides and prepared a question and answer part to better attract the audience's attention. As expected, the teacher recognized my efforts. I've never been particularly motivated to do better in the third presentation.
>
> (Li's reflective account)

With regard to cognitive engagement, the stimulated recalls indicated that Li took notice of 29 out of 40 teacher feedback points. Apparently, Li did not have an extensive understanding of teacher feedback. This was probably because, on the one hand, he did not listen attentively to teacher feedback provided on his first oral presentation, as he confessed: "My teammates had done everything, including searching for supporting materials and making the PPT slides. They even prepared the whole speech for me. Thus, I only paid attention to the feedback addressed to me as the speaker, after which I just played with my cellphone" (1st stimulated recall with Li). On the other hand, Li's cognitive disengagement was because that Li might have misunderstood the teacher's intentions behind certain feedback. For example, it was found that a term (i.e., rational concept) was still not clarified in his revised PPT slides of second oral presentation. In fact, the teacher recalled that she had intended to raise Li's awareness of audience needs through her feedback. Although the teacher explained that a clear definition of this term was necessary, Li refused to modify: "I thought it was a common phrase used in English. There was no need to clarify this term. Everybody knows it because you can find it on the internet" (2nd stimulated recall with Li). That being said, Li failed to take on board this feedback information and it was disappointingly observed that he still did not clarify this term in his third oral presentation.

Despite his inadequate English listening and comprehension skills, Li was surprisingly successful in recognizing the corrective force of teacher CF. Li often made connections between the CF strategy of elicitation with previous in-class grammar instruction to ascertain the teacher's corrective intention: "When I finished reading a passage or answering a question, the teacher would ask me 'how to say this word in English?' or 'Please read this word for us.' Usually, this was the case where I had mispronounced the word. It's the teacher's common CF practice" (Final interview with Li). This cognitive operation was also found in other cases where Li analyzed the specific locations of his pronunciation errors. In the oral CF episode 5, the teacher combined elicitation, recast, and metalinguistic clue to help Li detect the error treated.

Oral CF Episode 5

Amelia: (The teacher is writing the word "therapy" on the blackboard)

Chapter 5 Student Engagement with Teacher Feedback on Oral Presentations

How do we say this word in English? [→elicitation]

Li: /ˈθeirəpi/ [→uptake with no repair]

Amelia: /ˈθerəpi/.需要用单元音。[→recast + metalinguistic clue in Chinese]

(Amelia's feedback—To Li—Presentation 2)

In the stimulated recall, Li indicated that the teacher's use of L1 (i.e., Chinese) facilitated his diagnosis of the pronunciation error. Li successfully identified the vowel error by connecting his erroneous output (/ˈθeirəpi/) with the modified output (/ˈθerəpi/) by the teacher.

Researcher: What was worng with your pronunciation of this word?

Li: Um, the vowel. It should be /e/ not /ei/.

Researcher: Well, how did you know that?

Li: The teacher explained it to me in Chinese. She also pronounced this word. When I compared her pronunciation with my own, it was easy to detect that I had used the wrong vowel.

(2nd stimulated recall with Li)

In addition to making connections, reasoning in terms of metalinguistic analysis was also a cognitive operation used by Li to diagnose the error and identify the error source. Oral CF episode 6 is an example of Li retrieving his metalinguistic knowledge to identify the error (see Figure 5.4).

Oral CF Episode 6

Okay. Title. (The teacher is hovering the computer mouse over the title "Conclude") …Pay attention to the small details here. So, better noun not verb. Okay? [→metalinguistic clue]

(Amelia's feedback—To Li—Presentation 3)

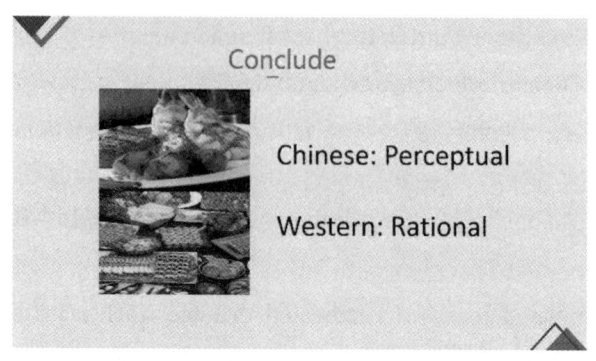

Figure 5.4 Excerpt of PPT slide—Li—Presentation 3

Li diagnosed the part of speech error by retrieving his metalinguistic knowledge about the derivational form (d→s+ion) of the verb "conclude". As he stated, "When I heard the two words 'noun' and 'verb', I realized that the problem was the word 'conclude' itself. It should be 'conclusion'" (3rd stimulated recall with Li).

Another cognitive operation that Li used was making predictions when processing unfamiliar words in teacher feedback. In his third oral presentation, the teacher suggested that Li enlarge the font size of texts on PPT slides: "I am not so sure about the font size here. (The teacher is pointing to the written texts on the slide) It is still small. It should be at least 24 points." Although Li did not understand the word "font", he used information conveyed through the teacher's nonverbal language to figure out the teacher's intention.

>Researcher: Did you understand what the teacher said?
>Li: Yes. She said font size for these words should be at least 24 points.
>Researcher: The teacher did not use "word" in her feedback. She used "font" instead. Did you know the word "font"?
>Li: Um, I did not know it. But when she commented on the slide, she hovered the computer mouse over these words. What else could it be?
>(3rd stimulated recall with Li)

Li's cognitive engagement was also manifested in his use of the metacognitive operation of monitoring. When revising the PPT slides, Li checked the accuracy of the possible revisions that had been suggested by the teacher. There was one excerpt that particularly revealed his thoughts when monitoring a revision operation: "Although the teacher said 'heat' should be replaced with 'calorie', I was still not sure about the correction. I then decided to consult the Youdao (i.e., an on-line dictionary). It turned out that the teacher was right because 'calorie' is a more suitable word to measure the energy value of food" (Li's reflective account). This indicates that Li engaged in the deep processing of specific lexical choice and applied strategies by confirming with external sources.

With regard to behavioral engagement, Li not only generated revisions to the PPT slides of three oral presentations but also improved his presentation delivery. Table 5.2 summarizes his revision operations in response to different foci of teacher feedback. Out of 24 teacher feedback (excluding compliments) points in total, Li acted upon 18 (75%) feedback points. A careful analysis revealed that four out of the six teacher feedback points unaddressed were given in response to Li's first oral presentation. As mentioned earlier, Li did not even listen attentively to Amelia's feedback on his first presentation let alone making revisions accordingly. It appeared that Li's revision operations were closely related to the level of attention he paid to specific teacher feedback.

Table 5.2　　Li's revision operations induced by teacher feedback

Focus of feedback	Language	Content	Organization	Presentation aid
Feedback point	7	7	3	7
Correction	5	5	2	6
No change	2	2	1	1
Feedback in total	24			
Total correction	18			
Revision rate	75%			

Note. The feedback excludes teacher compliments.

In addition to using artifacts (e.g., downloading pictures from Baidu Image and referring to the Youdao dictionary) in his revision processes, Li also approached his roommate for assistance. Li stated that this decision was made because he ran out of ideas about how to revise the conclusion of his second oral presentation. That being said, Li's contribution was merely repeating the teacher's feedback rather than generating concrete revision operations.

> Although my roommate was not in the same class with me, I still decided to seek help from him...I told him that the teacher said the conclusion should be a summary and I should not bring up new ideas that had not been covered in the presentation... He simply let me explain the contents of my second presentation to him in Chinese. Then, he rewrote the conclusion for me in English.
>
> (Li's reflective account)

Another aspect of Li's behavioral engagement with Amelia's feedback was reflected in his changing modes of presentation delivery. As shown in the video-recordings, Li read his speech manuscript word-for-word throughout the first presentation; he then memorized and recited the full speech in the second presentation; finally, he managed to deliver the third presentation in a structured conversational style. On the one hand, this behavioral engagement was driven by Li's intrinsic motivation to perform better each time. As Li stated, "When I performed a little bit better than the last time, it was a kind of progress for me" (Final interview with Li); on the other hand, Li's development of self-efficacy prompted him to take actions: "I attempted to tell myself that I could perform better as long as I was fully prepared for the task ahead" (Final interview with Li).

In conclusion, to the researcher's surprise, although Li was a lower-proficiency student, he was relatively successful in terms of processing teacher feedback as well as generating revision operations and improving presentation skills. His successful cognitive and behavioral engagement was closely related to his regulation of negative emotions and use of external sources (e.g., material and human artifacts) while engaging with feedback.

5.2 Engagement with Teacher Feedback: Student Cases from Gwen's Class

5.2.1 Wu: A High-Proficiency Student's Engagement with Teacher Feedback

5.2.1.1 Wu's Background

The high-proficiency student in Gwen's class was Wu, a female sophomore majoring in English Language and Literature and minoring in International Trade. Wu had ranked the highest in the oral English placement test in the previous academic year. The field notes showed that Wu was very active in class in terms of volunteering to answer Gwen's questions and participating in group discussions. It appeared that Wu had intrinsic motivations to speak English. For one thing, she was interested in the rhythm of English which she found quite different from Chinese. For another, Wu claimed that she found speaking English enjoyable and was willing to chat with her classmates in English after class: "I spend a lot of time at the English Corner where I can make new friends. It's fun" (1st interview with Wu).

Wu liked making oral presentations in class because, in her own words, "It was an opportunity to practice oral English and communicate ideas" (1st interview with Wu). Wu believed that oral competence and presentation skills were superior to content and organization. In line with this learning belief, Wu highly valued Gwen's oral CF: she thought that error correction was part of L2 learning and wanted to learn metalinguistic knowledge about the target L2 structures. Wu also believed that oral CF helped her detect learning weaknesses in terms of linguistic accuracy and she preferred to conduct self-correction of linguistic errors.

5.2.1.2 Wu's Engagement with Teacher Feedback

The analysis yielded a total of 31 teacher feedback points provided on Wu's three oral presentations, and the majority of feedback centered on incorrect language use (i.e., pronunciation and lexical errors). Although Wu claimed that she welcomed the teacher's error correction, she was stunned by the amount of CF given by Gwen, especially on her first oral presentation.

> Researcher: How did you feel after the teacher's error correction?
> Wu: Um, I was shocked. I certainly knew that my presentation cannot be error-free, but how could I possibly make so many mistakes? I was disappointed in myself.
> (1st stimulated recall with Wu)

The excerpt above indicated that the amount of teacher oral CF exceeded Wu's expectation, which probably led to her suffering from disappointment. Wu explained that some of the errors were made because she did not know the correct forms from the outset. Others were due to slips of the tongue. At the end of the stimulated recall, Wu expressed her resolution to shake off the negative emotions, as she commented, "After all I can learn from the teacher's correction. Next time when I make more careful preparations, I am sure the number of errors will decrease" (1st stimulated recall with Wu).

With regard to cognitive engagement, her verbal reports during the stimulated recalls indicated that Wu detected all thirteen CF points provided to her. Her successful recognition of the corrective intentions behind teacher CF was closely related to the corrective practices of Gwen who often began his error correction by saying, for example:

> Now, I would like to call your attention to some pronunciation problems…
> Again, I'd like to point out some of your improper pronunciations…
> Here, you used the wrong word…
> (Gwen's feedback—To Wu—Presentation 1)

Chapter 5 Student Engagement with Teacher Feedback on Oral Presentations

As illustrated in the quotes above, Gwen liked to use such words as "problem", "improper", and "wrong" before making further corrections. This practice facilitated learner awareness of teacher corrective intent. As Wu claimed, "Once the teacher said something was wrong with my blah, blah, blah, this was the signal for her error correction" (Final interview with Wu).

Wu was able to accurately provide reasons for almost all errors treated by CF, and only three errors were not explained, which indicates Wu's deep processing of teacher oral CF. In the processes of working out underlying rules of treated errors, Wu was, on the one hand, facilitated by the teacher's detailed metalinguistic explanations; on the other hand, she resorted to the use of two cognitive operations: reasoning and activating background knowledge. In terms of reasoning, Wu employed the metalinguistic rules that she had learned to identify the error sources and generate further revision operations. The excerpt below is an example illustrating how Wu conducted the metalinguistic analysis of a non-target-like L2 structure.

> *Oral CF Episode 7*
> *On the other hand, it makes us be embarrassed.*
> Gwen: Yeah, This slide. Here. Please read this sentence again. It makes us? [→elicitation]
> Wu: (Wu read the sentence again without making any corrections). [→uptake with no repair]
> (Gwen's feedback—To Wu—Presentation 2)

In this case, Wu did not initially make a successful repair of the error. However, she later succeeded in generating the revision and deleted the word "be" when she handed in the revised PPT slides. As she remarked:

> The error cannot be the word "makes" because the verb and subject must agree in person. The subject is "it", so the verb should be "makes"…I

remember my high school English teacher said "make sb do sth" or "make sth+adjective". The adjective serves as the complement of the word "make". The word "be" should be deleted. It is unnecessary here.

(Wu's reflective account)

In the excerpt above, Wu not only identified the error source by conducting an analysis of the linguistic rule (i.e., the agreement between verb and subject) but also retrieved previous metalinguistic knowledge about the use of an adjective as an object complement.

In addition, a striking difference was found between Wu's processing of form-focused feedback and content-related feedback. While Wu's cognitive engagement with teacher oral CF was extensive, she unconsciously disengaged from feedback on content and organizational issues in her presentations. Wu's lack of understanding could be due to the mode of collaboration at the task preparation stage. As mentioned in section 3.3.1, Gwen required students to give presentations in pairs. When interviewed, Wu stated that she and her teammate had been responsible for different jobs: her teammate searched for supporting materials and organized these materials in a Microsoft Word document, while Wu made the PPT slides and wrote the presentation speech manuscripts. Consequently, Wu showed a very limited understanding of teacher feedback provided on the content matters.

When the teacher asked me whether there were other ways of protecting the environment, my mind went completely blank. I did not know the answer because the information was not searched by me. Thanks to my teammate, she immediately responded to the teacher's question.

(2nd stimulated recall with Wu)

Behaviorally, Wu revised the PPT slides of all three rounds of presentations. Table 5.3 summarizes her revision operations in response to teacher feedback. Wu mostly acted upon teacher feedback on presentation aids in such aspects of reducing bullet points and texts on PPT slides and using background and text colors well. Given that Wu cognitively disengaged from content feedback, it was hardly surprising that she did not make any of the suggested revisions to the content and organizational issues in oral presentations.

Table 5.3   Wu's revision operations induced by teacher feedback

Focus of feedback	Language	Content	Organization	Presentation aid
Feedback point	13	2	0	5
Correction	3	0	0	4
No change	10	2	0	1
Feedback in total	20			
Total correction	7			
Revision rate	35%			

Note. The feedback excludes teacher compliments.

However, it was unexpected that Wu's revision operations in response to teacher CF were also very limited. The results (see Table 5.3) showed that Wu only repaired three out of these thirteen linguistic errors. Wu's lack of revision operations might be partially attributed to her lack of opportunity for follow-up learner repair. After Wu failed to repair non-target-like L2 structures in the first place, Gwen tended to either explicitly correct errors or only provide metalinguistic comments without offering further opportunities for learner repair.

To summarize, Wu was able to regulate her negative emotions upon receiving teacher CF. Moreover, despite her deep cognitive engagement with teacher language form-focused feedback, her revision operations in this regard were not as extensive as expected.

5.2.2 Chen: An Intermediate-Proficiency Student's Engagement with Teacher Feedback

5.2.2.1 Chen's Background

Chen was also a female sophomore in Gwen's class. She was identified as an intermediate-proficiency student as she ranked tenth in the oral English placement test in the previous academic year. Born and raised in a small town in Shandong province, Chen complained that she lacked opportunities to practice English listening and speaking at primary and secondary schools. She had difficulties in understanding the teachers' lessons and participating in class discussions in the first year of her undergraduate studies. While Chen attempted to catch up with her classmates, her efforts appeared to be in vain. Chen appeared to be demotivated to enhance her oral English proficiency at the time of the study. As she remarked, "I have seized every opportunity to practice listening and speaking, but the learning outcomes were not as good as I expected. I still did not get high scores in the oral English placement test" (1st interview with Chen). Chen stated that she only wanted to pass the TEM4 and TEM8. In line with this learning goal, Chen, unlike Wu, did not consider oral competence to be the foundation of successful English learning: "These tests (TEM4 and TEM8) do not necessarily have an oral procedure. I only need to excel in grammar, reading comprehension, translation, and writing" (1st interview with Chen).

In her opinion, the main purpose of an in-class oral presentation was to enable the presenter to share subject content-related knowledge in an organized manner to the teacher and student peers. Linguistic accuracy was considered by Chen to be secondary to presentation content. Chen also placed great emphasis on effective oral presentation structure and PPT slide layout, which helped presenters to stay on topic and allow the audience to keep up with them: "If the PPT slides are made in a logical and clear way, the audience will easily take away the messages" (1st interview with Chen).

5.2.2.2 Chen's Engagement with Teacher Feedback

Chen commented that she was not satisfied with Gwen's feedback practices since she expected that the teacher would provide more content-focused feedback. Indeed, the feedback analysis revealed that 40 teacher feedback points were provided to Chen, among which only 15 feedback points focused on the contents and organization of her presentations, whereas much of the remaining teacher feedback was targeted at Chen's non-target-like L2 structures. For example, Chen recalled after her first oral presentation:

Chapter 5　Student Engagement with Teacher Feedback on Oral Presentations

　　Researcher: How did you feel at the moment of receiving the teacher's feedback?

　　Chen: So many mispronunciations were pointed out. It's embarrassing.

　　Researcher: Didn't you like these corrections?

　　Chen: No. I did not feel like opening my mouth and speaking English again. I thought the teacher might comment on whether the contents of this presentation were complete or not, or something like that. However, the teacher only summarized the presentation.

(1st stimulated recall with Chen)

　　On the one hand, Chen felt embarrassed about receiving too much error correction and her confidence in public speaking decreased. On the other hand, Chen appeared to be disappointed, which was probably because the teacher had not shown explicit care for and recognition of her work. As she remarked later in the stimulated recall, "My teammate speaks English better than I do, so we discussed that she wrote the speech for both of us and I searched for relevant information and made the PPT slides". Like Wu, Chen also appeared to collaborate poorly with her teammate when they prepared for the task, thus contributing to her dissatisfaction with teacher feedback. Unfortunately, it has been found that Chen and her teammate continued to adopt this collaborative manner in their second and third oral presentations.

　　Probably because she was emotionally upset, Chen's cognitive engagement with teacher CF was not very extensive. Out of the 15 errors treated by teacher CF, Chen recognized the corrective intentions behind eleven CF points. This can be attributed to Gwen's employment of elicitations and clarification requests as main CF strategies. Below is an example showing that Chen misunderstood Gwen's intention of providing CF.

Oral CF Episode 8

　　Gwen: How do you say 唐宋时期 in English?[→elicitation]

　　Chen: Tangsong Dynasty.[→uptake with no repair]

Gwen: You used the Chinese phonetic alphabet. How to say it in English?[→elicitation]

Chen: (silence) [→no further uptake]

(Gwen's feedback—To Chen—Presentation 2)

In the CF episode above, the teacher asked Chen to use English to express a proper noun in Chinese (唐宋时期) because the teacher noticed that Chen had said it incorrectly in her presentation. However, for Chen, the teacher's elicitation was intended for her answering a general question instead of prompting self-correction. As Chen recalled:

Chen: I thought the teacher did not hear me clearly while I was presenting, so he asked me to repeat it.

Researcher: Well, did you know why the teacher asked you to say it again in English?

Chen: I had no idea why. Isn't the Chinese phrase 唐宋时期 called Tang-song Dynasty in English?

(2nd stimulated recall with Chen)

Furthermore, Chen was only able to explain eight errors that she recognized as being treated by teacher CF. Her understanding of and explanations for CF was facilitated by Gwen's specific metalinguistic comments. When processing these metalinguistic explanations, Chen often made connections between her L1 (i.e., Chinese) and L2 (i.e., English) and was able to work out the teacher's intentions and generate revision operations. For example:

Oral CF Episode 9

Gwen: How to pronounce this word when it is used as a noun? (The teacher is writing "content" on the blackboard) [→elicitation]

Chen: /kən'tent/[→uptake with no repair]

Chapter 5 Student Engagement with Teacher Feedback on Oral Presentations

Gwen: You put the stress on the second syllable. [→metalinguistic clue]

Chen: (silence) [→no further uptake]

Gwen: 重音在后一个音节上时是形容词，意思是满意的。当重音在前面时，才是名词，对吧?[→metalinguistic clue in Chinese]

Chen: /'kɒntent/ [→successful repair]

(Gwen's feedback—To Chen—Presentation 3)

When prompted, Chen recalled that she initially did not know the meanings of the two words "stress" and "syllable". However, after the teacher provided metalinguistic clues in Chinese, she connected these two English words with their Chinese counterparts "重音" and "音节", and managed to repair this mispronunciation /kən'tent/.

It was worth noting that there was one particular case where Chen used the cognitive operation of rote memorization while revising the PPT slides. The teacher pointed out the grammatical error through explicit correction.

Oral CF Episode 10

It has a positive effective on our mental states.

I don't think this is the correct word. It should be positive "effect" not "effective", right?[→explicit correction]

(Gwen's feedback—To Chen—Presentation 1)

Although Chen revised "effective" into "effect" in her revised PPT slides, she did not know the specific reason for this revision. Chen merely memorized the correct target L2 form without understanding the error correction. As she wrote in her reflective account,

…To me, this phrase (i.e., positive effective) is correct, but the teacher said "effective" should be changed into "effect". I had better not defy my teacher.

(Chen's reflective account)

With regard to behavioral engagement, Chen revised the PPT slides of all three presentations. As shown in Table 5.4, Chen was not very successful in addressing linguistic errors: she only repaired or revised eight errors, which was closely related to her lack of noticing and understanding of the errors.

Table 5.4　　Chen's revision operations induced by teacher feedback

Focus of feedback	Language	Content	Organization	Presentation aid
Feedback point	15	6	3	5
Correction	8	6	1	5
No change	7	0	2	0
Feedback in total	29			
Total correction	20			
Revision rate	69%			

Note. The feedback excludes teacher compliments.

Chen's behavioral engagement was mostly manifested in her use of teacher feedback to improve presentation contents and format presentation slides. While there was no evidence in the data indicating Chen's employment of metacognitive or cognitive operations during her revising the two aspects above, she resorted to external sources, such as using the internet to find pertinent supporting materials and watching online videos about how to design PPT slides.

In sum, Chen was dissatisfied with teacher feedback in general and felt particularly embarrassed when receiving teacher CF. When attending to teacher CF, she only noticed and successfully explained eight out of fifteen errors, reflecting her superficial level of cognitive engagement in this regard. Consequently, Chen did not conduct extensive revisions related to linguistic errors, either. Two cognitive operations were used by Chen to explain and revise errors: making connections and memorization. She also used external sources to revise presentation contents as well as format of PPT slides.

5.2.3 Han: A Lower-Proficiency Student's Engagement with Teacher Feedback

5.2.3.1 Han's Background

Han was a male sophomore who ranked sixteenth in class and was placed at the lower-proficiency level after taking the oral English test. Han's backgrounds were different from those of other participants in this study in that he was neither interested in nor motivated to study English. Han described himself as a high academic achiever at high school, but he failed to give his best performance at the College Entrance Examination. When asked about his reasons for studying the major of English Language and Literature, Han remarked that he originally applied for the major of Computer Science but were transferred to the English major. Han added that he was lucky to be able to study computer science again as he had elected it as his minor. He commented:

> There is a good saying that misery can be accompanied with happiness. On the one hand, I really don't like learning English, but my father says I have to learn English because it is always to have more skills. On the other hand, I want to study computer science because I hope to be a games producer in the future.
>
> (1st interview with Han)

Regarding his goal of learning English, Han stated that he had no ambition to be top of the class: "My priority is to pass the English exams. I do not expect very good test scores" (1st interview with Han). Moreover, Han was not a self-regulated language learner and he confessed that he did not do extra learning exercises after class. Instead, he spent most of the after-class time studying his minor of Computer Science.

When interviewed, Han appeared to show no preferences for English writing and speaking; he emphasized the importance of reading comprehension in terms of acquiring vocabulary and knowledge of grammar: "Adequate grammar and vocabulary increase my chance of passing the exams, although the scores may not be high" (1st interview with Han). Thus, it was not surprising that Han did not show much enthusiasm for the task of oral presentation. In fact, as he confessed in the final interview, much of the task preparation had been made by his teammate who was a good friend of his: "All I did was searching for a few supporting materials and gave them to my teammate. Then, I just needed to read the speech he had prepared beforehand" (Final interview with Han).

5.2.3.2 Han's Engagement with Teacher Feedback

Han received 39 teacher feedback points in total, among which twelve feedback points dealt with his problematic L2 linguistic forms. To the researcher's surprise, Han was delighted to receive teacher CF in that error correction indicated his weaknesses in linguistic competence. As he commented in his own words, "I am happy that the teacher corrects me and explains to me why these linguistic forms are wrong. Probably one day I will encounter them when taking a test and I will give the correct forms" (Final interview with Han). Accordingly, Han's preference for teacher CF was in line with his learning belief about the importance of linguistic competence. In contrast, Han affectively disengaged from other types of teacher feedback (such as feedback on content and presentation aid) and claimed that he did not have particular feelings upon receiving them. This emotional detachment resonated with his perception.

> I thought it (teacher feedback on content and presentation aid) was not addressed to me because it was my teammate who decided upon the presentation topics and what we would say about these topics. He also searched for most of the supporting materials and made the slides. So, why bothered with such feedback?
>
> (Han's reflective account)

While the teacher indicated Han's errors in an implicit manner, Han was extremely successful in noticing teacher CF and recognizing the teacher's corrective intent. It was found that Han detected all of Gwen's CF. For example, when

Chapter 5　Student Engagement with Teacher Feedback on Oral Presentations

asked how he showed awareness of teacher CF, he claimed:

> Mr. Gwen liked to ask the students, not just me, to re-pronounce words that he wrote on the blackboard. I knew exactly his intention; that is, I made a mistake and he was going to correct it.
>
> (1st stimulated recall with Han)

As indicated by the quote above, Han made connections between Gwen's current CF and his prior CF practices to realize the corrective force behind teacher CF. This cognitive operation was also used by the student participant of Li in Amelia's class.

Out of the twelve teacher CF points, Han was able to provide accurate reasons for nine errors. Specifically, he combined the cognitive operations of reasoning and activating previous knowledge to identify and explain these errors. In the example below, the teacher first asked Han to re-pronounce the word "desert", but after Han's unsuccessful repair, the teacher provided the explicit correction without giving any metalinguistic clues. In the last turn, Han successfully repaired this phonological error by producing its correct form.

Oral CF Episode 11

Gwen: (The teacher is writing "desert" on the blackboard) Excuse me? How to pronounce this word in English? [→clarification request + elicitation]

Han: /dɪˈzɜːt/ [→uptake with no repair]

Gwen: /ˈdezət/ not /dɪˈzɜːt/, right? [→explicit correction]

Han: /ˈdezət/. Um, I mistook it for the word "dessert". [→successful repair]

Gwen: Yes.

(Gwen's feedback—To Han—Presentation 3)

149

When prompted, Han remarked:

>Han: When the teacher gave the explicit correction /'dezət/, I was comparing it with my own pronunciation /dɪ'zɜːt/. It turned out that I put the stress on the wrong syllable, and also the second letter "e" was mispronounced as /i/.
>Researcher: Well, you re-pronounced it. This time it was correct.
>Han: Yeah. I suddenly realized that I confused "desert" with "dessert". I mispronounced the word "desert" as /dɪ'zɜːt/
>
>(3rd stimulated recall with Han)

The excerpt above showed that Han activated previous metalinguistic knowledge (i.e., stress and vowel sound), which facilitated his diagnosis of the error, and then he conducted an accurate metalinguistic analysis to repair his non-target-like pronunciation.

In the following case, without providing the metalinguistic explanation, the teacher merely made an explicit correction of the lexical error (i.e., expect) by saying "it should be except, right?"

>...*expect for this scenic spot*, ...

In the stimulated recall, Han showed his non-understanding of this correction because he had not heard the correction.

>Researcher: Did you know why the teacher corrected you?
>Han: Um, he said it should be, um... (Han attempted to pronounce "except", but he failed). In fact, I did not hear it clearly. Yeah, I did not hear the word.
>
>(2nd stimulated recall with Han)

Chapter 5 Student Engagement with Teacher Feedback on Oral Presentations

With regard to behavioral engagement, there is a striking difference between his responses to teacher oral CF and other types of feedback (see Table 5.5). On the one hand, Han made successful revisions to almost all of the linguistic errors.

Table 5.5　　Han's revision operations induced by teacher feedback

Focus of feedback	Language	Content	Organization	Presentation aid
Feedback point	12	5	4	5
Correction	9	0	0	0
No change	3	5	4	5
Feedback in total	26			
Total correction	9			
Revision rate	34.6%			

Note. The feedback excludes teacher compliments

On the other hand, Han did not generate revision operations with regard to feedback provided on presentation content and organization, presentation aid, and delivery. That being said, Han did not produce revised versions of the PPT slides, nor did he use the teacher's suggestions to improve his presentation delivery. As Han explained in the final interview, this decision was highly contextualized.

Han: As you know, there are tons of courses and assignments for students taking double-majors. I did not have spare time to revise PPT slides. Most importantly, the teacher did not require us to hand in the revised versions.

Researcher: How about the delivery of presentation? The teacher suggested that you make eye contact with your classmates.

Gwen: It's the same reason. I did not have time to recite the whole speech, and if I looked at my classmates, I would definitely forget what I was going to say.

(Final interview with Han)

To summarize, while Han held negative attitudes towards the task of oral presentation, he particularly welcomed teacher CF. Han's cognitive engagement with teacher feedback ran parallel with his behavioral engagement. Han understood most of the errors and successfully repaired them, whereas he did not pay attention or respond to teacher feedback provided on other aspects of oral presentations.

5.3 Factors Influencing Student Engagement with Teacher Feedback

The data analysis shows that a number of factors might influence the processes through which the students engaged with teacher feedback on their oral presentations: individual differences between students, characteristics of teacher feedback practices *per se*, teacher-student interactional patterns and interpersonal relationships, and teacher's teaching agenda.

5.3.1 Learner Individualization

A set of individual learner factors, involving learner L2 proficiency, learner beliefs about L2 speaking and the task of oral presentation they were undertaking, as well as learning goals and motivation, exerted great influence on students' engagement with teacher feedback. With regard to L2 proficiency, students with high proficiency levels (e.g., Deng and Wu) were better able to understand teacher feedback information in both classes. In the case of Deng, apart from certain feedback she intentionally ignored, her cognitive engagement was relatively successful and deep: she used three cognitive operations (i.e., predicting, making connections, and visualization) to reflect on and interpret teacher feedback. For Wu, she identified all teacher CF and provided reasons for almost all of her linguistic errors.

Although high L2 proficiency was found to facilitate students' cognitive engagement with teacher feedback, similar patterns were not identified with regard to behavioral or affective engagement. For example, as a high-proficiency student in Amelia's class, Deng did not revise any PPT slides and only responded to teacher feedback on presentation delivery. However, Li, the lower-proficiency student in the same class, made relatively extensive revisions in response to teacher feedback. In terms of affective engagement, it was interesting that lower-proficiency students (Li and Han) reported fewer negative feelings, whereas the high-proficiency student (Wu) and intermediate-proficiency students (Wang and Chen) suffered from more negative emotions, such as anger, upset, embarrassment, etc.

Students' beliefs about L2 speaking and making in-class oral presentations also influenced their engagement by mediating their processing and use of teacher feedback. This can be illustrated by the student participants of Wu and Chen in Gwen's class. As mentioned earlier, Wu prioritized oral competence, especially oral linguistic accuracy, over content and structure while delivering oral presentations, believing that "an oral presentation is transmission of ideas through accurate pronunciation of words and appropriate use of vocabulary. How you use language is more important than the non-language related aspects such as content and organization" (Final interview with Wu); conversely, Chen thought and said, "Interesting contents and clear structure hold the keys to a successful oral presentation" (1st interview with Chen). Owing to their respective views, Wu successfully identified and explained almost all of thirteen teacher CF points and had no intention of responding to content-related feedback. In contrast, Chen only recognized and explained eight out of fifteen errors treated by teacher CF but managed to generate substantial content and organization revision operations.

Students' goals and motivations in terms of EFL learning were also found to influence their engagement with teacher feedback. Han and Li were perhaps the least motivated participants in this study; they disliked learning English and regarded passing exams as the ultimate learning goal. This demotivation contributed to Han's minimal efforts in preparing for the task and using teacher content-related feedback. However, for Li, he was initially demotivated in English learning and making oral presentations, but later he became highly motivated in these two aspects. This motivational trajectory was realized as the result of the provision of teacher feedback, which in turn mediated his engagement with teacher feedback. As he commented:

> The biggest change is that I do not loathe this task (oral presentation) now. I find that if I use the teacher's suggestions to improve certain aspects of my presentation, the teacher will recognize them and praise me. Consequently, I know these are effective oral presentation tips and I should regard them as guidelines for oral presentations.
> (Final interview with Li)

5.3.2 Characteristics of Teacher Feedback Practices

Also influencing learner engagement were the characteristics of teachers' feedback practices *per se*, including the focus of feedback and strategies employed to give feedback. As indicated in Chapter 4, Amelia was mostly concerned with the content and structure of oral presentation in her feedback, whereas Gwen's feedback predominantly focused on language use. However, it appeared that the student participants (except for Li and Chen) were more cognitively and behaviorally engaged with teacher feedback on linguistic forms rather than content and structural issues. This finding indicates that linguistic forms can be more easily attended to and responded to while students are processing teacher feedback. Wang served as a typical case in this regard: she comprehended language-form feedback and repaired all linguistic errors accordingly, but she reacted to few content and structural issues (see section 5.1.2.2). This decision was well-explained by Wang:

> I don't worry about grammar because I've been through the *Gao Kao* (National Tertiary Matriculation Examination) and my performance on linguistic accuracy won't be too poor. The linguistic errors can easily be fixed, whereas content incompleteness and poor linking of ideas are difficult to tackle. For example, the teacher suggested that I make connections between an

Chapter 5 Student Engagement with Teacher Feedback on Oral Presentations

argument and its supporting evidence, but I did not know how to do the linking. I've never been trained in this regard before.

(Final interview with Wang)

Moreover, teacher correction of students' non-target-like L2 structures indicates the teachers' orientation to linguistic accuracy, which in turn reinforces the students' perception about the importance of linguistic forms. As Wu remarked, "The teacher pointed out so many errors in my speech, so it meant oral accuracy was important in an oral presentation" (1st stimulated recall with Wu). This partly explained why Wu often attended to the CF provided by Gwen.

As part of teacher feedback characteristics, the teachers' use of feedback strategies also mediated students' cognitive engagement. It was found that the CF strategies of elicitations and metalinguistic feedback mostly facilitated students' understanding of the reasons behind CF as well as their successful repair of linguistic errors. In addition, the feedback strategy of using L1 (i.e., Chinese) also mediated Li's and Chen's successful identification and explanation of linguistic errors, during which the cognitive operation of making connections was usually adopted. That being said, the students made connections between the two languages, i.e., English and Chinese to work out sources of errors. Finally, Amelia's provision of nonverbal clues that accompanied her feedback was also shown to facilitate Li's noticing of problematic areas in oral presentations. As indicated in section 5.1.3.2, Li noticed the teacher hovering the computer mouse over written texts on PPT slides and immediately realized that the font size needed to be enlarged.

5.3.3 Teacher-Student Interactional Patterns and Interpersonal Relationships

Another factor concerned the interactional patterns and personal relationships that the teachers and students in this study constructed when they engaged in the process of giving and receiving feedback. In this study, it was found that the teachers attempted to create interactional spaces for students to respond to them. This was reflected by the teachers' use of prompts such as elicitations and clarification requests as CF strategies, as well as the teachers' probing of content issues with open-ended questions. As illustrated in previous sections, most of the teachers' prompts led to successful student uptake and repair; however, the open-ended questions led to few follow-up interactions between teachers and students. These contrasting interactional patterns partially accounted for some students' limited engagement with teacher content- and organization-focused feedback. For example, Wang stated that she was unwilling to argue with Amelia about unsettled content and structural issues due to her shyness and embarrassment; for Wu and Han, they did not respond to Gwen's questions mainly because they were unfamiliar with the contents of their presentations and did not know how to make proper responses.

Moreover, the types of interpersonal relationships were directly linked to the emotions and attitudes induced by teacher feedback in general, as well as CF in particular. While the two teachers did not claim being authoritative evaluators of students' presentation performance, some student participants were somehow intimidated by the teachers' authoritative power. For example, Wang, Wu, and Chen thought much of a teacher's role as an assessor and considered their teachers' CF and critical comments as indications of dissatisfaction with their understanding and performance. This perception of a teacher's assessor role in learning could explain why the three students suffered from negative emotions such as embarrassment, upset, and disappointment upon the receipt of teacher feedback.

By contrast, Deng considered a teacher as an audience of her oral presentation: "The teacher is the same as other students who sit below the stage and watch my performance" (1st interview with Deng). In line with this view, Deng did not show intense mood swings when responding to either positive or negative teacher feedback, as indicated in section 5.1.1.2. Deng also mentioned that she valued student peers' responses to her oral presentation. She said:

> Sometimes, the classmates may hold different views about my oral presentation performance, compared with those of the teacher. In this situation, I tend to value their views and responses. After all, there are many

Chapter 5 Student Engagement with Teacher Feedback on Oral Presentations

students in the class and there is only one teacher.

(1st interview with Deng)

Therefore, it was not surprising that Deng had an awareness of the student audience when she cognitively engaged with Amelia's feedback on her presentation delivery.

Two student participants, i.e., Li and Han developed relatively positive interpersonal relationships with their teachers and perceived a teacher as a facilitator or motivator who showed care for and attention to their learning. As Li commented, "Miss Amelia did not put me off with lousy feedback because of my lower proficiency. Instead, she gave me specific feedback that benefited me" (Final interview with Li). Han echoed the same idea that Gwen did not treat him differently from other students and attended to his oral presentations seriously. Han said:

> To be honest, I did not expect the teacher to give me much feedback, but he not only corrected me but also explained to me the metalinguistic rules behind these errors. Besides, while the teacher was correcting me, he was really patient, so I did not experience constant negative emotions.
>
> (Final interview with Han)

As indicated above, within the same classroom context, the students confronted their teachers differently and constructed three kinds of interpersonal relationships with them: assessor and assessee, audience and performer, as well as facilitator and learner, which could possibly explain the students' differing emotions induced by teacher feedback.

5.3.4 Teaching Agenda

Finally, the findings indicated that students' engagement with teacher feedback could also be influenced by the teaching agenda, including the course requirements and task design. These two courses (i.e., *An Introduction to Intercultural Commu-*

nication and *Communicative English II*) were not intended for the instruction of public speaking, and oral presentation was only part of the teaching agenda. Therefore, teachers and students could not focus solely on this oral task. Also, since presenting the same topic anew and revising the PPT slides were not mandated by the two teachers, the students (i.e., Deng and Han) thought there was no need to revise their PPT slides. Although the teachers directly pointed out the problematic aspects on their PPT slides, they still did not make revisions accordingly, which indicates their intentional disengagement at the behavioral level. However, in Wang's case, she did not revise the slides of her first oral presentation, claiming:

> The teacher only suggested that I use natural intonation patterns and raise my voice. The contents and structure of the first presentation were fine, and I did not remember there being mistakes on the slides. So, I perceived it unnecessary to make revisions.
> (Wang's reflective account)

Moreover, the students actually presented different topics in three oral presentations. Amelia required students to address Chinese culture in the first presentation, deal with Western culture in the second presentation, and finally make comparisons between the two in the third presentation. This was also the case with Gwen who claimed that the students probably did not like the idea of presenting same topic three times in succession. This design feature probably constrained students' use of teacher feedback. In Wang's case, she partially ascribed her lack of revision operations to the inconsistent presentation topics. She did not feel comfortable with this task design. She said:

> Revisions to content and organizational issues were pointless in a sense, because I did not need to deliver the same presentation next time.
> (Final interview with Wang)

For Chen, the fact that she held unfavorable attitudes to receiving teacher correction of linguistic errors was closely related with her dissatisfaction about Gwen's task arrangement. When interviewed, she explicitly stated that she did not appreciate this task design, remarking:

> Each time I presented a different topic idea, the teacher mostly corrected the language-related errors that occurred in oral presentations. I did not know why the teacher always focused a great deal on linguistic errors. I think the success of an oral presentation lies in its content and structure.
> （Final interview with Chen）

From the quotes above, we can see that delivering an oral presentation in this study was a "one-off" act. Unlike the multiple-drafting approach in L2 writing, a student presenter did not have a second chance to present the same topic in class, which could partly explain Wang's unsuccessful use of teacher content feedback and Chen's negative emotions toward teacher CF.

5.4 Summary of Chapter

This chapter has first presented the narratives of six student participants （Deng, Wang, and Li in Amelia's class and Wu, Chen, and Han in Gwen's class） to explore their affective, cognitive, and behavioral engagement with teacher feedback. In Amelia's class, Deng engaged with teacher feedback on presentation delivery. Wang mostly engaged with feedback on linguistic forms and presentation aids but engaged less with content-related feedback. Li, despite being a lower-proficiency student, engaged with teacher feedback most extensively among the three students, which was closely related to his motivational change when engaging with feedback. In Gwen's class, while Wu's and Han's engagement processes were mainly manifested with teacher CF on linguistic forms, there were some differences among them: Wu noticed all the CF but generated few revision operations because she was provided with few opportunities for follow-up learner repair during teacher interactional CF. By contrast, Han successfully repaired most of the linguistic errors because compared with Wu, he took a further step by initiating self-repair after the teacher's CF. Unlike Wu's and Han's mere engagement with teacher CF on linguistic forms, Chen also generated revisions in presentation content, organization, and aids.

Despite these differences among the students' engagement patterns, there were also similarities in terms of student engagement with feedback. Firstly, the students had few difficulties recognizing the corrective intent behind teacher CF and explaining their linguistic errors, probably because they were often explicitly corrected and provided with metalinguistic clues. Also, despite the teachers using prompting error correction techniques, most students still realized that they had been implicitly corrected in that the students employed the cognitive operation of making connections (e.g., they connected previous experiences of receiving elicitations with current ones). Secondly, the students resorted to external resources, such as student peers, online dictionaries, and the internet to generate revision operations.

Having explored the six students' engagement with teacher feedback, the factors that can influence their engagement processes have also been discussed in this chapter. It was found that individual students with different levels of L2 proficiency, learning beliefs, goals and motivation, as well as the characteristics of teacher feedback, and the multi-layered contexts (teacher-student interactional patterns and interpersonal relationships and teaching agenda) jointly mediated the students' cognitive, behavioral, and affective engagement with teacher feedback.

Chapter 6 Discussion

This chapter presents the discussion of the findings reported in Chapter 4 and Chapter 5. It first discusses the two teachers' decision-making in providing feedback on students' oral presentations. It then moves on to discuss the six students' cognitive, behavioral, and affective engagement with teacher feedback, as well as how learner and contextual factors interact and influence student engagement. Based on the findings and discussion of this study, the chapter also presents a revised conceptual framework of teacher feedback on EFL learning and task-based oral performance.

6.1 Understanding Teacher Feedback on Oral Presentations in the Chinese EFL Context

While most previous studies on EFL teachers' feedback on oral presentations were conducted in experimental or quasi-experimental settings, this study has extended previous research and shed light on how EFL teachers relate their feedback to the sociocultural and instructional context of naturalistic university-level EFL classrooms. The findings illustrate the diversity of teachers' feedback practices with respect to feedback focus, function, and strategy. It has been revealed that the teachers were predisposed to give lengthy comments to improve student oral presentation performance rather than conducting summative assessment that focuses on outcome-based feedback in previous experimental studies (e.g., Cheng & Warren, 1999, 2005; Saito, 2008; Saito & Fujita, 2009). Regarding focus of teacher feedback, the findings of this study add to the research literature that teacher feedback on EFL oral presentations is not confined to addressing students' oral linguistic proficiency, and it also deals with non-language related aspects such as students' abilities to handle subject content, structural development, visual aids, etc. Furthermore, due to their instructional beliefs in the two courses, Amelia and Gwen differed the focus of their feedback practices in students' oral presentations. Students in the course of *An Introduction to Intercultural Communication* study intercultural knowledge, so Amelia mostly emphasized the content and organization of oral presentation. By contrast, Gwen taught the language skill-oriented course of *Communicative English (II)* and was mostly concerned with language-related aspects, including speech as well as written texts on PPT slides. Therefore, this study echoes the findings of previous studies that teachers' beliefs about language teaching often guide their feedback practices (e.g., Mori, 2011; Roothooft, 2014).

Moreover, the two teachers in this study mostly gave positive-oriented feedback and considered praise and suggestion as main functions of their feedback on oral presentations. This particular finding coincides with Hattie and Yates's (2014) insights that teachers avoid negative feedback for fear of embarrassing students and creating an unfavorable classroom climate. This finding further indicates the intriguing possibility of positive teaching which underlies the teachers' pedagogical belief that praise is far more effective than punishment. Notably, however, although the two teachers in this study perceived the value of beneficial praise, criticism was also shown to be a predominant function of Gwen's feedback. This was probably due to Gwen's frequent use of the praise-criticism-suggestion triad in his oral feedback. This "sandwich pattern" merits our attention because it not only mitigates the critical force of feedback by putting criticism in the middle of this pattern, but also entails ways for improvement manifested through suggestion in the last step. This finding supports the view that criticism is not necessarily detrimental to student learning when provided in a constructive context (F. Hyland & K. Hyland, 2001).

With regard to feedback strategies, the teachers in this study used a variety of error correction techniques, resorted to L1 and nonverbal behaviors, and incorporated peer feedback and self-feedback into teacher feedback. Interestingly,

Gwen liked to prompt students to conduct self-correction either through elicitations or a combination of elicitations with metalinguistic clues. These CF strategies gain theoretical support from Swain's (1985, 1995) Output Hypothesis that output production provides opportunities for learner language acquisition. As argued by Lyster and Ranta (1997), this output-pushing approach can trigger students' noticing linguistic errors and lead to their further responses (known as learner uptake).

In addition, while the strategic use of L1 and nonverbal language only served as two specific types of oral CF (also known as translation and nonlinguistic signal, respectively) in previous teacher feedback studies (e.g., Ahangari & Amirzadeh, 2011; Lee, 2016; Mori, 2002), the findings of this study add to the literature that L1 can also be used to provide subject knowledge, as exemplified in Amelia's feedback, and to maintain social communications with students and facilitate understanding, as perceived by Gwen when he gave feedback. Moreover, Gwen's incorporation of peer feedback and self-feedback into teacher feedback is also shared by other researchers who argue that triangulating multiple feedback sources contributes greatly to learning reflection among students (Carroll, 2006), and encourages high-level engagement in the feedback processes on the part of students (Cheng & Warren, 2005).

In this study, the findings about CF strategies employed by the teachers also highlight the key claim of SCT, i.e., "corrective feedback needs to be 'graduated' to the level of the individual learner to enable them to self-correct" (Erlam, Ellis, & Batstone, 2013, p. 258). In this adjustment process, teachers provided scaffolding to support students' L2 learning and problem solving. One typical example that illustrates this mechanism is the oral CF episode 9 in section 5.2.2.2. In this CF episode, we can see how implicit these oral CF strategies (i.e., elicitation and metalinguistic clue) are. The teacher started by eliciting Chen to identify and correct the pronunciation error on her own, after which the teacher moved on to give a metalinguistic clue in English. When these two implicit CF moves failed to encourage learner uptake, the teacher finally provided a less implicit CF strategy, that is, making a metalinguistic comment in Chinese.

This very last implicit CF enabled Chen to self-correct her pronunciation error. It would seem that the teacher's scaffolding (i.e., a continuum of implicit CF strategies) was successful in enabling Chen to produce the correct L2 linguistic form on her own.

As revealed, a range of teacher, learner, and contextual factors was found to play a role in influencing teacher feedback practices. The findings of this study illustrate the situated nature of teachers' beliefs and feedback practices in relation to both cultural and educational contexts. Although research has emphasized the importance of contextual factors in understanding ESL writing teachers' feedback practices (e.g., Goldstein, 2006; Lee, 2008a), our study adds new evidence to support the mediating role that the Chinese cultures of learning context play in teachers' oral feedback practices in EFL classrooms. Different from writing instruction, the two teachers in this study interacted with students in a typical classroom setting where feedback was delivered not only face-to-face but also in front of the whole class. In other words, teachers and students participated in a shared learning environment of interpreting feedback. This unique situational classroom environment called for teachers' consideration of face-saving in the wider context of Chinese culture. Moreover, this finding is inconsistent with that of Yu, Lee, and Mak's (2016) study in which face-to-face peer feedback was not particularly influenced by the traditional Chinese culture. This is not surprising given that teachers in the Eastern educational cultural setting are supposed to be dominant and directive, while students are expected to be disciplined (Zhang, 2007). It is reasonable to assume that there is a larger power distance between teachers and students than between the students themselves. Therefore, the teachers may deem praise and suggestion as effective ways of reducing the power distance to foster harmonious and supportive student-teacher relationships. The finding also offers insights into how the combined effects of the micro-setting of the classroom and the macro-context of Chinese sociocultural discourse give rise to language teachers' indirectness in commenting on students' oral presentations. Overall, grounded in the sociocultural theoretical perspective of scaffolding instruction, this study extends the feedback literature to EFL students' task-based oral presentations. The findings of this study play an important role in further extending our understanding of the complexities of teacher feedback in the context of Chinese EFL classrooms.

6.2 Student Engagement with Teacher Feedback on Oral Presentations

6.2.1 Interrelatedness of Affective, Cognitive, and Behavioral Engagement

This case study involved six Chinese EFL students and explored how they affectively, cognitively, and behaviorally engaged with teacher feedback on oral presentations. The findings of this study illustrate the complexity of student engagement within its main construct, as well as across three sub-constructs at the affective, behavioral, and cognitive levels.

With regard to affective engagement, there is evidence that students' emotional responses to teacher oral feedback might be related with individual learner expectations, which corroborated the findings of Han and Hyland's (2015) study on learner engagement with written CF. For instance, Deng perceived her weakness in the aspect of rhetorical structure of oral presentation, so she felt happy when Amelia recognized her task improvement in this regard. As for Chen, she expected teacher content feedback, and thus she felt disappointed upon receiving CF. Moreover, when receiving negative feedback (e.g., teacher CF on linguistic errors and critical comments on content issues), Li and Wu were able to regulate negative emotions of upset and embarrassment into motivation, whereas Wang remained frustrated and upset. In fact, Wang's negative emotional responses were observed to be closely associated with her unsuccessful cognitive and behavioral engagement, indicating the interrelatedness of these three dimensions of student engagement.

Cognitive engagement in this study was conceptualized as the extent to which students understood teacher feedback (for example, noticing and explaining linguistic errors treated by teacher CF), and students' adoption of metacognitive and cognitive operations when processing teacher feedback. The findings offer insights into the role of learner attention in cognitive engagement processes. Upon receiving teacher oral feedback, some students paid no attention to certain types of feedback, which influenced their further cognitive processing of teacher feedback. For instance, Deng did not show cognitive responses to group or class feedback because she did not listen attentively to it. As argued by Price, Handley, and Millar (2011), immediate attention is a precursor to its next stage of cognitive response. Moreover, in line with the assumptions made by Nassaji (2009), who claimed that "elicitations can be equally (or even more) effective if learners already know the targeted forms or have declarative knowledge of those forms" (p. 441), the students in this study successfully recognized their corrective nature, as well as identified and explained the errors treated by elicitations. This can be explained by students' use of the cognitive operation of making connections. Specifically, since students were often corrected with this CF technique, they could easily connect their previous CF experiences with current elicitations to work out teachers' intents. Apart from making connections, another five cognitive operations were also generated in the processing and revision processes, including reasoning, predicting, activating previous knowledge, visualization, and memorization. In contrast, only two metacognitive operations (i.e., planning and monitoring) were limitedly employed by students to regulate their mental efforts and generate revisions, which calls for students' metacognitive development in the engagement processes.

The students' behavioral engagement with teacher feedback was manifested in terms of revision operations as well as strategies taken to generate revisions. On the one hand, the findings of this study show that students' behavioral engagement ran in parallel with their cognitive engagement, which was particularly true for Wang who often found the teacher's content feedback difficult to comprehend and act upon. On the other hand, inconsistencies were also found between these two dimensions of student engagement. It is worth noting that some intermediate- and lower-proficiency students could still successfully repair their non-target-like linguistic structures by drawing on teacher provision of metalinguistic clues, despite initially failing to understand the errors. Moreover, some students also resorted to external resources such as online dictionaries and resources and student peers to help generate revision operations. Considering these findings, this study suggests that L2 proficiency may not be the sole indicator of successful behavioral engagement as expected. The usable level of teacher feedback and the availability of external resources can also influence students' behavioral engagement.

6.2.2 Multiple Factors Influencing Student Engagement with Teacher Feedback

In this study, it was found that an array of learner, teacher, and contextual factors contributed to the complexity of students' engagement with teacher feedback. Learner factors included students' different levels of L2 proficiency, beliefs about L2 speaking and making oral presentations, learning goals and motivation. Teacher factors referred to the characteristics of teacher feedback practices, such as focus of teacher feedback (form vs. content) and feedback strategies that teachers adopted. Contextual factors are operating at three levels—the interactional level (i.e., teacher-student interactional patterns), the interpersonal level (i.e., teacher-student interpersonal relationships) and the instructional level (i.e., teaching agenda).

In terms of learner factors, high-L2 proficiency students' cognitive engagement was not necessarily extensive but rather deep, which can be exemplified in the cases of Deng and Wu. Although Deng intentionally neglected most teacher feedback, she was able to understand and reflect on the feedback to which she listened attentively. For Wu, she successfully noticed all teacher CF and provided reasons for nearly all. Similar findings have also been uncovered in Qi and Lapkin (2001), who reported that more proficient ESL students were able to identify and explain more errors. One possible reason for the relationship between L2 proficiency and depth of processing was that, according to Cohen (1987), students with higher proficiency may have a larger storage of cognitive and metacognitive operations, which can facilitate their deep processing of teacher feedback.

Moreover, it is interesting to observe that Deng, the high-proficiency student in Amelia's class, generated much fewer revision operations than her intermediate- and lower-proficiency peers (i.e., Wang and Li) did. This was probably because Li and Wang were willing to make revisions to the PPT slides while Deng was not. In Gwen's class, Han, the lower-proficiency student, improved his linguistic accuracy more than his high-proficiency counterpart, Wu did. One possible explanation was that during teacher-student interactions Wu sometimes did not initiate self-repair of errors; instead, Han was often pushed by Gwen to self-repair the errors. These findings suggest that L2 proficiency may not be regarded as a necessary indicator of students' effective revisions after receiving feedback. Overall, there appears to be a non-linear relationship between students' L2 proficiency and their engagement with teacher feedback.

In line with previous research findings (Han & Hyland, 2015; Han, 2017; Hyland, 2003; Storch & Wigglesworth, 2010), this study indicates that other learner factors like students' L2 learning beliefs, motivations, and goals also mediated their engagement by allocating their attention to different types of feedback, as well as shaping their emotional reactions and decisions to use teacher feedback. On the one hand, the students (Deng, Wu, and Han) who were more concerned about oral competencies or presentation skills had limited intentions of addressing the content and structural issues in their oral presentations. In contrast, Chen attached greater importance to content issues than linguistic accuracy, and thus she felt disappointed and upset about receiving error correction, which in turn constrained her deep processing of teacher CF. On the other hand, the students (Deng, Wang, and Wu) who were motivated to make oral presentations and had specific learning goals, had high expectations of receiving teacher feedback and took teacher feedback seriously upon receiving it. For the students (Chen and Han) who were less motivated and only had the goal of passing exams, they were not very enthusiastic about teacher feedback in general, although they did show expectations regarding certain types of teacher feedback. Here, the case of Li merits our special attention. Since the teacher acknowledged Li's task performance, Li transformed from "being demotivated" to "being motivated" in terms of engaging with teacher feedback as well as making oral presentations. Overall, the findings of this study support the importance of learner beliefs, goals, and motivation as individual characteristics mediating L2 learning (Dörnyei & Ryan, 2015).

With regard to teacher factors, this study has illustrated that the way in which feedback is given by teachers can mediate students' engagement with teacher feedback. In this study, even lower-proficiency students (i.e., Li and Han) were able to identify problematic areas and generate accurate revision operations. This was closely related to teachers' strategic use of metalinguistic clues, L1, and nonverbal behaviors. From the sociocultural perspective, it is plausible that these feedback strategies can be a fit to the ZPD of lower-proficiency students who are equipped with less metalinguistic knowledge (Aljaafreh & Lantolf, 1994).

The findings of this study add to the growing body of research (Goldstein, 2004; 2006; Han & Hyland, 2015; Lee, 2008a, 2008b) which argues that not only teachers' provision of feedback, but also students' receiving, processing, and using feedback is a social activity mediated by a cluster of contextual factors. At the interpersonal level, this study offers insights into the concept of power distance in constructing teacher-student relationships (Zhang, 2007). Although nearly all of the six students had no objection to teachers being representatives of truth, authority, and knowledge, there were still differences in the students' perceptions of the roles and identities of their teachers. These different perceptions possibly accounted for the students' varied emotional reactions to teacher feedback.

At the interactional level, the findings further our understanding of the value of interactional CF provided on EFL students' task-based oral presentations. The teachers and students cooperated in building oral conversations and negotiating meanings, which impacted students' subsequent revision operations. In line with the findings of Weissberg's (2006) study on oral scaffolding in L2 writing, the two teachers in this study also made a set of discourse mechanisms based on the text analysis of teacher feedback. For example, they used elicitations and clarification requests to prompt learner uptake of feedback with repair. When the teachers failed, they attempted to keep the ball rolling by immediately giving metalinguistic clues, using L1, or providing nonverbal clues to facilitate students' understanding of feedback information.

At the instructional level, this study has revealed a range of contextual constraints that impact students' engagement with teacher feedback. The findings provide reasons for students' unsuccessful or lack of revision in response to teacher feedback, which have not been reported in previous research (Goldstein, 2004, 2006; Han & Hyland, 2015), including the lack of mandated revisions required by teachers, dissimilar task topics, and the inaccessibility of teacher oral feedback in terms of keeping records.

6.2.3　Learner Agency and Engagement with Teacher Feedback

As mentioned in section 6.2.2, individual learner and contextual factors work together to mediate students' engagement with teacher feedback, but it remains unclear how these factors relate to one another in this study. It is argued that learner agency comes into play by underlying the engagement processes. As noted by Winstone, Nash, Parker, and Rowntree (2017), students are expected to play the role of "proactive recipients" (p. 17) of teacher feedback by actively engaging with feedback processes. In this study, the students made decisions about whether and how to engage with feedback as a result of the multiple factors acting together. The relationship between learner factors and contextual factors was particularly salient in the cases of Li and Wang. For instance, Li felt motivated to act upon the teacher's feedback by consulting his peer when he was confused about how to make revisions to the conclusion of his second oral presentation. By contrast, Wang did not choose to seek external help when she was upset about figuring out how to incorporate the teacher's content-related suggestions into her revisions. We can see that the two students' decisions regarding whether or not to engage with teacher feedback were based on perceptions of the potential opportunities and constraints afforded by the surrounding context, and their perceptions were underlined by their own individual traits.

Overall, although Ellis (2010a) identified the interactional relationships between learner and contextual factors, few empirical investigations (Han,

2016, 2017) were made to explore how they interact with each other and contribute to learner engagement with teacher feedback. The findings of this study have provided insights into the relationship between the theoretical construct of engagement and the multi-layered context in which engagement is situated.

6.3 An Exploratory Conceptual Framework of Teacher Feedback on Task-Based Oral Presentation Performance

Based on the findings reported in Chapter 4 and Chapter 5, as well as the discussion above, the researcher revised the original conceptual framework in section 2.5 and proposed an exploratory conceptual framework (see Figure 6.1) of EFL teachers' feedback on task-based oral presentation performance. Hopefully, this conceptual framework can be further refined in future research.

This exploratory framework is informed by a multi-dimensional research perspective (i.e., cognitivism, sociocultural theory, and social constructivism), which allows a holistic understanding of the phenomenon of EFL teachers' feedback on task-based oral presentation performance. The dotted lines in Figure 6.1 demonstrate the theoretical perspectives: cognitively, a teacher provides feedback as an input which is then processed by a student nurturing output and finalizing it in learning outcomes (i.e., language learning and oral presentation performance). Through the sociocultural lens, feedback is given by means of scaffolding to support a student to the next stage (i.e., the student's ZPD) in which learning outcomes are achieved. The social constructivism focuses on how a student is actively engaged in constructing the feedback information through his or her learner agency. On the one hand, learner factors underlie an individual student's potential capacity to regulate his or her engagement with teacher feedback, that is, learner agency. On the other hand, learner agency is mediated by the surrounding contexts. In fact, not all contextual properties can be perceived and used by the student. As Han (2016) argued, "only when the contextual properties are 'filtered through' (perceived, appreciated, and used) learner agency" (p. 249), can these contextual properties afford student engagement with teacher feedback. Thus, learner agency in this figure is represented by broken lines that connect learner factors and contextual factors to show its changing and dynamic nature.

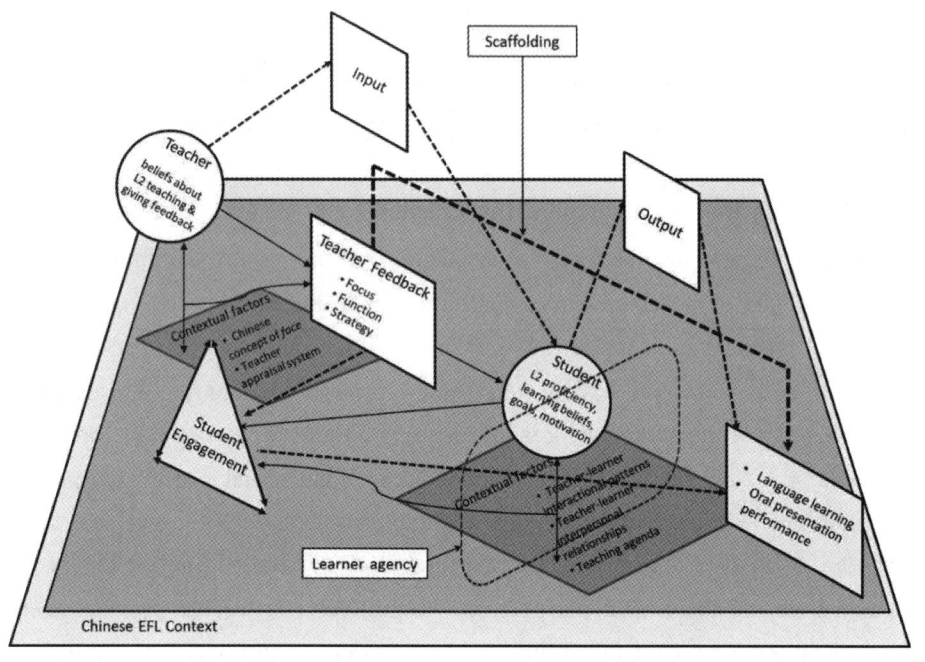

Figure 6.1　An exploratory conceptual framework of teacher feedback on EFL learning and task-based oral presentation performance

　　Moreover, this conceptual framework (see Figure 6.1) is further refined on the basis of the tentative conceptual framework (see Figure 2.3). Based on the findings of this study, it is concluded that the two constructs—teacher feedback practices and student engagement with teacher feedback are influenced by an array of mediating teacher, learner, and contextual factors. The solid lines in Figure 6.1 show how these two constructs are influenced by the mediating factors. To be more specific, a teacher's feedback practices can be examined in three aspects: feedback focus (i.e., what to say in the feedback), function, and strategy (i.e., how to give the feedback). Teacher feedback practices are not only influenced by the teacher's beliefs about L2 learning and giving feedback, but also mediated by the Chinese sociocultural context of face-saving and the institutional context of teacher appraisal system. With regard to student engagement with teacher feedback, it is a multi-faceted construct composed of the three interrelated (represented by the double-headed arrows) sub-constructs of cognitive engagement, behavioral engagement, and affective engagement. That being said, when a student engages with teacher feedback, the three dimensions unfold simultaneously and inseparably. A student's engagement with teacher feedback is influenced by his or her L2 proficiency, learning beliefs, motivation and goals, as well as mediated by the contextual factors of teacher-student interactional patterns, interpersonal relationships, and teaching agenda. It is worth noting that the multitude of factors — teacher factors and contextual factors dynamically interact and jointly influence a teacher's giving feedback in the real-life Chinese EFL classroom. Likewise, the multitude of learner factors and contextual factors exerted the joint influence on a student's engagement with teacher feedback in an authentic Chinese EFL classroom. These joint influences are represented by the solid curves in Figure 6.1.

To better showcase this complexity, the researcher illustrates this framework with the student participant of Han. As shown in section 5.2.3, Han understood most of the teacher's CF on linguistic forms and successfully repaired these linguistic errors, which partly resulted from the teacher's CF strategy of explicit corrections. More importantly, Han employed cognitive operations of reasoning (i.e., conducting metalinguistic analysis) and activating previous metalinguistic knowledge. In addition, Han did not feel upset or embarrassed upon the receipt of CF, because he preferred learning grammar knowledge and developed a "learner-facilitator" type of interpersonal relationship with the teacher when engaging with teacher feedback. By contrast, Han had a relatively inadequate understanding of the teacher's content feedback, which was constrained by the free riding in group work. In fact, most of the pertinent research materials used in pair presentations were found by Han's teammate. Moreover, the institutional context, particularly the voluntary revisions of PPT slides required by the teacher, further contributed to Han's disengagement with content feedback, because Han lacked the motivation to make oral presentations and regarded passing exams as his primary learning goal. Overall, Han's willingness to engage with teacher feedback was mediated by the dynamic interaction between multiple learner and contextual factors, as well as the specific characteristics of teacher feedback *per se*.

6.4 Summary of Chapter

This chapter has argued for both a cognitive and social understanding of teacher feedback on task-based oral presentation performance. On the one hand, teachers' giving of feedback or students' engagement with feedback is largely an internalized cognitive process mediated by teacher-internal and learner-internal factors. On the other hand, teachers' practices of giving feedback and student engagement processes are also situated human activities, which can be mediated by a multitude of contextual factors. An exploratory framework has been proposed to account for how teachers give feedback on students' oral presentations, as well as how students cognitively, behaviorally, and affectively engage with teacher feedback in the context of authentic Chinese EFL classrooms.

Chapter 7　Conclusion

Chapter 7 concludes the present study by first summarizing the main findings in accordance with the four research questions. It then highlights the significance and limitations of this study. This chapter ends with implications for EFL teaching and suggestions for future research.

7.1　Summary of Main Research Findings

This study has adopted a multiple-case study research design to investigate teachers' feedback on task-based oral presentations, as well as students' engagement with such feedback in Chinese university-level EFL classrooms. Specifically, this study involved two Chinese EFL teachers from two different classes and six Chinese EFL English-majored undergraduates with different levels of L2 proficiency (i.e., three students from each of the two classes). Multiple sources of qualitative data were collected over a period of one academic semester, including classroom observations, the researcher's field notes, video-recordings of students' oral presentations, transcripts of teachers' oral feedback, semi-structured interviews, stimulated recalls, students' reflective accounts, as well as a variety of class documents. Taking place in naturalistic classroom settings, this case study attempted to (ⅰ) explore what feedback the teachers provided to students' oral presentations and the reasons that influenced their feedback practices; and (ⅱ) investigate how the students affectively, cognitively, and behaviorally engaged with the teachers' feedback and the reasons underlying their engagement processes.

Regarding teacher feedback practices, text analysis of transcripts of teacher oral feedback revealed that the delivered feedback explicitly focused on five main aspects pertaining to the task of oral presentation: use of language (both speech and written texts on PPT slides), content of oral presentation, organization of oral presentation, presentation aid (e.g., PPT format, background, etc.), and presentation delivery. The results of descriptive statistics showed that Amelia mostly focused on content and organizational issues, whereas Gwen was mainly concerned with linguistic forms. Moreover, it was found that both Amelia and Gwen combined criticisms with either praise or suggestions to soften the negativity of critical feedback. In this study, Amelia opted for input-providing CF strategies and made strategic use of students' L1 (i.e., Chinese) and nonverbal language, whereas Gwen other than using L1 preferred output-prompting CF techniques and resorted to generating other feedback sources (i.e., peers and self).

Referring to reasons underlying the two teachers' feedback practices, five main factors were revealed based on data analysis of transcripts of interviews and stimulated recalls. They were teacher beliefs about feedback and the task of oral presentation, constraints of limited time and energy, individual student performance, face-saving policy, and teacher appraisal system. It is worth noting that these factors were intricately related to each other and jointly influenced teacher feedback practices.

Student engagement with teacher feedback manifested on three interrelated dimensions: affective, cognitive, and behavioral engagement. With regard to affective engagement, although the six students held positive attitudes towards teacher feedback in general, they reported experiencing different emotions, such as positive emotions of happiness, motivation, and appreciation and negative emotions of embarrassment, upset, anger, etc. These emotions were closely related to students' individual differences and were sometimes subject to self-regulation: some students (e.g., Wang and Chen) resented being corrected too much by teachers, whereas others (e.g., Li and Han) were quite happy to receive CF and could convert negative feelings into positive ones. In terms of cognitive engagement, students showed individual differences in respect to the depth of processing and the use of metacognitive and cognitive operations. In contrast with students' frequent adoption of cognitive operations when processing feedback, such as reasoning, predicting, activating background knowledge, making connections, visualization, and memorization, only two metacognitive operations (i.e., planning and monitoring) were conducted which enabled students to regulate their revision operations. Behavioral engagement with feedback referred to students' use of teacher feedback in the revision processes, actions taken to apply teacher feedback to subsequent oral presentations, and revision strategies (such as using external resources). In general, most students (except for Li and Chen) chose to behaviorally engage with teacher CF on linguistic forms rather than content-related feedback.

A cluster of learner, teacher, and contextual factors was identified as playing a role in influencing the students' engagement with teacher feedback. Learner factors included students' different levels of L2 proficiency, beliefs about L2 speaking and making oral presentations, learning goals, and motivation. These learner factors were found to mediate students' depth of processing of feedback, their emotions in response to different types of feedback, and how much effort they were willing to make to conduct revision operations. Moreover, characteristics of teacher feedback *per se* also mediated students' selection of cognitive operations when processing feedback. As for the contextual factors, the data analysis showed that teacher-student interpersonal relationships influenced students' attitudes and emotions upon receiving teacher feedback, especially teacher CF. Teachers' teaching agenda also impacted whether or not, as well as how students chose to generate revisions in response to different types of teacher feedback.

7.2 Significance of the Study

The current study makes contributions to the research on teacher feedback in EFL education in terms of the following aspects. First, a multi-dimensional theoretical perspective (i.e., cognitive, sociocognitive, and social constructive) has been identified in this study, which provides a theoretical basis for teacher feedback on EFL learning because it indicates that learning and understanding are socially constructed and contextualized rather than being a pure mental mechanism. Through this theoretical lens, the phenomenon of teachers giving feedback and students engaging with teacher feedback is well explained. In addition, an exploratory conceptual framework (see section 6.3) has been proposed in this study to help gain a holistic view and understanding of the phenomenon of Chinese EFL teachers' feedback on task-based oral presentation performance. This conceptual framework may allow researchers to examine the interactive relationship between teacher feedback and learner development and encourage students to productively engage with teacher feedback to develop their EFL learning.

Secondly, while most previous teacher feedback studies focused exclusively on the particular form of CF on form-focused oral activities in EFL classrooms, the findings of this study extend previous research by examining teachers' overall feedback practices in meaning-oriented EFL oral tasks. More importantly, this study addressed the research gap whereby the construct of learner engagement, which links the provision of feedback and learning outcomes, has been underexplored. On the one hand, the findings of this study offer insights into the engagement processes through which students deal with teacher feedback on EFL oral tasks. On the other hand, the findings of this study provide empirical evidence of the complex and dynamic relationship between affective, cognitive, and behavioral engagement with teacher feedback (Ellis, 2010a). As shown, these three dimensions often interact with one another, which indicates that any separate understanding of learner engagement with feedback would be insufficient.

Thirdly, since this multiple-case study focused on teacher feedback on group/pair presentations and involved Chinese university-level EFL teachers and English-majored undergraduates, it highlighted the particularities of this sociocultural, institutional, and instructional context. They are: (i) the Chinese cultural issues of face-saving and power distance, which influenced how teachers formulated feedback as well as how students perceived the teacher's role in negotiating feedback, and (ii) the fact that students lacked sufficient understanding of collaborative learning in terms of pair or group work. While the purpose of this qualitative case study is not to generalize the research findings across contexts, it can offer insights for researchers and teachers who work in similar sociocultural contexts.

7.3 Limitations of the Study

Before providing the implications of this study, an acknowledgement needs to be made in terms of its limitations. First, the demerits of this study are inherently related to the issue of generalizability. Since this case study involves two EFL teachers and six English-majored undergraduates at one particular Chinese university, the findings may not be generalized to other EFL populations (such as students enrolling in other study programmes) and contexts (such as other universities in the mainland of China). For example, only two EFL students with lower levels of L2 proficiency participated in this study. This small number of data collection units makes it difficult to represent the larger population units and achieve the so-called statistic generalization. That being said, generalizability is not the main goal of the researcher in this study. While the methodological approach of case study lies in the particularity, it is hoped that through the thick description of this study, readers can determine what can be transferred to their own contexts (Lincoln & Guba, 1985).

Another inherent limitation of this study concerns the specific data collection methods employed. The stimulated recall method is criticized for having "the potential for secondary ordering of the cognitions and the potential for bias in the responses" (Lyle, 2003, p. 871), and therefore may not thoroughly elicit teachers' and students' mental thoughts when giving or receiving feedback. Moreover, the processes of students' revisions to PPT slides were not observed or video-recorded in the present study. Students were told by the researcher to record their revision processes in their reflective accounts, which runs the risk of students not reporting detailed actions taken in their revisions.

Finally, it was difficult to confirm the accuracy of students' understanding of as well as their revision operations generated in response to teacher feedback on the content and organizational matters in oral presentations. This difficulty is associated with the lack of measures of so-called content or structural accuracy because the teachers in this study only encouraged students to make revisions but did not provide further feedback on students' revised PPT slides. This limitation made it difficult to obtain a comprehensive picture of students' engagement with teacher content-focused feedback.

7.4 Pedagogical Implications

This study provides several useful implications for both teacher feedback practices in Chinese EFL classrooms and similar pedagogical contexts and language teacher training and education programmes. First, there is a need to raise language teachers' awareness of the multi-faceted nature of teacher feedback. As oral presentations are different from grammar and vocabulary exercises, the study has shown that teacher feedback, if limited to focusing on linguistic forms, appeared to be insufficient for students' improvement of task performance. Useful corrections of oral errors in students' speeches or written errors on their PPT slides may take place during feedback on oral presentations. However, perhaps more importantly, teachers should also provide useful information about students' abilities to organize presentations and develop ideas in a logical manner, along with effective use of communication tools (e.g., presentation aids in this study) and presentation delivery (e.g., eye contact, volume, rate, etc.). These abilities can be regarded as a set of macro-level communicative strategies (Canale & Swain, 1980), exerting dramatic impacts on the effectiveness of oral presentation performance. In other words, when giving feedback on communicative language tasks, teachers need to not only pay attention to the linguistic aspects of language learning, but also consider learner development of macro communication skills.

The findings of this study reveal that L1 of Chinese is an important mediating tool in teacher oral feedback because it can help enhance students' understanding of teacher feedback. As Storch and Aldosari (2010) stated, "to restrict or prohibit the use of L1 in L2 classes is to deny learners the opportunity of using an important tool" (p. 372). Moreover, this study provides evidence that nonverbal behavior is also an important facet of L2 teachers' feedback act. It is therefore suggested that teachers increase the effectiveness of their feedback in L2 by accompanying it with L1 and nonverbal behaviors.

Another pedagogical implication that can be drawn from this study is that teachers should bear in mind the specific sociocultural context in which feedback is situated. The Chinese sociocultural context which emphasizes face-saving and maintaining harmony in communication exchange is of great prominence in this study and it has profound implications for how teachers should formulate and conduct their feedback on oral tasks in Chinese EFL classrooms. For example, Gwen's "feedback sandwich" in which criticisms are sandwiched between praises and suggestions is in line with principles of good feedback (Molloy, 2010) and softens negative comments. Besides, linguistic softeners like hedges of modal expression (e.g., could and might) and vague language can also be used when teachers intend to mitigate the negativity in their public feedback.

In addition, the study has demonstrated that the six students engaged with teacher feedback differently with regard to their emotional and attitudinal responses to teacher feedback, the depth of processing, metacognitive and cognitive operations that they employed, the revision operations and other actions taken to use teacher feedback. These differences can be attributed to individual differences between students' L2 proficiency, learning beliefs, goals and motivation. Thus, teachers should recognize individual learner differences in terms of engagement with teacher feedback and should not become disappointed if some students failed to fulfill their expectations of deep and extensive engagement with teacher feedback.

That being said, the lingering question is how teachers can help students enhance their engagement with teacher feedback. Some concrete suggestions are proposed as follows. First, as indicated in this study, when the CF strategy of explicit correction was provided, students were able to notice its corrective force and explain it; whereas some students were stuck in the first place of identifying the implicit oral CF such as elicitation (see oral CF episode 7 in section 5.2.1.2 for review), let alone generating further engagement with it. Therefore, teachers can give students explicit instruction of CF strategies before error correction and help students acquire the knowledge in this regard. In this case, students are more likely to make the connection between teacher CF and previous instruction and produce corrections.

Second, teachers need to suggest some learning strategies and resources that can facilitate students' engagement with teacher feedback. For example, since some students (for example Wang) in this study lacked relevant knowledge and strategies about how to act upon teacher feedback, particularly feedback on macro-level issues such as content and organization of oral presentation, teachers can consider showing students authentic videos, websites and books so that students know how to prepare effective oral presentations rather than relying on intuitions. Instruction about oral presentation evaluation rubrics that help students to understand what are expected in terms of task performance can be helpful as well.

Aside from providing students with instruction, resources and strategies, teachers should raise students' awareness of collaborative learning. It was found that some students in this study (e.g., Deng in Amelia's class and Han in Gwen's class) paid more attention to just-for-me feedback than group feedback and thus generated few revision operations in this regard. Therefore, it is suggested that teachers increase students' willingness to collaborate and contribute as a team. On one hand, teachers need to make sure that collaboration runs through the pre-task, during-task and post-task phases so that students value group work and feedback in the first place. On the other hand, teachers need to communicate with individual students as well as the whole group and balance these two kinds of feedback. Teachers should also create opportunities for students to negotiate feedback information with them. For example, out-of-class conferencing can be organized where students have private conversations with teachers to voice their non-understanding of teacher feedback; this would allow teachers to provide specific clarifications to explain their feedback. Moreover, if possible, revisions to PPT slides can be externally mandated after teachers verbally comment on students' oral presentation performance. This approach allows students to use and reflect upon teacher feedback so that feedback is not reduced into "dangling data"

(Sadler, 1989, p. 121).

Last but not least, in order to enable teachers to make more informed decisions about providing feedback on oral tasks, what seems to be needed is supportive teacher training programmes that can contribute to productive feedback practices. A series of activities such as workshops, seminars and classroom observations, in which teachers read related literature and communicate with researchers in the field of teacher feedback, can be organized to develop teachers' beliefs and knowledge of feedback and equip teachers with effective feedback strategies.

7.5 Suggestions for Future Research

While the current research presents an exploratory study adopting the naturalistic multiple-case study approach and involving only eight study participants (i.e., two Chinese EFL teachers and six English-majored undergraduates), the findings can serve as tentative hypotheses that suggest directions for future research.

One possible line of further research would be to explore differences among teachers of different cultural backgrounds in terms of providing feedback on oral tasks. As mentioned in section 7.3, one limitation of this study concerns the issue of generalizability: the research findings can only be transferred to similar contexts. Since this study only took place in the specific sociocultural context of the mainland of China where collectivism, group harmony, and face-saving are deeply rooted (Nelson & Carson, 2006), future comparative case studies can be conducted to emphasize comparisions across contexts; for instance, selecting teacher cases from the United States where directness and individualism is more common than in Asia.

In terms of student engagement, future research could narrow down its scope of inquiry to a specific type of feedback provided on tasks of oral presentation. Given that oral CF and content feedback co-occurred after students' presentations, it is possible that these two types of feedback compete for students' cognitive resources. There is a need for research that separately investigates students' engagement with either type of feedback. Such investigations are meaningful in that more fine-tuned pedagogical implications can be drawn for teachers in improving students' linguistic accuracy and task performance in general.

In addition, future studies could also investigate student engagement with peer feedback on oral presentations. In this study, since the phenomenon of interest is teacher feedback, the researcher did not explore how students engaged with peer feedback on their oral presentations, although Gwen elicited a certain amount of peer feedback in his own feedback practices. This is an important issue to study because Chinese students generally believe in a teacher's authority as the sole knowledge holder, which probably leads to different engagement patterns from those with teacher feedback.

As regards issues in methodology, other investigation paradigms can be used in future research. Given that students in this study activated prior knowledge about oral CF to ascertain the teachers' intention behind current CF, it may be illuminating if future researchers were to combine descriptive and experimental paradigms. For instance, teachers could give pre-feedback instruction in terms of oral CF strategies, as well as train students to use the provided feedback. This line of research would allow us to examine both the process and product in terms of student engagement.

7.6 Summary of Chapter

In summary, this multiple-case study has investigated Chinese EFL teachers' feedback on students' task-based oral presentation performance, as well as students' engagement with teacher feedback. This study has also indicated that both teacher provision of feedback and student engagement with feedback can be influenced by the interrelated teacher, learner, and contextual factors. The findings of this study enrich our understanding of teacher feedback and learner engagement in communicative EFL classrooms. This study provides implications for EFL teachers to enhance their feedback practices and support students to productively engage with feedback. It is hoped that this study will throw light upon future directions of research into teacher feedback in EFL teaching and learning.

Appendices

Appendix A Informed Consent Form for Teacher Participants

Chinese EFL teachers' feedback on task-based oral presentations

Information sheet for teacher participants
PURPOSE OF THE STUDY

This research study aims to investigate how EFL (English as a foreign language) teachers in China give feedback to English-majored undergraduate students in their in-class oral presentations, and how the students understand, use, think of, and react to teacher feedback. The study also aims to identify factors that may influence how teachers give feedback on students' oral presentations, as well as how students understand, use, think of, and react to teacher feedback.

PROCEDURE

The study will last for 18 weeks over a period of one academic semester.

As part of your normal class:

- All the oral presentations that students make will be observed and video-recorded, together with your oral feedback that you provide to them after their performance. Your written feedback to students and scores if provided to them will also be collected.

Out of class:

- You will be invited to attend two face-to-face semi-structured interviews with the researcher in a quiet room in the university, each of which will last approximately 60 minutes. The first interview will take place before students' first round of oral presentations and the second interview will take place after students finish their third oral presentations. You will be audio-recorded during this procedure.

- You will take part in a stimulated recall in a quiet room in the university, after each occasion of you providing feedback on your students' oral presentations. Each stimulated recall will last approximately 20 to 30 minutes. You will be asked to recall and think about your thoughts when providing feedback. You will be audio-recorded during this procedure.
- During the research period, the researcher may collect a range of documents, including the course syllabus, lesson plans, grading rubrics for oral presentations if there are any, students' original and revised PowerPoint slides, their drafts of speech, or any other related aspects of your students' oral presentations.

POTENTIAL BENEFITS

As a result of your participation in the study, you will have a better understanding of the nature and role of teacher feedback in the process of English language learning and have opportunities to reflect on your feedback practices as a feedback giver. This reflection may help you to improve your teaching skills.

POTENTIAL RISKS

There is very little possibility of discomfort throughout your participation in this study.

CONFIDENTIALITY

The information that will be collected from this study will be kept confidential and will be used for research purposes only. Pseudonyms will be used when reporting the findings in any publication.

PARTICIPATION AND WITHDRAWAL

Your participation is voluntary. That means you can choose to stop at any time without negative consequences. You will have the right to decide whether to allow the researcher to observe and video-record your students' oral presentations, as well as audio-record your discussions with the researcher in the stimulated recalls and semi-structured interviews. Furthermore, you can also decide which part of the audio-recorded interviews and stimulated recalls you would like to share with the researcher.

****

Informed Consent
Reply Slip

I _____ (name of participant) understand the procedures described above and agree to participate in this study.

_____   _____
   Signature of the teacher   Date

Appendix B   Informed Consent Form for Student Participants

Chinese EFL teachers' feedback on task-based oral presentations

Information sheet for student participants

PURPOSE OF THE STUDY

This research study aims to investigate how EFL (English as a foreign language) teachers in China give feedback to English-majored undergraduate students in their in-class oral presentations, and how the students understand, use, think of, and react to teacher feedback. The study also aims to identify factors that may influence how teachers give feedback to student oral presentations, as well as how students understand, use, think of, and react to teacher feedback.

PROCEDURE

The study will last for 18 weeks over a period of one academic semester.

As part of your normal class:

- You will make three oral presentations as instructed by your teacher. All the oral presentations that you make will be observed and video-recorded, together with the teacher's oral feedback provided to you after your performance. Teacher written feedback to you and scores if provided will also be collected.

Out of class:

- You will be invited to attend two face-to-face semi-structured interviews with the researcher in a quiet room in the university, each of which will last approximately 60 minutes. The first interview will take place before your first oral presentation and the second interview will take place after you finish the third oral presentation. You will be audio-recorded during this procedure.
- You will take part in a stimulated recall in a quiet room in the university, after each occasion of teacher's feedback on your oral presentation. Each

stimulated recall will last approximately 20 to 30 minutes. You will be asked to recall and think about your thoughts and feelings when receiving teacher feedback. You will be audio-recorded during this procedure.

- You will be asked to write a reflective account as part of a take-home task, which covers your experiences and thoughts about receiving your feedback and making revisions if there are any. This will be no less than 350 words, either in English or in Chinese. The reflective account will not be graded by the teacher.

- During the research period, the researcher may collect a range of documents, including your PowerPoint slides and the revised slides if there are any, your drafts of speech, or any other related aspects of your oral presentations.

POTENTIAL BENEFITS

As a result of your participation in the study, you will have opportunities to reflect on your engagement process as a feedback receiver and will therefore have a better understanding of teacher feedback as well as your engagement with teacher feedback. Such reflection may help you to improve your English language learning and oral presentation performance.

POTENTIAL RISKS

There is very little possibility of discomfort throughout your participation in this study.

CONFIDENTIALITY

The information that will be collected from this study will be kept confidential and will be used for research purposes only. Pseudonyms will be used when reporting the findings in any publication.

PARTICIPATION AND WITHDRAWAL

Your participation is voluntary. That means you can choose to stop at any time without negative consequences. You will have the right to decide whether or not to allow the researcher to observe and video-record your oral presentations, as well as to audio-record your discussions with the researcher in the stimulated recalls and semi-structured interviews. Furthermore, you can also decide which part of the audio-recorded interviews and stimulated recalls you would like to share with the researcher.

****

Informed Consent
Reply Slip

I _____ (name of participant) understand the procedures described above and agree to participate in this study.

_____   _____
    Signature of the student   Date

Appendix C Sample Verbatim Transcripts of Student Speech in Oral Presentations

(Wang—Presentation 2—Week 9—lasting for 5 minutes 41 seconds)

Good morning, everyone. In the last presentation, our topic is attitude of love in Chinese culture. Today we are going to talk about attitude of love in western countries. We divide this presentation into three parts. The first part is the position of love in western people's mind. The second part is the expression of love in western countries. In the last part, we talk about the reasons why most of the westerners have such view of love. The first part. Position of love in western people's mind. Most of the westerners are influenced by religions. They think love is sacred and supreme. They admire the freedom of love. They think the choice and marriage of each other should be based on love, regardless of the family background, social status, age, religion and other factors. We have an example of Kahlil Gibran. Gibran is an outstanding poet in the 20th century and he did not marry throughout his life. However, he has a very toughing love story with Merry who was ten years older than him. They fell in love with each other deeply. For Gibran, Merry was not only his teacher but also his love. Merry loved him very much and helped him selflessly and did not want to restrict his development. So, she refused Gibran's proposal. The second part is the expression of love in western countries. Western way of expressing love is always in straightforward words and specific actions. They express their feelings in a very open way. Here is an example. It is one of Heine's poems. You are like a flower. [a period of silence lasting 10 seconds] This poem is a very direct expression of the author's emotion. We can see that the expressions in western countries are very direct. However, when they say I love you, they just express their feelings which can express how deep he loves you at present, but not promising for the future. In the last part, we focus on the reasons why most westerners think in this way. The first reason is the thinking patterns. Most westerners think in a very clear, logical and rational way. They pursue for love and personal freedom. They think it's their right to do so. The second reason is the social background. Most western countries have more democratic and individualistic societies, so they had the social background to do so. Individualism is an important cultural phenomenon in western countries. That's all. Thank you. Next time, we will talk about the comparison between Western and Chinese attitude of love. Thank you.

Appendix D Sample Verbatim Transcripts of Teacher Oral Feedback

(Amelia—To Wang—Presentation 2—Week 9—lasting for 6 minutes)

(*After Wang's presentation, Amelia began to provide oral feedback in both English and Chinese*)

Amelia: Just brief comments on the presentation. Ok. This time, the volume of the voice is fine and the speed and the rhythm is really good. But, still something about the contents, that is, the attitude of love. [Amelia is turning to PPT slide 2] Alright. About these three parts: "the position of love", "the expression of love", "analyze the reasons". Quite clear structure. But, let us look at the details of each part. [Amelia is turning to PPT slide 3]So, first part. Better put the subtitle also on that slide, right? You are familiar with your contents, but the audience are not, right? So, first part, that is, "the position of love". "Sacred" means holy, right? Put it in Chinese, that is 神圣的。Ok. Next one. "Supreme". "Freedom of love". "Based on love". Yes, you are talking about love. But, look at those words. I mean, "based on love", what's love? "Freedom of love". This part is Ok. But, think about it. You just like lingering on the surface of this topic, but you never try to go deeper into this topic. What is love? It is a kind of emotion, right? Think about this concept. So, Ok. "Based on love". Then, what kind of love? Love between males and females? Or love between two males? Or love between two females? Come on. This topic could be more interesting and it should cover lots of contents. Not just like this one, quite generally. Some bullet points here. Ok? The good side is that this group gives us some examples and tries to illustrate it. But, about those examples, could you find interesting pictures or something interesting to put it on your slide so that your audience could be attracted to your presentation? Just some suggestions here.

Amelia: [Amelia is turning to PPT slide 4] Ok. This one. Part two. I couldn't remember the contents of part two. Ok. "The expression of love". Ok. Just like the method of what they have used in their first presentation about Chinese love. "Straightforward words", then "specific actions". Yeah, there is a grammatical mistake here. Right? It should be "open ways" not "opening ways". Ok. "Open ways".

Amelia: [Amelia is turning to PPT slide 5] But, there is no specific illustration. Just one poem here. Look at this poem. Wang, I think you should read it out for your audience so that they could follow your thoughts, Ok? So, they will read the poem with you. [Amelia is reading the poem: *You are like a flower, Tender and pure and beautiful. As soon as I see you, The sorrow goes into my heart. I think I should touch your head with my hands. May god keep you pure, beautiful and tender forever.*] You mentioned the author of this poem, the title, and the name of this poem, right? I suggest you write it down here so that we know whether this is a famous poet or not. But, I don't appreciate the poem here. Look at the expressions. Are they really straightforward? You said it's straightforward, but look at here, i.e., *You are like a flower*. How about "You are just beautiful"? *Tender and pure and beautiful*. Is love sweet? Or, isn't love sweet? Why the sorrow goes into my heart? What's kind of situation here? Or, what happened here? *I think I should touch your head with my hands*. [Amelia is turning back to PPT slide 3 and pointing to the word "straightforward"] Is this love this one or this one? [Amelia is writing the word "sacred" and the phrase "freedom of love" on the blackboard] So, what's love? Think about it. Then, why do you think this poem is really straightforward? How is it related to your point? Think about it. Or, would you like to choose another literary work to replace this poem? Ok. Anyone in your group could answer this question? Do you think it's a proper poem here?

A student in Wang's group: No, I don't think so.

Amelia: Next time, when you are choosing your data, be more careful. Don't make this kind of mistake. The data and also your point are actually contradictory. Ok? 是矛盾的吧？你们自己仔细分析一下，别光把材料摆在这儿就完了，你们有没有仔细想过？

Amelia: Ok. About the third part. "Analyze the reasons". Or, just say

"Analysis of the reasons", Ok? Because you use noun phrases in the title part. [Amelia is turning to PPT slide 6] Ok. So "thinking pattern" and "social background". Let me see. Still for the first reason, it's just a little bit far from this point, i.e., thinking pattern. And there should be a punctuation mark, a comma between the words "logical" and "rational". They are thinking patterns, something like this. [Amelia is drawing two lines (a spiral and a straight) on the blackboard] So, what's the relationship between thinking pattern illustrated by the two lines and the topic of love? What's the relationship between those thinking patterns and love? You haven't made it clear. Maybe you could illustrate your point. Try to say more about it. Do the linking. Ok? Do the connection work.

Wang: But, we tend to think that the westerners like flirting around and hooking up. [The whole class is laughing]

Amelia: You need to do more work. They also tend to be practical, even more practical than we Chinese are. When they are talking about love and marriage, maybe the first love is blind, but after that they tend to be quite practical. 我跟大家说一下啊,《中西方比较》这门课我们还要讲这个点,西方人对于爱情观比中国人来的还务实,并不是你们脑子里想的,噢,西方人相当浪漫,怎么怎么样。一夜情他们可能不怎么考虑,但那不是他们长久的 partner, 不是他的 husband and wife. 但是一旦涉及到要以结婚为目的的,或者是一辈子不结婚,永久性的 partner 的时候,他们想法比中国人还务实,这是我跟你们要强调的。所以你们这一组的资料还是浮于咱们平时想法里的,这个想当然的,不是真正的去深入调查了,西方的婚恋观念并非是这样子的。

Amelia: Ok. 所以我说你们提到的 thinking pattern, 起码第一反应是黑板上的直线和螺旋线. Your topic is love. 这到底中间有个什么 linking 呀? 你最多说他们的 life style. 最多有时候说是荷尔蒙的影响,但是真正的不是这个情况啊,所以你的 love 都没有界定清楚, So, is love just a period of rush or something long-lasting? Ok? 到底是夫妻之间的长久的关系还是说只是一时的冲动。想清楚。

Amelia: Ok. Next one. Social background. This part is Ok, but I think there should be more. If you really want to explore the reasons. First, life style and also their expression style. So, they tend to be quite direct, straightforward and nothing else. If it's a period of rush, then it's Ok. They tend to be blind and think nothing about it. After that, how many people will get divorced? Think about it. Alright. So, when you are trying to say something or organize some ideas about the reasons, about the analysis of your topic, then be cautious. Better find some supporting statements from academic writing or from some internet data. Find something more reliable. Ok? 找一些比较可靠的资源，去论证，别只是靠自己总结。然后需要再具体展开。To be more specific. Try to explain more about those points. Try to explain the linking, the connection between your points and your illustration. Then, you will say that I think it's that way. That's how the presentation works, and how the logic and the content work here. Think about it. So much about my feedback.

Appendix E   Teacher Semi-Structured Interview Guide

Personal experiences of English teaching and use of oral presentations

1. Tell me about your English teaching experience. For example, how long have you been teaching English at the university? What courses do you currently teach?
2. How do you use oral presentations in your classroom teaching?
3. What do you think is the role of using oral presentations in facilitating students' English language learning?

Teacher beliefs about English learning and teaching of oral English

4. What do you think are the objectives of the English major undergraduate programme at the university? What should students achieve?
5. What do you think is the role of oral English skills in developing students' English language proficiency?
6. What do you believe are the strengths and weaknesses of your students' oral competence?

Teacher beliefs about giving feedback and their feedback practices in oral presentations

7. What is your purpose/intent in providing feedback on students' oral presentations?
8. How do you see the role of your feedback on students' oral presentations?
9. How do you usually give feedback on students' oral presentations? What forms does your feedback typically take?
10. What areas do you usually focus on while providing feedback on students' oral presentations? For example, do you focus on students' oral English, the contents and topics of presentations, the logical structures of presentations, or any other issues? Why?
11. How do you usually address students' errors in their oral presentations? Which specific errors should be corrected? Why?
12. There are many types of oral corrective feedback, like explicit correc-

tion, giving metalinguistic explanations, etc. Do you have a preferred type of oral corrective feedback? Why do you prefer this type of oral corrective feedback?

13. What types of comments do you usually make? For example, do you provide judgments on students' presentation performance or offer suggestions to improve their presentation performance? Or both? Why?

14. Do you tailor your feedback to different learners? Why so or why not?

15. If you tailor your feedback to different learners, in what ways do you do that?

16. When providing feedback on students' oral presentations, what factors do you consider?

17. What are some major constraints that you face when giving feedback on students' oral presentations?

18. What do you expect students to do with your teacher feedback?

19. If students do not use your feedback as expected, what do you do?

Reflections upon teacher feedback

20. Looking back at your experience of providing feedback over the semester, what would you have done differently?

21. How do you assess the effectiveness of your own feedback practices over the semester?

22. A new teacher seeks your advice about improving the way he/she gives feedback on his/her students' oral presentations. What advice or suggestions would you give to him/her?

23. Do you have any further comments or reflections on your feedback practices?

Appendix F Sample Verbatim Transcripts of Teacher Semi-Structured Interview

Interviewer：Researcher（R）	**Interviewee**：Gwen（G）
Week：Week 18	**Place**：Room 327
Span of time：15 minutes 20 seconds	**Language**：Chinese and English

R：这学期您布置了三次口语展示任务。您能谈一下是怎么考虑的？而且您用的是两人一组的形式。

G：首先从安排的次数角度来看，有这样几方面的考虑。第一，从教学内容角度，让他们选取和课文中某一个单元相关的话题，来做展示。涉及三次主要是想让他们更多地去展示吧。另一层考虑是去检测学生，在前面一次展示之后，他们到底有没有去记下来老师的点评，有没有针对性地去做改进，在下次展示时，会不会把老师给的点评用到。出现的一些问题，尽量去避免。扬长避短吧，好的地方继续坚持。相对是一个进步的过程吧，希望能看出来。

R：嗯。

G：还有就是相当于我们取平时成绩一样，避免一次考试定终身。

R：嗯。我观察到有的学生在每一次口语展示后还上交 PowerPoint 的修改稿。

G：对。我没有硬性规定他们必须上交。但就是我会根据情况，比如我在我点评之后，他们根据我的点评他们把其中出现的一些问题，做了修改，之后再提交给我修改稿的话，我会考虑给他们增加一些分数。

R：这么做有什么考虑呢？

G：作为一种激励和约束吧。

R：激励？

G：就是老师给我点评后，老师给我的建议，我是否采纳。这样可以反映出他们学习的态度和积极性。给他们点评，然后他们如果提交修改稿，感觉就是一种动机吧。让他们利用我的反馈在以后的口头展示表现地更好。

R：嗯。那您的点评有什么标准吗？还是说就是凭借自己的第一印象？

G：标准。嗯。我觉得是有一些参考点的。主要是我在前期也看了，结合一些演讲啦。再加上要是给分数的话，需要一些客观性。我看了针对口语展示的评价，包括网上的资源，还有别的老师的一些之前的做法。基本上就是这样。

R：嗯，您能具体展开讲讲这些参考点吗？

G：好。主要是语言方面。

R：是的。我观察到您给学生的这三次口语展示，给了很多语言方面的反馈，包括单词的发音，重音问题。包括 PowerPoint 上的一些语言问题。内容上面并没有点评特别多。

G：其实一开始在我预期当中更多的是关注他们的内容啊，知识分享啊。或者是口语展示实际过程当中的表现等。但后来发现，经过第一轮口语展示，他们本来不应该出现的一些语言错误挺多的。我觉得好多错误不应该是英语专业的学生，作为专门学习英语的同学，不应该犯的错误。

R：比如呢？

G：像一些时态的错误啦，单复数的错误啦。

R：您指的是什么语言？口语还是 PowerPoint 上的语言？

G：PowerPoint 上的语言。但是口语的话，他们也有很多问题。第一就是语音上面的不准确。比如非常基本的一些单词就会出现错误。

R：嗯。我注意到在第一次访谈您时，您当时没有把 PowerPoint 作为您反馈的关注点，包括动画啊，图片之类的。

G：嗯。主要是口语展示这项活动的教学目的，跟这个有关。我一开始是觉得口语展示主要是知识分享，这一点占的比例更多一些。但后来发现他们的语言连我的预期都达不到。所以在实际反馈时，我就转向了语言。给语言方面的反馈比较多。比如，我们刚才提到的单词重音问题，一些很简单的词语，一些并不难发音或者在他们展示中很关键的词，他们的发音都没有掌握住。所以就点评他们出现的一些代表性的，或者重复出现的语言错误。这是后来关注的。

R：嗯。

G：然后 PowerPoint 呢，一开始没有想到他们会出现错误，但在他们口语展示时，我发现 PowerPoint 上出现的错误还不少。不应该出现的错误都挺多。而这样的话，考虑到现场记笔记，出现的错误，我无法有效地把它们都记下来。所以后来，我要求他们把 PowerPoint 可以提前发给我。真的是有些根本就不应该犯的错误，他们竟然就这么放在 PowerPoint 上。

R：比如说？

G：就像刚才说的，第三人称单数不加 s，不会用复数。还有一些就是时态的混用。包括 PowerPoint 中同一级标题不一致，有的用了动名词，有的用了动词原形，有的是名词结构，有的是动词结构，这种混用的情况很多。说明他们没有这种一致性或者说统一性这种语言意识。

R：嗯，我在课堂观察也发现了。

G：对。就是类似这种基本语言常识。PowerPoint 中的目录页。Table of Contents。很多同学就用的单数 Content 而没有用 Contents，这种错误是很明显的。第一感觉就是不应该，很不舒服。在看到这种基本错误都很多的情况下，觉得再过多点评口语展示的内容就好像没有意义了。

R：下一个问题是，我观察到您给学生反馈时，没有给太多批评。有时候看起来应该是批评的，但好像也没有。经常您反馈的时候就是 shinning points。学生表现好的地方说一下，坏的地方，对了，您不说"坏的地方"。您在点评时称作 weakness。之后，您就开始给建议。您这样的反馈形式是为什么？

G：首先在我看来，他们现在已经是大学生了，不应该再像中学生或小学生的老师去批评他们，那是很正常的。他们年龄也大了，自主学习的能力也是有的。然后呢，也有一定的面子考虑。包括我个人的性格，自己也不大希望去直观地批评学生。我觉得，嗯，一种探讨式的或者叫协商式的，给一些建议去提高，这么做会更好一些。

R：您觉得批评有用吗？

G：肯定是有用。这么说吧，批评他们在一段时间会给他们压力。他们会想"我没有做好啦，老师生气啦，我不应该犯这样的错误啊"。是会给他们一定压力，让他们去改进。但是我是觉得只是批评，而不给出他们建议的话，他们不知道努力的方向在哪儿。有可能想改，但是我到底怎么改，他们不知道。他们可能不知道怎么把老师的批评去改变成我自己的一种行为。

R：嗯，除此之外，还有其他考虑吗？

G：有啊。就是目前，从我们学校老师出发，还有另外一层原因。现在都是提倡以学生为中心的教学理念。老师们感觉现在学生在课堂上。怎么说呢，我们有时候就会说学生现在像"顾客"一样（Gwen 尴尬地笑）。老师是给他们提供服务的人员，那你服务地好与不好啊，学生们可以进行，因为现在有学生评教嘛，学生可以在学期末给你打分，然后教务处会给学院反馈。这样老师们在评职称的时候，评教成绩会作为一个参考，如果评教成绩不是很理想，排名比较靠后，可能会影响老师职称晋升。所以现在老师们很严厉地批评学生或者直接向学生吼过去，或者言辞激烈地批评学生，现在并不常见。所以这也是一方面考虑吧。怕影响评教成绩。

R：好的。我看您在反馈时，也会点评学生 presentation 的 delivery，比如学生是否脱稿？看不看观众？之前第一次跟您访谈时，您也没有特别说需要关注这一点。您有什么考虑吗？

G：是这样。之前这部分没有作为我关注的重点，是因为当时我读本科的时候，教室里面没有多媒体，就是黑板和粉笔这么一种教学形式。当时我们同学做口语展示时，基本不会拿稿子上到讲台，没有什么可以借助的，像现在有幻灯片和电脑投影作为一种辅助手段。就是单纯靠自己去讲，也不会说拿着稿子来直接去念。这在我们上大学时候，是很正常的一件事情。

R：是的，现在都是要多媒体教学。

G：对，这就是说为啥要叫 oral presentation，它不是阅读性质的。但现在不是有多媒体嘛，因为我要教这个课程，要设计教学任务，我就看了一些这方面的教程，国外一些大学他们的成功做法，怎么要求学生做口语展示。我觉得他们讲的非常有道理。比如，在口语展示当中，其它的都是辅助手段，包括多媒体。主要还是学生自己的讲解，跟观众这种面对面的交流。

R：就像 TED 演讲一样？

G：对。那些演讲者也会使用 PowerPoint，但不会让下面的观众一句一句地读屏幕上的大段文字，那是不可能的。PowerPoint 只起到一种提示性、纲领性的作用。你可以用它作为 notes 或者说是提示演讲者的思路。反正不应该是照着 PowerPoint 一句一句读，一句一句讲，那是不行的，那不是一个好的口语展示。

R：您觉得学生做到您刚才说的这种脱稿的方式了吗？

G：在这学期前几周我给学生放了视频，告诉他们好的口语展示是什么样子，跟他们强调要和观众有眼神交流等等。其实每一次口语展示结束，我给他们点评的时候都会去说这一点。

R：嗯。

G：还是有很多同学做不到，还是照着稿子来念。我觉得这一方面还真是一个问题。以前自己上学时不觉得是一个问题，但对现在的学生却是一个问题。学生们对这个电脑和投影还是非常依赖。其实我们老师们课下互相交流时，也提到在讲课时没有 PowerPoint 不行，只有 PowerPoint 也不行。很多学生上课时也就是看为主，不去听老师讲。

Appendix G Student Semi-Structured Interview Guide

Personal experiences of English learning and making oral presentations

1. Tell me about your learning experiences of English (oral English in particular) in high school.
2. Tell me about your learning experiences of English (oral English in particular) so far at the university.
3. How do English teachers at the university help you improve oral skills?
4. Share with me your experiences of making oral presentations so far.

Learner beliefs about and attitudes toward English learning, oral skills, and oral presentations

5. What is your goal of English learning in college?
6. What are the strengths and weaknesses of your own English learning?
7. What role do you think English plays in your future life and career after graduation?
8. How important are oral skills as part of your English learning?
9. In your opinion, what qualities should a good oral presentation have?

Learner beliefs about, use of, and attitudes toward teacher feedback

10. In your opinion, what does the "ideal" teacher feedback on oral presentations look like?
11. What do you think is the main reason why your teacher gives feedback on your oral presentations?
12. To what extent do you usually understand the teacher's feedback on your oral presentations?
13. Have you ever found the teacher's feedback confusing or unclear to you? If so, what are the reasons why teacher feedback is sometimes difficult to understand? Can you give me an example?
14. What do you do with certain teacher feedback that you do not understand?
15. What resources and strategies do you usually use to improve your oral presentations?
16. How do you feel when you receive feedback from your teacher on your

oral presentations?

17. Do you think the teacher's feedback is helpful for your performance of oral presentations? Why or why not? Can you give me an example of useful feedback?

18. If your teacher wants to improve the way he/she gives feedback to your oral presentations, what advice or suggestions would you give him/her?

Appendix H Sample Verbatim Transcripts of Student Semi-Structured Interview

Interviewer：Researcher（R）	**Interviewee**：Wang（W）
Week：Week 18	**Place**：Room 327
Span of Time：10 minutes 7 seconds	**Language**：Chinese and English

R：你能再谈一下对口语展示这项课堂活动的看法？

W：我反正就是结合我自己准备，然后还有我借鉴比较我们班同学，也就是其他组的同学，我这方面就没他们那么好，其他组的同学准备材料的时候就分工特别明确，然后他们上去讲的那个人会提前把稿子写好，上去的时候根据 PowerPoint 上的内容随性发挥，就是不会特别按稿子上的内容来死记硬背。然后，我感觉这种形式就比较好。从这三次的过程中就一直比较想效仿他们，因为我感觉这种方式就比较好。

R：这个为啥好呢？

W：就是你能够心态更好一点儿，不紧张，然后随性一点，以防有什么突发事件，跟同学交流可以让气氛变好，口语展示也比较自然。不然像我第一次和第二次那样背稿子特别明显的话，就感觉没有那种效果，就感觉你在台上背，台下的同学也没有兴趣听，也就是老师在听嘛。即使你准备再多，气氛活跃不起来，效果就不是特别好。

R：那除此之外，比如说脱离稿子以外，还有哪些要素来组成一个好的口语展示呢？

W：其他要素的话，我感觉，比如说内容，内容要贴近生活，还有就是表达时的方式。比如说我们班那两个男生，就比较幽默，会表达地比较好。有时候我自己说话比较平淡，这样就提不起大家的兴趣。

R：表达方式？比如说有一个 PowerPoint，你的意思是说读 PowerPoint？

W：对，就比如说播放 PowerPoint 首页时，就有的组介绍地特别好。就是先介绍自己，然后说感谢我的组员。大家印象比较深然后大家也比较感兴趣。

R：除此之外呢，你感觉 PowerPoint 呢？

W：就里边的内容？

R：嗯。PowerPoint 的这种设计吧，和老师一直强调你们的这些对吧？

W：嗯，PowerPoint 首先是要清晰，不要太花，不要为了好看插太多的图片，千万要注意坐在台下面的同学能看清字。有时在电脑上能看清楚，但在投影的大屏幕上就看不清了。条理还要清晰，不能把东西都放到一起，对比的时候要有对比，比较的时候要有比较，要条理清晰。

R：OK，下一个问题就是，你能谈一下你对在课上做口语展示的态度吗？

W：在台上讲时，尤其是第一次的时候，真的特别特别紧张。本来我就容易紧张，然后超出正常的紧张，本来我口语表达就不是太好，然后对上去讲的话题也比较陌生，老师又是我们班主任，第一年又没跟她接触太多，面对班主任，心理压力特别大，超紧张。

R：为啥心理压力大，还超级紧张？

W：就感觉她是我们的班主任，就有特别大的压力。她对我们的要求还是很高的，我的口语不是特别好，我上去讲时就有点紧张，然后她又是我的班主任，她对我们的要求有点高，就感觉更紧张一点。

R：你为啥觉得自己口语不好，口语那么多方面，你觉得哪儿不好？

W：就是比如说要表达一个东西吧，我要用英语表达的话我要想一会儿，我不能立刻表达出来，当场想说什么就能立即说出来一个句子，就是这种能力不强。还有就是一些单词的发音不准。

R：除此之外呢？

W：还有就是音调，在上边做演讲声音小。

R：嗯。那你对口语展示这项活动的态度，我们会讲你是一种 positive，还是 negative？

W：可能紧张也有好处吧，我第一次汇报的时候就提前了很长时间准备。我感觉我就特别积极，一直准备，跟我一组的剩下两位同学就不能理解，她们不是特别积极，我们也发生了一些分歧。

R：分歧在哪儿呢？

W：在我们第一次口语展示时，引用了三首中国古诗去说明中国文化中的爱情，但我就不是特别理解它们和主题之间的关系，然后我就问，她们解释的时候就有点儿牵强吧，但我还是听她们的了，然后我就说让她们找个英文版的。

R：嗯。之前你说过你们小组的分工是她俩负责找资料，你要写讲稿，上台进行展示。

W：对。她俩找了个英文版的诗歌，然后她们又说要录视频采访学生对爱情的态度，然后我就说录视频不太好，汇报展示总共就几分钟，视频时间肯定不能那么长，并且采访的还都是我们班女生，我感觉就是有点应付那个意思，我不是特别同意。但是我也没想出更好的办法，她们周四晚上九点跟我说，视频还没有弄好，当时星期六和星期天还有事就没法再弄其他的，就用这个视频。但最后她们也没有给我这个采访视频。

R：所以我想问你，对这门课上做 oral presentation 的态度是什么？

W：我做我自己负责的部分是很积极的。但是第一次上台展示之后，老师点评后，其实当时感觉情绪有点儿低沉吧，有一点点低沉，因为视频那个事儿的原因。虽然说有点儿想责怪她们俩，就感觉，唉，特别烦。

R：嗯。那总体来说，在整个学期你是持一个积极的还是消极的态度呢？

W：总体讲，我感觉我还是比较积极，我有积极准备材料，无论是上去讲，还是下来听老师点评，还是我自己准备资料的时候都是比较积极，不会说特别烦的。

R：你为什么要积极的对待这项任务呢？

W：首先对我来说，不说别人，我本来这方面就比较差嘛，也算给我这次机会去锻炼。有机会锻炼为什么不好好把握？还有就是在这个过程中学到了很多知识，并且可以从中找到自己的不足。如果消极对待的话，你还是需要去做汇报，而且会让自己感觉特别烦。

R：你享受这个过程吗？

W：百分之七十多的享受吧，准备过程会遇到各种困难，有时候就不知道那个结构，不知道怎么弄的时候，心理上就感觉特别烦。

R：在台上的时候，享受这个过程吗？

W：第一次没有，自己做得越好越会享受，跟以前相比会越来越享受。

R：就是你会感觉以后自己越来越好，对吧？

W：对。

Appendix I Prompts of Stimulated Recall with Teachers and Students

Prompt for teacher

I am investigating how EFL (English as a foreign language) teachers in China give feedback to English-majored undergraduate students in their in-class oral presentations, and identifying factors that may influence how teachers give feedback on students' oral presentations.

You are going to watch the video-recordings of students' oral presentations, along with your feedback afterwards. I will point to each piece of feedback that you provided to students. While I could hear your oral feedback, I do not know what you were thinking at the time you were providing feedback on their performance. Please tell me what's on your mind THEN, rather than now. I am also interested in the reasons why you provided such feedback and your expectations for students who received feedback. You may choose to recall in Chinese, English, or a mixture of both. Do you have any questions so far? If not, let's start now.

Prompt for student

I am investigating how Chinese EFL (English as a foreign language) students engage with teacher feedback on tasks of in-class oral presentations. The study also aims to identify factors that may influence how students engage with teacher feedback on their oral presentations.

You are going to watch the video-recordings of your oral presentations, along with teacher feedback afterwards. I will point to each piece of feedback that you received from your teacher. While I could hear the teacher's oral feedback, I do not know what you were thinking at the time you were receiving feedback on your oral presentation performance. Please talk about how you understand, use and think of teacher feedback. Please tell me what's on your mind THEN, rather than now. You may choose to recall in Chinese, English, or a mixture of both. Do you have any questions so far? If not, let's start now.

Appendix J Sample Verbatim Transcripts of Stimulated Recall with Teacher

Interviewer：Researcher（R）	Interviewee：Amelia（A）
Week：Week 12	Place：Room 327
Span of Time：7 minutes 33 seconds	Language：Chinese and English

R：我们先来听您给 Wang 同学第三次口语展示的点评。您随时可以按暂停键，告诉我您的想法。

（video-recordings of Amelia's feedback）

Amelia：First they met some problems. [Amelia is turning to slide 1] I think it's the computer problem because this group sent their slides to me earlier and I saw it was not like this. Anyway，if the audience couldn't see the title of your presentation，you'd better tell them and then continue or start with your presentation.

A：她今天早上 7 点多把 PowerPoint 发给我，我在 iPad 上面看是没有问题的。这就是属于 technical problem. 但是在课堂上她就视而不见，直接就翻到第二页 PowerPoint 去了。

R：这样不好？

A：我觉得这样没有礼貌。相当于你刚上来做汇报就出现一点失误，不应该对大家表示歉意吗？我们同学可能不知道这种情况该怎么办，哪怕用汉语解释一下也可以。但是遗憾的是没有任何表示。

R：您为什么会关注这样的技术问题？按常理说这跟内容和语言都不相关。

A：我觉得是一种交际策略吧。这门课叫做《跨文化交际》，最终落脚点在交际上面。现在就出现了一个现实问题，需要我们同学用语言策略去解决，可是我们同学什么都没有做。

R：嗯。您觉得给这条点评是想提高学生口语展示的哪方面？

A：我觉得是表现的能力。怎么说呢？我可以用英文吧？

R：当然可以。

A：the way in which students actually deliver their presentations.

R：presentation delivery?

A：对。

R：您是怎么看待 presentation delivery?

A：因为 oral presentation 像又不像传统的写作任务，用笔和纸来传达意义。展示的内容和逻辑结构很重要。但是都需要我们同学 deliver 或者说是 perform 出来。它很强调多种模态的结合，演讲者有语言、动作、眼神、肢体还要考虑到观众的视觉和听觉。像今天这样的状况就是我们同学没有用有效的策略去展示出来。

R：嗯。那我们接着往下听您的反馈。

（video-recordings of Amelia's feedback）

Amelia: Still, in the second part, [Amelia is turning to slide 8] you quote some literature and you try to read it for us, which is good. But, I haven't got the meaning here. Why do you cite this poem that comes from this famous Chinese play The Peony Pavilion? Why this one is implicit and why that one, Romeo and Juliet, is explicit? Why? I could not see it actually. In which part is love expressed in this poem in The Peony Pavilion? Please tell me. Where? Which sentences show they fall in love? So, you'd better do your work and do the analysis a little bit further. Yes, you are trying, but you still need to read between the lines and do a little bit analysis.

R：您给这条反馈建议是怎么想的？

A：这个问题一直贯穿这三次口语展示。她这次还好的一点是吸取前两次的教训，在台上不是说让我们自己去看，她给我们读了一遍。但你把牡丹亭这三个字给我抹掉，我是看不出来 PowerPoint 上放的这首诗歌，跟她要论证的观点 manners of expressing love in China is implicit 之间的关系。到底哪句诗歌说爱情？哪句诗歌暗示了我们中国爱情观？或者你再给我们继续解释一下。无法看出来到底哪儿体现出来这个 implicitness。

R：嗯。

A：还有牡丹亭旁边这个节选。Romeo and Juliet.也是仅仅给我们读一遍，也没告诉我们到底是 Romeo 想念 Juliet 还是 Juliet 想念 Romeo？这个感情的抒发，你至少要给我们在台下坐着的观众解释一下。后来我在点评时，带着大家读一遍这首诗歌，才知道是 Juliet 想念 Romeo。

R：所以你希望她怎么做？

A：就比如说给大家说这个确实是关于爱情的。要结合具体的诗句比如"良辰美景奈何天"反应了爱情的什么？既然她把这个例子放到 PowerPoint 上面，说明她对这个例子很熟悉，那就应该给我们进行解析啊。

Appendix K　Sample Verbatim Transcripts of Stimulated Recall with Student

Interviewer：Researcher（R）	**Interviewee**：Li（L）
Week：Week 11	**Place**：Room 327
Span of Time：12 minutes 45 seconds	**Language**：Chinese and English

R：我们还是像上次一样，我播放 Amelia 老师的点评，然后针对每一条反馈，你告诉我你的想法。

（video-recordings of Amelia's feedback）

Amelia：Here are some brief comments. So first，something about language. Ok，Li，how to say 唯一的 in English?

Li：Unique ['ju: ni:k]

Amelia：你这个重音不对。[ju:'ni:k].

Li：[ju:'ni:k]

L：老师提问后，我其实愣了一下，我当时在想哪个单词是"唯一的"，是 only，还是？后来我一想，应该是之前口语展示刚开始的时候，用了 unique 那个词，可能发音不对嘛。

R：那你回答的时候，第一次发音还是读错了。

L：对。

R：那你之前一直是读这个音吗？

L：好像也有人纠正过，但一直以来就这么读，顺口了，就一直这么读了，没有刻意去改。

R：你知道这个单词你的发音问题在哪儿吗？

L：重音。应该在最后一个音节。

R：你是怎么知道的？

L：老师不是用汉语解释了一下，说我的重音不对。再说了，老师把正确的读音说了一下，对比我之前的发音。很容易就知道我把重音放错音节了。

R：好的。

L：其实这个词我在下面准备时都查词典了，然后老师当时不是说了，这个词我上去的时候没读对嘛，当时也不知道咋回事，我就没读对。放到句子里面一连串说的时候，如果你不是十分注意它的发音，就很有可能读错，但是如果单独把它提出来，让我读的话，就能读对。

R：好的。我们继续听下面老师的点评。

（video-recordings of Amelia's feedback）

Amelia：And next one，how to say this word. Um，where is it? Ok. This one. [Amelia is pointing at the word "aroma" on slide 5].

Li：[əˈroʊmə]

Amelia：Good. [əˈroʊmə]. Do you know its meaning?

Li：芳香。

Amelia：直接上中文了哈，嗯，这个中文蛮简单的，香。注意最后一个 syllable，发音是[ə]. 你上来的时候发的不是[ə]的音。

R：这个单词你的读音是对的。

L：我应该在讲稿中也把它的音标写下来了。但不知道怎么在台上读错了，可能还是对这个单词读音不熟悉，没有到自然而然就读对的地步。

R：嗯。下面老师进行了一些 summary，然后对 rational concept 这个词组提出疑问。我们来看一下视频。

（video-recordings of Amelia's feedback）

Amelia：I like the first part. You lead us through a brief review about what you have done up till now and then come to today's topic：the western dietary culture. Give us a brief introduction. In the brief introduction，you told us the unique characteristics of the western dietary culture and also the rational concept. [Amelia is turning to slide 4] Do you all agree with the idea that it is a rational concept? What do you mean by rational concept? [There are no responses from the class，so Amelia continues to say] Ok. It's not like that in China. We pay attention to，um，we focus on all these four aspects：aroma，color，shape，taste. But，maybe in this way，westerners focus more on the calorie and vitamin contained by food and also protein，right? So，maybe give more explanation to this term. So，let this be more self-explanatory. I mean，make this term clearer so that your audience will get it quite easily. Not when I read this phrase，I am thinking what this rational concept means here. Ok. So，you may just say healthy concept or emphasizing health. Something like this. Or，westerns will put health in the first place when it comes to food. Ok?

R：那你知道老师在说什么？

L：就是老师的意思是直接在这儿放一个 rational concept 就显得让人有点摸不到头脑，或者是观众看了之后没法一目了然知道你在讲什么，就感觉不够清晰，就这么单独的一个词组放到这儿，感觉显得有点太突兀吧，这种感觉，或者需要在后面再加点东西，让它的表述更清楚点，让观众看完一眼就明白。

R：你同意老师的观点吗？

L：怎么说呢。因为这个 PPT 不是我做的，我后来在网上查了，发现网上很多资料都提到这么一个词组。网上很多资料都用了这个词组。这个词组还挺常用的吧，我觉得不用单独解释。

R：嗯。我们继续。

（*video-recordings of Amelia's feedback*）

[Amelia is turning to slide 6] *Maybe change a word，not "heat" but "calorie". Something like this，alright?*

R：你看第 6 页 PPT，图片上面你用的英文单词是 heat.

L：对，老师说让我用 calorie 这个单词。

R：那你当时怎么想的呢？

L：我当时觉得，感觉都可以吧，因为之前在网上也有人用 heat 这个词。我觉得 heat 不能算错，但是可能 calorie 表达起来更好点。大概就这么想的，然后以后就用 calorie。

R：那既然 heat 没错，你为什么要用 calorie？

L：那老师既然提出来了，那不就证明了 calorie 表达比 heat 更清楚一点，heat 可能，会不会有什么歧义啥的。

R：你觉得会有什么歧义？

L：我觉得没有啊，放在食物里面不就是热量嘛，我也不知道。

R：那你会同意老师的改法，还是坚持自己的？

L：同意吧，因为我之前也有考虑过是用 calorie 还是 heat，然后当时也是在网上看别人用了 heat，然后当时也懒得改成卡路里了，就没有改，因为我觉得 heat 也可以，不能算错。那 heat 本来放到食物里面就是热量的意思嘛。

R：所以你觉得放在这儿 Ok。

L：对。

R：我再问一下，你总是提到在网上看别人的用法，那你的资料来源是？

L：我们组成员找的资料。有些资料是中文，需要翻译，然后有时去维基百科上去找一找，搜一下 western dietary culture，因为别的文章介绍这些东西不是都很长嘛，各个方面，各个点涵盖的太多了，就得从这些文章里面找一些，有代表性的点，拿出来说一下，不能全说，全说的话太长了，那根本一节课都说不完。

Appendix L Prompt of Reflective Account and Sample

Prompt of reflective account

Please write an account to describe how you understand and respond to teacher feedback on your oral presentation performance. You can also record how you use teacher feedback to improve your oral presentation performance, such as revising PowerPoint slides and enhancing delivery of oral presentation. Any factors that may influence your understanding, feeling, and use of teacher feedback can also be included. The reflective account should be no less than 350 words long. You can write either in Chinese or in English. You can either hand in a hard copy or email it to me.

Sample reflective account: Deng from Amelia's class

针对老师的点评，我有以下反思和改变：

在语速方面，在第一次的点评中，老师花了很大的功夫，以向班上同学提问的方式，点出了我的语速过快。在她点评的那一瞬间，我觉得我的语速是没有问题的，但是看到同学们举手表决时，我又觉得自己的语速确实有些快了。在这个 delivery 当中，我们不仅仅要考虑老师还要考虑同学，看看她们是否能跟得上。

在 PPT 结构方面，有时候自己可能不能正确认识到自己的不足。重新看了看之前的 PPT，我发现相比较第一和第二次的 PPT，第三次确实有了很大程度的提高。之前两个 PPT 都是我自己做的，小组成员可能就是搜集了一点资料，至于到底是因为第三次换人做 PPT 了还是积累了两次经验才能将 PPT 完善至此，我也不知道。可能多一个人多一份力，思路相比较一个人更开阔。然后第三次我主要是提出了思路框架，后期再提出 PPT 修改意见，然后组员再协助修改，不同人员的精力集中到不同地方，效果会好很多。

在手势方面，其实第一次老师说我在做 presentation 的时候手一直在动，是因为紧张或者是试图保持自己的一种节奏，都不是的。因为第一次是把这个汇报当作演讲的形式来准备的，所以觉得手势是必要的。到后两次可能就觉得要把它当作一个汇报展示，就少了许多肢体语言。

口语展示的逻辑方面，提升比较大，这当然也表现在 PPT 结构上。其实我回看了一下之前的视频，发现第一次和第三次的框架基本是一样的，第二次的内容也是从学校到家庭教育。但比较三次的 PPT，很明显发现结构分层有很大差异。尤其第二次，五个小标题，三四个都是学校教育的分支内容，但就是和家庭教育凑在了一起。

在听到老师的批评指正意见之后，可能最开始我会想着这一点是有失偏颇的，坚持认为自己是对的并想要去争辩。但是随着时间的变化，我会慢慢想通，明白当时那些意见是对的，并且是有道理的。当然，我还是坚持着一些自己的观点，至于对待老师的肯定或者是表扬的评价，我内心也不会有太大波澜，可能一方面是因为对自己要求严格，觉得没做好是不应该的；另一方面，也是觉得现在的表扬都是建立在之前的批评上的，例如之前某个地方不好，现在弄好了。但对于逻辑这方面的肯定我很开心，因为渴望在这方面有所提高。

另一点要说的是，通过哪些方面让我记住老师的评价，理解并且想要提高。那就是老师的评价比较到位，不会只关注你好的一面，也不会局限在差的部分。老师的点评比较细致，首先她很仔细地听我的口语展示，然后点评的方面也很多，并且据实。尤其是第三次点评，真的觉得她很关注细节，那么在老师能够认真地给你做出点评之后，你肯定也会想要认真改进。因为其他课老师点评的机会也不多，真的很感动。

Appendix M Scripts of Sample Ready-Made PowerPoint Slides Used to Teach Oral Presentations

Slide 1: Before you begin (I)
- The communication process: multi-directional
  - Source (speaker), message (language and ideas), receiver (audience), channels (media and/or speaker's voice), noise, nonverbal information, feedback
- Determining your purpose
  - Informative presentations (to investigate, expose, or inform about a new phenomenon, etc.)
  - Persuasive presentations (to persuade or convince an audience about an argument, ideology, or opinion, or to refute a claim)

Slide 2: Before you begin (II)
- Selecting a topic: relevant and important to both you and your audience
- Outlining the speech: a speech can be thought of as a well-structured oral essay; select an appropriate organizational pattern
- Documenting your sources: to avoid plagiarism and enhance credibility
- What to cite?
  - periodical (cite the title and data)
  - books (author, author's credentials, title, and year)
  - polls and studies (who conducted? When?)
  - literature (title and author)

Slide 3: Research and supporting material
- The research process: obtain as much information and support as possible

- Supporting material:
  - Hard evidence (news item, statistics/studies, factual descriptions, definitions, government documents, etc.)
  - Soft evidence (narrative, personal experiences, analogies and metaphors, historical examples, art/literature/movies/TV, etc.)
- Tips for using internet:
  - Be cautious and cite websites with their *URLs*

Slide 4: Organizing your presentation (I)

- Thesis statement
- Example: informative presentation
  - Topic: Computers
  - Purpose: To inform the audience about new advances in computer technology
  - Possible Thesis: Recent advances in the computer industry have revolutionized the way that we live our daily lives

Slide 5: Organizing your presentation (II)

- The body of the speech:
- By and large, most presentations will contain two to three major body areas and should address the major issues of the speech, including the following major questions:
  - What or where is the problem/issue?
  - Who is involved?
  - Why does it exist?
  - Why should your audience care?
  - If it is a problem, what can or should be done to solve it?
  - What are the implications?
- Patterns of organization: chronological pattern, spatial pattern, topical pattern, causal pattern, problem/cause/solution design…

Slide 6: Using language effectively (I)

- Oral style vs. written style: oral speech vs. written texts on slides
- For example:
    - and vs. moreover, in addition…
    - so vs. therefore, thus, consequently…
    - or vs. in other words, put simply…
    - but vs. however, nevertheless, in spite of that…

Slide 7: Using language effectively (II)

- Useful phrases to introduce your presentation: get the attention of your audience
- For example:
    - Good morning and welcome. Let me introduce myself …
    - Today I'm going to talk about …
    - This morning I'd like to explain …
    - The purpose of my presentation today is to …

Slide 8: Using language effectively (III)

- Useful phrases for the body of your presentation: present main points one by one
- For example:
    - Let's start by looking at …
    - I'd like to start by …
    - So, let me start by …
    - The first issue is in relation to …

Slide 9: Using language effectively (IV)

- Useful phrases for the conclusion and audience questions
- For example:
    - To sum up …
    - In conclusion …
    - To recap the main points …
    - That concludes my presentation.
    - Thank you. Are there any questions?

- Thank you for listening. Does anyone have any questions?

Slide 10: Using presentation aids (I)

- What are presentation aids?
  - the resources beyond the speech words and delivery that a speaker uses to enhance the message conveyed to the audience
- Types of presentation aids
  - visual aids: pictures, diagrams, charts and graphs, maps, etc.
  - audible aids: musical excerpts, audio speech excerpts, etc.

Slide 11: Using presentation aids (II)

- Using presentation software (Microsoft PowerPoint) and designing PPT slides:
- Restrict the number of slides and the material on each slide
  - Put only the bare essentials on the main slides.
  - Use landscape and large font.
  - Convey one message per slide.
    - ✓ Summarize the message in the headline.
    - ✓ Use at most ten bullet points to deliver the message.
    - ✓ Restrict each bullet point to one line.
- Plan to say everything that is on the slides
  - Go beyond what is on the slides (explanation, example, discussion).

Slide 12: Using presentation aids (III)

- Make figures, graphs, and tables accessible
- Design each figure to convey one message summarized in the title
  - Label the axes and the curves clearly.
  - Use large font (typically at least 24).
- Keep tables simple
  - Put only the numbers that you plan to talk about.
  - If you need more than 10 numbers, consider turning the table into a figure.

Slide 13: Delivering an effective speech

- Vocal style
- Nonverbal elements: eye contact, volume, rate, gestures, text movement, posture, facial expression
- Modes of delivery
  - Impromptu
  - Manuscript
  - Extemporaneous
  - Memorized

Appendix N Course Information for *An Introduction to Intercultural Communication*

Course Name	*An Introduction to Intercultural Communication*		
Department	Department of English Language and Literature, College of Foreign Languages		
Hours	36	Credits	2
Semester/School Year	1st semester/Year 2	Course Types	Compulsory
Instructor	Amelia		
Students	Year 2 English majors		

Course Description:

The context of globalization requires English-majored undergraduates not only to be good at English as a language, but also be gifted with the humanistic quality of intercultural exchange and communication. In line with the talent internationalization, the course entitled as *An Introduction to Intercultural Communication* is set to help students adapt to the environment of international business and cultural communication. With the teaching methods like lead-in lecture and case study, this course aims to facilitate students with the definition, evolvement and significance of intercultural exchanges, and guide them to understand diverse cultural values, to compare Chinese culture and those abroad, to acquire social etiquette and to discuss effective ways of cultural adaptation. Being practical is a great feature of this course.

Appendix O Course Information for *Communicative English* (II)

Course Name	*Communicative English* (II)		
Department	Department of English Language and Literature, College of Foreign Languages		
Hours	64	Credits	4
Semester/School Year	1st semester/Year 2	Course Types	Compulsory
Instructor	Gwen		
Students	Year 2 English majors		

Course Description:

Communicative English (II) is an integrated course centering on such skills as listening, speaking, reading, writing, translating, etc. The course of *Communicative English* is run at two stages, with the first two academic years as the intermediate stage and the third as the advanced. Each stage features a diversity of theme-related topics as the teaching materials, which aims at cultivating students' productive skills of the language. The course revolves around issues of current interest, incorporating systematically the application of linguistic knowledge into the training process and putting the development of students' critical thinking as the top priority. The course can help students acquire the knowledge of diverse kinds, enhance the communicative competence, and participate in social interactions for certain academic purposes.

Appendix P   Abbreviations

CF	Corrective Feedback
CLT	Communicative Language Teaching
EFL	English as a Foreign Language
ESL	English as a Second Language
FL	Foreign Language
L1	First Language
L2	Second Language
PPT	PowerPoint
SCT	Sociocultural Theory
SLA	Second Language Acquisition
TBLT	Task-based Language Teaching
TEM	Test for English Majors
ZPD	Zone of Proximal Development

Appendix Q Author's Scholarship in Relation to This Book

1. Journal Articles

[1] Wang, B., Teo, T., & Yu, S. (2017). Teacher feedback to student oral presentations in EFL classrooms: A case study. *Journal of Education for Teaching*, 43 (2), 262-264. DOI: 10.1080/02607476.2016.1257507

[2] Wang, B., Yu, S., & Teo, T. (2018). An exploratory case study into Chinese EFL teachers' commentary practices in oral presentations. *Taiwan Journal of TESOL*, 15 (2), 65-94. DOI: 10.30397/TJTESOL. 201810_15 (2).0003

[3] Wang, B., Yu, S., & Teo, T. (2018). Experienced EFL teachers' beliefs about feedback on student oral presentations. *Asian-Pacific Journal of Second and Foreign Language Education*, 3 (12), 1–13. DOI: 10.1186/s40862-018-0053-3

[4] Wang, B., Yu, S., Zheng, Y., & Teo, T. (2022). Student engagement with teacher oral feedback in EFL university classrooms. *Language Teaching Research*. DOI: 10.1177/13621688221105772

2. Panel presentations

[1] Wang, B. June, 2017. *Understanding EFL teachers' commentary practices in oral presentations: A case study of three experienced tertiary teachers in Mainland China*. Paper presented at the 6th International Conference on English, Discourse and Intercultural Communication, Macau SAR, China: Macao Polytechnic Institute.

[2] Wang, B. September, 2017. *Investigating EFL teachers' commentary practices in student oral presentations*. Paper presented at the 7th National Conference on Foreign Language Teacher Education and Development, Changjun, China: Northeast Normal University.

References

Adams, R. (2007). Do second language learners benefit from interacting with each other? In A. Mackey (Ed.), *Conversational interaction in second language acquisition* (pp. 29-51). Oxford: Oxford University Press.

Advisory Board for the Education of English as a Specialty. (2020). *The national curriculum for English majors in Chinese tertiary institutions*. Beijing: Foreign Language Teaching and Research Press.

Ahangari, S., & Amirzadeh, S. (2011). Exploring the teachers' use of spoken corrective feedback in teaching Iranian EFL learners at different levels of proficiency. *Procedia Social and Behavioral Sciences*, *29*, 1859–1868.

Ahmad, S., & Rao, C. (2013). Applying communicative approach in teaching English as a foreign language: A case study of Pakistan. *Porta Linguarum*, *20*, 187–203.

Algarawi, B. S. (2010). *The effects of repair techniques on L2 learning as a product and as process: A CA-for-SLA investigation of classroom interaction*. (Unpublished doctoral dissertation). University of Newcastle, Newcastle.

Aljaafreh, A., & Lantolf, J. P. (1994). Negative feedback as regulation and second language learning in the Zone of Proximal Development. *The Modern Language Journal*, *78*, 465–483.

Ammar, A., & Spada, N. (2006). One size fits all? Recasts, prompts and L2 learning. *Studies in Second Language Acquisition*, *28*, 543–574.

Arts, J. G., Jaspers, M., & Joosten-ten Brinke, D. (2016). A case study on written comments as a form of feedback in teacher education: So much to gain. *European Journal of Teacher Education*, *39*, 159–173.

Bailey, K. M. (1990). The use of diary studies in teacher education programs. In J. C. Richards & D. Nunan (Eds.), *Second language teacher education* (pp. 215–226). Cambridge: Cambridge University Press.

Barcelos, A. M. F. (2003). Researching beliefs about SLA: A critical review. In P. Kalaja & A. M. F. Barcelos (Eds.), *Beliefs about SLA: New research approaches* (pp. 7–33). Dordrecht: Springer.

Basturkmen, H. (2012). Review of research into the correspondence between language teachers' stated beliefs and practices. *System, 40*, 282–295.

Basturkmen, H., East, M., & Bitchener, J. (2014). Supervisors' on-script feedback comments on drafts of dissertations: socialising students into the academic discourse community. *Teaching in Higher Education, 19*, 432–445.

Basturkmen, H., Loewen, S., & Ellis, R. (2004). Teachers' stated beliefs about incidental focus on form and their classroom practices. *Applied Linguistics, 25*, 243–272.

Benson, P. (2011). *Teaching and researching autonomy* (2nd ed.). Harlow, England: Pearson Education Limited.

Bitchener, J. (2012). A reflection on "the language learning potential" of written CF. *Journal of Second Language Writing, 21*, 348–363.

Bitchener, J., & Ferris, D. (2012). *Written corrective feedback in second language acquisition and writing.* New York, NY: Routledge.

Bitchener, J., & Knoch, U. (2008). The value of written corrective feedback for migrant and international students. *Language Teaching Research, 12*, 409–431.

Bitchener, J., Basturkmen, H., & East, M. (2010). The focus of supervisor written feedback to thesis/dissertation students. *International Journal of English Studies, 10*, 79–97.

Bitchener. J., & Knoch, U. (2009). The relative effectiveness of different types of direct written corrective feedback. *System, 37*, 322–329.

Borg, S. (2006). *Teacher cognition and language education.* London: Continuum.

Boud, D., & Molloy, E. (2013). *Feedback in higher and professional education: Understanding it and doing it well*. New York, NY: Routledge.

Breen, M. (1987). *Learner contributions to task design*. In C. Candlin & D. Murphy (Eds.), *Language learning tasks* (pp. 23–46). Englewood Cliffs, NJ: Prentice-Hall.

Brookhart, S. M. (2008). *How to give effective feedback to your students*. Alexandria, VA: Association for Supervision and Curriculum Development.

Brooks, G., & Wilson, J. (2014). Using oral presentations to improve students' English language skills. *Kwansei Gakuin University Humanities Review, 19*, 199–212.

Bruton, A. (2009). Improving accuracy is not the only reason for writing, and even if it were… *System, 37*, 600–613.

Bunch, G. C. (2009). "Going up there": Challenges and opportunities for language minority students during a mainstream classroom speech event. *Linguistics and Education, 20*, 81–108.

Burnett, P. C. (2002). Teacher praise and feedback and students' perceptions of the classroom environment. *Educational Psychology, 22*, 5–16.

Butler, Y. (2015). English language education among young learners in East Asia: A review of current research (2004-2014). *Language Teaching, 48*, 303–342.

Canale, M., & Swain, M. (1980). Theoretical bases of communicative approaches to second language teaching and testing. *Applied Linguistics, 1*, 1–47.

Carroll, C. (2006). Enhancing reflective learning through role-plays: The use of an effective sales presentation evaluation form in student role-plays. *Marketing Education Review, 16*, 9–13.

Chandler, J. (2003). The efficacy of various kinds of error feedback for improvement in the accuracy and fluency of L2 student writing. *Journal of Second Language Writing, 12*, 267–296.

Cheng, W., & Warren, M. (1999). Peer and teacher assessment of the oral and written tasks of a group project. *Assessment & Evaluation in Higher Education*, *24*, 301–314.

Cheng, W., & Warren, M. (2005). Peer assessment of language proficiency. *Language Testing*, *22*, 93–121.

Cohen, A. D. (1987). Student processing of feedback on their composition. In A. L. Wenden & J. Rubin (Eds.). *Learner strategies in language learning* (pp. 57–69). Englewood Cliffs, NJ: Prentice-Hall.

Corder, S. P. (1980). Second language acquisition research and the teaching of grammar. *BAAL Newsletter*, *10*, 1–12.

Cortazzi, M., & Jin, L. (1996). Cultures of learning: Language classrooms in China. In H. Coleman (Ed.), *Society and the language classroom* (pp. 169–206). New York, NY: Cambridge University Press.

Cox, M. R. (2007). *What every student should know about preparing effective oral presentations*. Boston, MA: Pearson Education Limited.

Creswell, J. W. (2007). *Qualitative enquiry and research design: Choosing among five approaches* (2nd ed.). Thousand Oaks, CA: Sage publications.

Croker, R. A. (2009). An introduction to qualitative research. In J. Heigham & R. A. Croker (Eds.), *Qualitative research in applied linguistics* (pp. 3–24). London: Palgrave Macmillan.

Davies, M. (2006). Paralinguistic focus on form. *TESOL Quarterly*, *40*, 841–855.

De Grez, L. (2009). *Optimizing the instructional environment to learn presentation skills* (Unpublished doctoral dissertation). Ghent University, Belgium.

Dempsey, N. P. (2010). Stimulated recall interviews in ethnography. *Qualitative Sociology*, *33*, 349–367.

Denzin, N. K., & Lincoln, Y. S. (2000). Introduction: The discipline and practice of qualitative research. In N. K. Denzin & Y. S. Lincoln (Eds.), *Handbook of qualitative research* (2nd ed.) (pp. 1–30). Thousand Oaks, CA: Sage Publications.

Dilans, G. (2010). Corrective feedback and L2 vocabulary development: Prompts and recasts in the adult ESL classroom. *The Canadian Modern Language Review, 66,* 787–815.

Dörnyei, Z. (2007). *Research methods in applied linguistics: Quantitative, qualitative, and mixed methodologies.* Oxford: Oxford University Press.

Dörnyei, Z. (2011). *Research methods in applied linguistics: Quantitative, qualitative, and mixed methodologies* (2nd ed.). Oxford: Oxford University Press.

Dörnyei, Z., & Ryan, S. (2015). *The psychology of the language learner revisited.* New York, NY: Routledge.

Ellis, R. (2000). Task-based research and language pedagogy. *Language Teaching Research, 4,* 193–220.

Ellis, R. (2001). Non-reciprocal tasks, comprehension and second language acquisition. In M. Bygate, P. Skehan, & M. Swain (Eds.), *Researching pedagogic tasks: Second language learning, teaching and testing* (pp. 49–75). London: Longman.

Ellis, R. (2003). *Task-based language learning and teaching.* Oxford: Oxford University Press.

Ellis, R. (2007). The differential effects of corrective feedback on two grammatical structures. In A. Mackey (Ed.), *Conversational interaction in second language acquisition: A collection of empirical studies* (pp. 407–452). Oxford: Oxford University Press.

Ellis, R. (2009a). Corrective feedback and teacher development. *L2 Journal, 1,* 3–18.

Ellis, R. (2009b). A typology of written corrective feedback types. *ELT Journal, 63,* 97–107.

Ellis, R. (2010a). Epilogue: A framework for investigating oral and written corrective feedback. *Studies in Second Language Acquisition, 32,* 335–349.

Ellis, R. (2010b). Cognitive, social, and psychological dimensions of corrective feedback. In R. Batstone (Ed.), *Sociocognitive perspectives on lan-*

guage use and language learning (pp. 151–165). Oxford: Oxford University Press.

Ellis, R., & He, X. (1999). The roles of modified input and output in the incidental acquisition of word meanings. *Studies in Second Language Acquisition, 21,* 285–301.

Ellis, R., Sheen, Y., Murakami, M., & Takashima, H. (2008). The effects of focused and unfocused written corrective feedback in an English as a foreign language context. *System, 36,* 353–371.

Emerson, R. M., Fretz, R. I., & Shaw, L. L. (1995). *Writing ethnographic fieldnotes.* Chicago, IL: University of Chicago Press.

Erlam, R., Ellis, R., & Batstone, R. (2013). Oral corrective feedback on L2 writing: Two approaches compared. *System, 41,* 257–268.

Faraco, M., & Kida, T. (2008). Gesture and the negotiation of meaning in a second language classroom. In S. G. McCafferty, & G. Stam (Eds.), *Gesture: Second language acquisition and classroom research* (pp. 280–297). London: Routledge.

Feagin, J. R., Orum, A. M., & Sjoberg, G. (1991). *A case for the case study.* Chapel Hill, NC: University of North Carolina Press.

Ferris, D. R. (1997). The influence of teacher commentary on student revision. *TESOL Quarterly, 31,* 315–339.

Ferris, D. R. (2002). *Treatment of error in second language student writing.* Ann Arbor, MI: University of Michigan Press.

Ferris, D. R. (2004). The "grammar correction" debate in L2 writing: Where are we, and where do we go from here? (and what do we do in the meantime...?) *Journal of Second Language Writing, 13,* 49–62.

Ferris, D. R. (2010). Second language writing research and written corrective feedback in SLA. *Studies in Second Language Acquisition, 32,* 181–201.

Ferris, D. R., & Roberts, B. (2001). Error feedback in L2 writing classes: How explicit does it need to be? *Journal of Second Language Writing, 10,* 161–184.

Ferris, D. R., Pezone, S., Tade, C. R., & Tinti, S. (1997). Teacher commentary on student writing: Descriptions and implications. *Journal of Second Language Writing*, *6*, 155–182.

Fetterman, D. M. (2010). *Ethnography: Step-by-step* (3rd ed.). Thousand Oaks, CA: Sage Publications.

Gall, M. D., Gall, J. P., & Borg, W. R. (2003). *Educational research: An introduction* (7th ed.). Boston, MA: Allyn and Bacon.

Gao, Y. (2009). Sociocultural contexts and English in China: Retaining and reforming the cultural habitus. In J. L. Bianco, J. Orton, & Y. Gao (Eds.), *China and English: Globalisation and the dilemmas of identity* (pp. 56–78). Bristol, UK: Multilingual Matters.

Gass, S. M., & Mackey, A. (2000). *Stimulated recall methodology in second language research*. New York, NY: Routledge.

Gass, S., & Varonis, E. (1994). Input, interaction, and second language production. *Studies in Second Language Acquisition*, *16*, 283–302.

Girard, T., Pinar, M., & Trapp, P. (2011). An exploratory study of class presentations and peer evaluations: Do students perceive the benefits? *Academy of Educational Leadership Journal*, *15*, 77–94.

Goldin-Meadow, S. (1999). The role of gesture in communication and thinking. *Trends in Cognitive Sciences*, *3*, 419–429.

Goldstein, L. M. (2004). Questions and answers about teacher written commentary and student revision: Teachers and students working together. *Journal of Second Language Writing*, *13*, 63–80.

Goldstein, L. M. (2006). Feedback and revision in second language writing: Contextual, teacher, and student variables. In K. Hyland & F. Hyland (Eds.), *Feedback in second language writing: Contexts and issues* (pp. 185–205). New York, NY: Cambridge University Press.

Han, Y. (2016). *Learner engagement with teacher written corrective feedback in Chinese tertiary-level EFL classrooms: A sociocognitive perspective* (Unpublished doctoral dissertation). University of Hong Kong, Pokfulam,

Hong Kong SAR.

Han, Y. (2017). Mediating and being mediated: Learner beliefs and learner engagement with written corrective feedback. *System*, *69*, 133–142.

Han, Y., & Hyland, F. (2015). Exploring learner engagement with written corrective feedback in a Chinese tertiary EFL classroom. *Journal of Second Language Writing*, *30*, 31–44.

Harmer, J. (1983). *The practice of English language teaching*. London: Longman.

Hattie, J. A., & Yates, G. C. (2014). Using feedback to promote learning. In V. A. Benassi, C. E. Overson, & C. M. Hakaia (Eds.), *Applying science of learning in education: Infusing psychological science into the curriculum* (pp. 45–58). Retrieved from the Society for the Teaching of Psychology website: http: //teachpsych.org/ebooks/asle2014/index.php

Hattie, J., & Timperley, H. (2007). The power of feedback. *Review of Educational Research*, *77*, 81–112.

Heath, C., Hindmarsh, J., & Luff, P. (2010). *Video in qualitative research*. Los Angeles: Sage Publications.

Hedgcock, J., & Lefkowitz, N. (1994). Feedback on feedback: Assessing learner receptivity in second language writing. *Journal of Second Language Writing*, *3*, 141–163.

Hood, M. (2009). Case study. In J. Heigham & R. A. Croker (Eds.), *Qualitative research in applied linguistics* (pp. 66–90). London: Palgrave Macmillan.

Hostetter, A. B., & Alibali, M. W. (2004). On the tip of the mind: Gesture as a key to conceptualization. In K. Forbus, S. Gentner, & T. Regier (Eds.), *Proceedings of the Twenty-Sixth Annual Conference of the Cognitive Science Society* (pp. 589–594). Chicago, IL: Erlbaum.

Howatt, A. P. R. (1984). *A History of English language teaching*. Oxford: Oxford University Press.

Hu, G. W. (2002). Recent important developments in secondary English-language teaching in the People's Republic of China. *Language, Culture and Curriculum, 15*, 30–49.

Hu, G. W. (2005). Contextual influences on instructional practices: A Chinese case for an ecological approach to ELT. *TESOL Quarterly, 39*, 635–660.

Hu, G. W., & McKay, S. L. (2012). English language education in East Asia: Some recent developments. *Journal of Multilingual and Multicultural Development, 33*, 345–362.

Hunt, K. W. (1965). Grammatical structures written at three grade levels. *NCTE Research Report No. 3*. Champaign, IL: NCTE.

Hyland, F. (1998). The impact of teacher written feedback on individual writers. *Journal of Second Language Writing, 7*, 255–286.

Hyland, F. (2003). Focus on form: Student engagement with teacher feedback. *System, 31*, 217–230.

Hyland, F. (2010). Future directions in feedback on second language writing: Overview and research agenda. *International Journal of English Studies, 10*, 173–185.

Hyland, F., & Hyland, K. (2001). Sugaring the pill: Praise and criticism in written feedback. *Journal of Second Language Writing, 10*, 185–212.

Hyland, K. (2000). *Disciplinary discourses: Social interactions in academic writing*. London: Longman.

Hyland, K. (2013). Student perceptions of hidden messages in teacher written feedback. *Studies in Educational Evaluations, 39*, 180–187.

Hyland, K., & Anan, E. (2006). Teacher perceptions of error: The effects of first language and experience. *System, 34*, 509–519.

Hyland, K., & Hyland, F. (2006a). Contexts and issues in feedback on L2 writing: An introduction. In K. Hyland & F. Hyland (Eds.), *Feedback in second language writing: Contexts and issues* (pp. 1–19). New York, NY: Cambridge University Press.

Hyland, K., & Hyland, F. (2006b). Interpersonal aspects of response: Constructing and interpreting teacher written feedback. In K. Hyland & F. Hyland (Eds.), *Feedback in second language writing: Contexts and issues* (pp. 206–224). New York, NY: Cambridge University Press.

Jean, G., & Simard, D. (2011). Grammar teaching and learning in L2: Necessary, but boring? *Foreign Language Annals, 44,* 467–494.

Jeon, I., & Hahn, J. (2006). Exploring EFL teachers' perceptions of task-based language teaching: A case study of Korean secondary school classroom practice. *Asian EFL Journal, 8,* 123–143.

Jiang, Y. (2003). English as a Chinese language. *English Today, 19,* 3–8.

Jin, L., & Cortazzi, M. (2002). English language teaching in China: A bridge to the future. *Asia Pacific Journal of Education, 22,* 53–64.

Jin, L., & Cortazzi, M. (2006). Changing practices in Chinese cultures of learning. *Language, Culture and Curriculum, 19,* 5–20.

Jin, L., & Cortazzi, M. (2011). Introduction: Contexts for researching Chinese learners. In L. Jin & M. Cortazzi (Eds.), *Researching Chinese learners: Skills, perceptions and intercultural adaptations* (pp. 1–18). Basingstoke, UK: Palgrave Macmillan.

Jonassen, D. H. (1991). Evaluating constructivist learning. *Educational Technology, 31,* 28–33.

Junqueira, L., & Kim, Y. (2013). Exploring the relationship between training, beliefs, and teachers' corrective feedback practices: A case study of a novice and an experienced ESL teacher. *Canadian Modern Language Review, 69,* 181–206.

Junqueira, L., & Payant, C. (2015). "I just want to do it right, but it's so hard": A novice teacher's written feedback beliefs and practices. *Journal of Second Language Writing, 27,* 19–36.

Kepner, C. G. (1991). An experiment in the relationship of types of written feedback to the development of second-language writing skills. *The Modern Language Journal, 75,* 305–313.

King, J. (2002). Preparing EFL learners for oral presentations preparing. *Dong Hwa Journal of Humanistic Studies, 4,* 401–418.

Kluger, A. N., & DeNisi, A. (1996). The effects of feedback interventions on performance: A historical review, a meta-analysis, and a preliminary feedback intervention theory. *Psychological Bulletin*, *119*, 254–284.

Koike, D., & Pearson, L. (2005). The effect of instruction and feedback in the development of pragmatic competence. *System*, *33*, 481–501.

Koosha, M., & Yakhabi, M. (2013). Problems associated with the use of communicative language teaching in EFL contexts and possible solutions. *International Journal of Foreign Language Teaching and Research*, *1*, 63–76.

Kulhavy, R. W. (1977). Feedback in written instruction. *Review of Educational Research*, *47*, 211–232.

Kumar, V., & Stracke, E. (2007). An analysis of written feedback on a PhD thesis. *Teaching in Higher Education*, *12*, 461–470.

Lantolf, J. P. (1996). SLA theory building: "Letting all the flowers bloom!" *Language Learning*, *46*, 713–749.

Lantolf, J. P., & Thorne, S. L. (2007). Sociocultural theory and second language learning. In B. van Patten & J. Williams (Eds.), *Theories in second language acquisition: An introduction* (pp. 693–701). Mahwah, NJ: Lawrence Erlbaum Associates, Inc.

Lee, H. H., Leong, A. P., & Song, G. (2017). Investigating teacher perceptions of feedback. *ELT Journal*, *71*, 60–68.

Lee, I. (2004). Error correction in L2 secondary writing classrooms: The case of Hong Kong. *Journal of Second Language Writing*, *13*, 285–312.

Lee, I. (2008a). Understanding teachers' written feedback practices in Hong Kong secondary classrooms. *Journal of Second Language Writing*, *17*, 69–85.

Lee, I. (2008b). Student reactions to teacher feedback in two Hong Kong secondary classrooms. *Journal of Second Language Writing*, *17*, 144–164.

Lee, I. (2009). Ten mismatches between teachers' beliefs and written feedback practice. *ELT Journal*, *63*, 13–22.

Lee, I. (2011). Bringing innovation to EFL writing through a focus on assessment for learning. *Innovation in Language Learning and Teaching*, 5, 19–33.

Lee, I. (2014). Revisiting teacher feedback in EFL writing from sociocultural perspectives. *TESOL Quarterly*, 48, 201–213.

Lee, I., Mak, P., & Burns, A. (2015). EFL teachers' attempts at feedback innovation in the writing classroom. *Language Teaching Research*, 20, 248–269.

Leki, I. (1991). The preferences of ESL students for error correction in college-level writing classes. *Foreign Language Annals*, 24, 203–218.

Li, S. (2010). The effectiveness of corrective feedback in SLA: A meta-analysis. *Language Learning*, 60, 309–365.

Lightbown, P. M., & Spada, N. (1999). *How languages are learned* (2nd ed.). Oxford: Oxford University Press.

Lincoln, Y. S., & Guba, E. G. (1985). *Naturalistic inquiry*. Beverly Hills, CA: Sage Publications.

Loewen, S., & Nabei, T. (2007). Measuring the effects of oral corrective feedback on L2 knowledge. In A. Mackey (Ed.), *Conversational interaction in second language acquisition: A collection of empirical studies* (pp. 361–377). Oxford: Oxford University Press.

Long, M. H. (1983). Native speaker/non-native speaker conversation and the negotiation of comprehensible input. *Applied Linguistics*, 4, 126–141.

Long, M. H. (1985). A role for instruction in second language acquisition. In K. Hyltenstam & M. Pienemann (Eds.), *Modelling and assessing second language acquisition* (pp. 77–99). Clevedon Avon: Multilingual Matters.

Long, M. H. (1996). The role of linguistic environment in second language acquisition. In W. Ritchie & T. Bhatia (Eds.), *Handbook of second language acquisition* (pp. 413–468). San Diego, CA: Academic Press.

Lyle, J. (2003). Stimulated recall: A report on its use in naturalistic research. *British Educational Research Journal*, 29, 861–878.

Lyster, R. (2004). Differential effects of prompts and recasts in form-focused instruction. *Studies in Second Language Acquisition*, 26, 399–432.

Lyster, R., & Ranta, L. (1997). Corrective feedback and learner uptake. *Studies in Second Language Acquisition*, 19, 37–66.

Lyster, R., & Saito, K. (2010). Interactional feedback as instructional input: A synthesis of classroom SLA research. *Language, Interaction and Acquisition*, 1, 276–297.

Lyster, R., Saito, K., & Sato, M. (2013). Oral corrective feedback in second language classrooms. *Language Teaching*, 46, 1–40.

Mackey, A. (2006). Feedback, noticing and instructed second language learning. *Applied Linguistics*, 27, 405–430.

Mackey, A., & Gass, S. M. (2005). *Second language research: Methodology and design*. Mahwah, NJ: Lawrence Erlbaum Associates.

Mackey, A., & Philp, J. (1998). Conversational interaction and second language development: Recasts, responses, and red herrings? *The Modern Language Journal*, 82, 338–356.

Mackey, A., Gass, S. M., & McDonough, K. (2000). How do learners perceive interactional feedback? *Studies in Second Language Acquisition*, 22, 471–497.

Maxwell, J. A. (1996). *Qualitative research design: An interactive approach*. Thousand Oaks, CA: Sage Publications.

McMartin-Miller, C. (2014). How much feedback is enough? Instructor practices and student attitudes toward error treatment in second language writing. *Assessing Writing*, 19, 24–35.

Merriam, S. B. (2001). *Qualitative research and case study applications in education*. San Francisco, CA: Jossey-Bass Publishers.

Merriam, S. B. (2009). *Qualitative research: A guide to design and implementation* (3rd ed.). San Francisco, CA: Jossey-Bass Publishers.

Miles, M. B., & Huberman, A. M. (1994). *Qualitative data analysis: A sourcebook of new methods* (2nd ed.). Thousand Oaks, CA: Sage Publications.

Molloy, E. K. (2010). The feedforward mechanism: a way forward in clinical learning? *Medical Education, 44*, 1157–1159.

Mori, R. (2002). Teachers' beliefs and corrective feedback. *JALT Journal, 24*, 48–69.

Mori, R. (2011). Teacher cognition in corrective feedback in Japan. *System, 39*, 451–467.

Morita, N. (2000). Discourse socialization through oral classroom activities in a TESL graduate program. *TESOL Quarterly, 34*, 279–310.

Muñoz, A. P., & Álvarez, M. E. (2010). Washback of an oral assessment system in the EFL classroom. *Language Testing, 27*, 33–49.

Nassaji, H. (2009). Effects of recasts and elicitations in dyadic interaction and the role of feedback explicitness. *Language Learning, 59*, 411–452.

Nelson, G., & Carson, J. (2006). Cultural issues in peer response: Revisiting 'culture'. In K. Hyland & F. Hyland (Eds.), *Feedback in second language writing: Contexts and issues* (pp. 42–59). New York, NY: Cambridge University Press.

Nicol, D. (2010). From monologue to dialogue: improving written feedback processes in mass higher education. *Assessment & Evaluation in Higher Education, 35*, 501–517.

Nicol, D. J., & Macfarlane-Dick, D. (2006). Formative assessment and self-regulated learning: A model and seven principles of good feedback practice. *Studies in Higher Education, 31*, 199–218.

Nipaspong, P., & Chinokul, S. (2010). The role of prompts and explicit feedback in raising EFL learners' pragmatic awareness. *University of Sydney Papers in TESOL, 5*, 101–146.

Nunan, D. (1989). *Designing tasks for the communicative classroom*. Cambridge: Cambridge University Press.

Nunan, D. (2004). *Task-based language teaching*. Cambridge: Cambridge University Press.

Oliver, R. (2000). Age differences in negotiation and feedback in classroom and pair work. *Language Learning*, *50*, 119–151.

Oxford, R. (2006). Task-based language teaching and learning: An overview. *Asian EFL Journal*, *8*, 94–121.

Palincsar, A. S. (1998). Social constructivist perspectives on teaching and learning. *Annual Review of Psychology*, *49*, 345–375.

Pittinger, K., Miller, M., & Mott, J. (2004). Using real-world standards to enhance students' presentation skills. *Business Communication Quarterly*, *67*, 327–336.

Pole, C., & Morrison, M. (2003). *Ethnography for Education*. Maidenhead: Open University Press.

Polio, C., Gass, S., & Chapin, L. (2006). Using stimulated recall to investigate native speaker perceptions in native-nonnative speaker interaction. *Studies in Second Language Acquisition*, *28*, 237–267.

Prabhu, N. S. (1987). *Second language pedagogy*. Oxford: Oxford University Press.

Price, M., Handley, K., & Millar, J. (2011). Feedback: Focusing attention on engagement. *Studies in Higher Education*, *36*, 879–896.

Qi, D. S., & Lapkin, S. (2001). Exploring the role of noticing in a three-stage second language writing task. *Journal of Second Language Writing*, *10*, 277–303.

Rahimi, M., & Zhang, L. J. (2015). Exploring non-native English-speaking teachers' cognitions about corrective feedback in teaching English oral communication. *System*, *55*, 111–122.

Ramaprasad, A. (1983). On the definition of feedback. *Systems Research and Behavioral Science*, *28*, 4–13.

Rao, Z., & Lei, C. (2014). Teaching English as a foreign language in Chinese universities. *English Today*, *30*, 40–45.

Rassaei, E. (2013). Corrective feedback, learners' perceptions, and second language development. *System*, *41*, 472–483.

Richards, J. C., & Rodgers, T. S. (2001). *Approach and methods in language teaching: A description and analysis. Cambridge: Cambridge University Press.

Roothooft, H. (2014). The relationship between adult EFL teachers' oral feedback practices and their beliefs. *System*, *46*, 65–79.

Roth, W. M. (2009). Epistemic mediation: Video data as filters for the objectification of teaching by teachers. In R. Goldman, R. Pea, & B. Derry (Eds.), *Video research in the learning sciences* (pp. 367–382). New York, NY: Routledge.

Sadler, D. R. (1989). Formative assessment and the design of instructional systems. *Instructional Science*, *18*, 119–144.

Saito, H. (1994). Teachers' practices and students' preferences for feedback on second language writing: A case study of adult ESL learners. *TESL Canada Journal*, *11*, 46–70.

Saito, H. (2008). EFL classroom peer assessment: Training effects on rating and commenting. *Language Testing*, *25*, 553–581.

Saito, H., & Fujita, T. (2009). Peer-assessing peers' contribution to EFL group presentations. *RELC Journal*, *40*, 149–171.

Saito, K., & Lyster, R. (2012a). Effects of form-focused instruction and corrective feedback on L2 pronunciation development of /ɹ/ by Japanese learners of English. *Language Learning*, *62*, 595–633.

Saito, K. & R. Lyster (2012b). Investigating the pedagogical potential of recasts for L2 vowel acquisition. *TESOL Quarterly*, *46*, 385–396.

Schmidt, R. (1990). The role of consciousness in second language learning. *Applied Linguistics*, *11*, 129–158.

Schmidt, R. (2001). Attention. In P. Robinson (Ed.), *Cognition and second language instruction* (pp. 3–32). Cambridge: Cambridge University Press.

Seidman, I. (2006). *Interviewing as qualitative research: A guide for researchers in education and the social sciences* (3rd ed.). New York, NY: Teachers College Press.

Sheen, Y. (2004). Corrective feedback and learner uptake in communicative classrooms across instructional settings. *Language Teaching Research*, *8*, 263–300.

Sheen, Y. (2006). Exploring the relationship between characteristics of recasts and learner uptake. *Language Teaching Research*, *10*, 361–392.

Sheen, Y. (2007). The effect of focused written corrective feedback and language aptitude on ESL learners' acquisition of articles. *TESOL Quarterly*, *41*, 255–283.

Sheen, Y., & Ellis, R. (2011). Corrective feedback in language teaching. In E. Hinkel (Ed.), *Handbook of research in second language teaching and learning*, Vol. 2. (pp. 593–610). New York, NY: Routledge.

Shimura, M. (2006). Peer- and instructor assessment of oral presentations in Japanese university EFL classrooms: A pilot study. *Waseda Global Forum*, *3*, 99–107.

Shuell, T. (1986). Cognitive conceptions of learning. *Review of Educational Research*, *56*, 411–436.

Skehan, P. (1998). *A cognitive approach to language learning*. Oxford: Oxford University Press.

Stake, R. E. (1995). *The art of case study research*. Thousand Oaks, CA: Sage Publications.

Stake, R. E. (2005). Qualitative case studies. In N. K. Denzin & Y. S. Lincoln (Eds.), *The Sage handbook of qualitative research* (3rd ed.) (pp. 443–466). Thousand Oaks, CA: Sage Publications.

Stam, G. (2006). Thinking for speaking about motion: L1 and L2 speech and gesture. *International Review of Applied Linguistics*, *44*, 145–171.

Storch, N. (2010). Critical feedback on written corrective feedback research. *International Journal of English Studies*, *10*, 29–46.

Storch, N., & Aldosari, A. (2010). Learners' use of first language (Arabic) in pair work in an EFL class. *Language Teaching Research*, *14*, 355–375.

Storch, N., & Wigglesworth, G. (2010). Learners' processing, uptake, and retention of corrective feedback on writing. *Studies in Second Language Acqui-*

sition, *32*, 303–334.

Stracke, E., & Kumar, V. (2010). Feedback and self-regulated learning: Insights from supervisors' and PhD examiners' reports. *Reflective Practice*, *11*, 19–32.

Strauss, A., & Corbin, J. (1990). Open coding. In A. Strauss & J. Corbin (Eds.), *Basics of qualitative research: Grounded theory procedures and techniques* (2nd ed.) (pp. 101–121). Thousand Oaks, CA: Sage Publications.

Swain, M. (1985). Communicative competence: Some roles of comprehensible input and comprehensible output in its development. In S. M. Gass & C. Madden (Eds.), *Input and second language acquisition* (pp. 91–103). Rowley, MA: Newbury House.

Swain, M. (1995). Three functions of output in second language learning. In G. Cook & B. Seidlhofer (Eds.), *Principle and practice in applied linguistics: Studies in honor of H. G. Widdowson* (pp. 125–144). Oxford: Oxford University Press.

Takimoto, M. (2006). The effects of explicit feedback on the development of pragmatic proficiency. *Language Teaching Research*, *10*, 393–417.

Tavakoli, P., & Foster, P. (2008). Task design and second language performance: The effect of narrative type on learner output. *Language Learning*, *58*, 439–473.

Thorndike, E. L. (1913). *Educational psychology. Volume I: The original nature of man*. New York, NY: Columbia University Press.

Truscott, J. (1996). The case against grammar correction in L2 writing classes. *Language Learning*, *46*, 327–369.

Tsui, A. (2003). *Understanding expertise in teaching: Case studies of ESL teachers*. Cambridge: Cambridge University Press.

Uddin, M. N. (2021, April). *Use of L1 in corrective feedback and learner uptakes in foreign language learning*. Paper presented at 9th International Conference on Second Language Pedagogies, Concordia University, Montreal.

Van Beuningen, C. (2010). Corrective feedback in L2 writing: Theoretical perspectives, empirical insights, and future directions. *International Journal of English Studies*, *10*, 1–27.

Van Lier, L. (2005). Case study. In E. Hinkel (Ed.), *Handbook of research in second language teaching and learning* (pp. 195–208). Mahwah, NJ: Lawrence Erlbaum Associates.

Vygotsky, L. S. (1978). *Mind in society: The development of higher psychological processes*. Cambridge, MA: Harvard University Press.

Vygotsky, L. S. (1979). Consciousness as a problem in the psychology of behavior. *Soviet Psychology*, *17*, 3–35.

Wang, B., Teo, T., & Yu, S. (2017). Teacher feedback to student oral presentations in EFL classrooms: A case study. *Journal of Education for Teaching*, *43*, 262–264.

Wang, B., Yu, S., & Teo, T. (2018). An exploratory case study into Chinese EFL teachers' commentary practices in oral presentations. *Taiwan Journal of TESOL*, *15*, 65–94.

Wang, W., & Loewen, S. (2016). Nonverbal behavior and corrective feedback in nine ESL university-level classrooms. *Language Teaching Research*, *20*, 459–478.

Weissberg, R. (2006). Scaffolded feedback: Tutorial conversations with advanced L2 writers. In K. Hyland & F. Hyland (Eds.), *Feedback in second language writing: Contexts and issues* (pp. 246–265). New York, NY: Cambridge University Press.

Willis, D. (1996). *A framework for task-based learning*. London: Longman.

Winstone, E. N., Nash, A. R., Parker, M., & Rowntree, J. (2017). Supporting learners' agentic engagement with feedback: A systematic review and a taxonomy of recipience processes. *Educational Psychologist*, *52*, 17–37.

Wood, D., Bruner, J. S., & Ross, G. (1976). The role of tutoring in problem solving. *Journal of Child Psychology and Psychiatry*, *17*, 89–100.

Yang, L., & Gao, S. (2013). Beliefs and practices of Chinese university teachers in EFL writing instruction. *Language, Culture and Curriculum, 26,* 128–145.

Yang, Y., & Lyster, R. (2010). Effects of form-focused practice and feedback on Chinese EFL learners' acquisition of regular and irregular past tense forms. *Studies in Second Language Acquisition, 32,* 235–263.

Yin, R. K. (2003). *Case study research: Design and methods* (3rd ed.). London: Sage Publications.

Yin, R. K. (2011). *Qualitative research form start to finish.* New York, NY: The Gulford Press.

Yoshida, R. (2008). Teachers' choice and learners' preference of corrective feedback types. *Language Awareness, 17,* 78–93.

Yu, S., Lee, I., & Mak, P. (2016). Revisiting Chinese cultural issues in peer feedback in EFL writing: Insights from a multiple case study. *The Asia-Pacific Education Researcher, 25,* 295–304.

Zamel, V. (1981). Cybernetics: A model for feedback in the ESL classroom. *TESOL Quarterly, 15,* 139–150.

Zamel, V. (1985). Responding to student writing. *TESOL Quarterly, 21,* 697–715.

Zhang, J. (2007). A cultural look at information and communication technologies in Eastern education. *Educational Technology Research and Development, 55,* 301–314.

Zhang, L. J., & Rahimi, M. (2014). EFL learners' anxiety level and their beliefs about corrective feedback in oral communication classes. *System, 42,* 429–439.

Zhang, Z. V. (2017). Student engagement with computer-generated feedback: A case study. *ELT Journal, 71,* 317–328.

Zheng, Y. (2012). Exploring long-term productive vocabulary development in an EFL context: The role of motivation. *System, 40,* 104–119.

Zheng, Y., & Yu, S. (2018). Student engagement with teacher written corrective feedback in EFL writing: A case study of Chinese lower-proficiency students. *Assessing Writing*, *37*, 13–24.

Zhou, N. (2015). Oral participation in EFL classroom: Perspectives from the administrator, teachers and learners at a Chinese university. *System*, *53*, 35–46.

Zhou, X., & Zha, M. (2020). Back to basics: A response to 'The English major crisis in China' (Chen, 2019). *English Today*, *36*, 24–29.